and t

The
Warrior
King

and the

Invasion of France

DESMOND SEWARD

PEGASUS BOOKS
NEW YORK LONDON

For Michael and Daphne Dormer

THE WARRIOR KING AND THE INVASION OF FRANCE

Pegasus Books LLC
80 Broad Street, 5th Floor
New York, NY 10004

ISBN: 978-1-60598-644-9

10 9 8 7 6 5 4 3 2 1

Printed in the United States of America
Distributed by W. W. Norton & Company, Inc.

Preface to the New Edition

When this book first came out during the 1980s it was noticeably less successful in Britain than in America, judging from reviews and sales. The reason was obvious enough. The British dislike an objective approach to the shortcomings of their country's national heroes and tend to reject out of hand any criticism of Henry V, whom they admire because, like Nelson and Wellington, he beat their old enemies the French.

Sir Winston Churchill (in his *History of the English Speaking Peoples*) verged on idolatry whenever he referred to Henry as 'the gleaming king', adding that he 'was more deeply loved by his subjects of all classes than any king had been in England.' Henry, said Churchill, was 'entirely national in his outlook: he was the first king to use the English language in his letters and his messages home from the front; his triumphs were gained by English troops; his policy was sustained by a Parliament that could claim to speak for the English people.' For Sir Winston, 'Agincourt ranks as the most heroic of all the land battles England has ever fought.'

Understandably, the critical judgement of Americans is not distorted by any such hang-up. In Britain, however, a strong bias in favour of Henry is still in evidence. It continues to influence academics of the highest calibre, although T. B. Pugh commented in *Henry V and the Southampton Plot* (1988) that 'he won unity for his realm and glory for himself at the price of immediate misery for France and eventual confusion for England.' Despite no new evidence having been found to change my view of King Henry since the first edition of this book in the 1980s, most studies by English historians since then are far less critical than mine.

The most important of these is undoubtedly Professor Christopher Allmand's *Henry V* (1992), which remains the definitive scholarly study. Without denying Allmand's exhaustive knowledge of the sources, one can disagree strongly with some of his major conclusions. As a keen admirer of the king and his gifts, Allmand tried to separate his success in France from his domestic achievements in England. Claiming that Henry's French conquests helped to unite his delighted subjects, he admitted that the 'venture' across the Channel had become a problem even before the king died—the English enjoyed conquering their ancient enemy and all the loot, but did not relish paying for the war effort—and turned into an increasing political and financial liability. On the other hand, Allmand insisted that at home Henry provided the English with outstandingly good and efficient government. Yet the king's policy in France cannot be separated from his policy in England, for the simple reason that he wanted the English to become, as far as possible, a society organised for war.

In *England's Empty Throne: Usurpation and the Language of Legitimisation, 1399-1422*, Paul Strohm (1998) uses textual criticism to suggest that Henry had hired chroniclers to promote his image, chroniclers who exaggerated the

Lollard conspiracy and the Southampton plot to supplant him with the Earl of March. An uninhibited American, Strohm certainly fuelled the debate, but does little to help us make up our mind about the king. If concerned with Henry as propagandist rather than ruler, he does at least note that he 'galvanised, rather than assuaged, the martial anger of the French.'

Another leading English medievalist, Gerald Harriss, showed himself among Henry's admirers in *Shaping the Nation* (2005), but without drawing a hard and fast line between Henry's behaviour in France and in England. Even so, he argued that, because the king hoped for a legal peace, he might have succeeded—'Had Henry V lived to establish this new order and embody it in his kingship, it might have acquired political legitimacy.' But then Harriss contradicted himself. 'Whether Frenchmen could have been persuaded to accept rule by their ancient enemy in these terms [those of a legitimate Christian king] is doubtful, though for a time some were prepared to do so.'

Keith Dockray in *Henry V* (2005) suggested that if the king had been content with the Duchy of Normandy, abandoning his claim to the French crown, 'in a settlement along the lines of the Treaty of Brétigny,' he might have secured its future under English rule. Yet the overtaxed Normans, plundered by English garrisons who wrecked their commerce, were bound to reject English government, in the same way the Poitevins of Edward III's Principality of Aquitaine (created by the Treaty of Brétigny) had rejected the Black Prince during the previous century.

Recently (2013), John Matusiak has continued to insist that the Dauphin might have been defeated, bringing 'a decisive peace founded upon a definitive victory'. Yet there were other Valois princes who would have continued the struggle and, as a far richer country with a population five times larger, once France had overcome her temporary disunity, the expulsion of the English was inevitable. Never again would they conquer territory across the Channel.

This author remains convinced that Henry V's ramshackle Anglo-French monarchy and duchy of Normandy were doomed from the start, even as they struggled on for thirty years. Both were created by a megalomaniac, who like Napoleon and Hitler did not know where to stop, and who, had he lived longer, could not possibly have found the men or the money needed to make his fantastic dream come true. Eventually, Henry's dream transformed itself into a nightmare for England. It ended in her final, complete, and humiliating defeat—the crown impoverished, the Wars of the Roses, and the destruction of the Lancastrian dynasty—with a deepening of that traditional French distrust of the English that lingers on even today.

—Desmond Seward, October 2014

Contents

List of Illustrations

Henry V, from a screen at York Minster begun about 1425. Like the statues of his immediate predecessors on the screen, this is undoubtedly a portrait.
(The Mansell Collection)

Henry V as a youth. From an early sixteenth-century copy of a lost original.

John, Duke of Bedford, kneels before St George, from the *Bedford Books of Hours* c. 1423. The small forked beard makes it highly probable that St George is a portrait of Henry V. (The British Library)

Thomas Montacute, Earl of Salisbury – Henry's most formidable commander – with fashionable military haircut. Note his poleaxe. (The British Library)

Henry V's father-in-law, King Charles VI of France, with his counsellors.
(François Martin)

Henry V's brother-in-law the Dauphin, when King Charles VII, as one of the Three Magi. From a miniature by Jean Fouquet. (Photographie Giraudon)

A room well known to Henry V – the ruins of the dining hall of Kenilworth Castle in Warwickshire. (John Cooke Photography)

The château of Lassay in Maine. Destroyed in 1417 to stop it being used as a base by the English, it was rebuilt in 1458 with cambered walls designed to resist siege artillery of the type used by Henry V. (S. Mountgarret)

A hunting scene of a sort very well known to Henry V. In the background is his favourite French residence, the castle of Bois-de-Vincennes. From the *Très Riches Heures du duc de Berry*. (Photographie Giraudon)

Henry V's official residence in Paris, the Louvre, as it was in his time. From the *Très Riches Heures du duc de Berry*. (Photographie Giraudon)

Line Illustrations

p. 34 Henry's seal as Prince of Wales and p. 147 The seal of Queen Catherine. (Sandford, F, *A genealogical history of the kings of England monarchs of Great Britain*, London 1671)

p. 194 Vincennes in 1576, still just as it had been in Henry V's time. The *donjon* (or keep) within the inner moat is where the king died in 1422. (Jacques Androuet du Cerceaux, *Les Plus Excellents Bastiments de France*).

Acknowledgements

It was Mr Michael Dormer who first suggested that I write this book. I am most grateful to him.

I am indebted to Count and Countess Pierre de Montalembert, and Count Artus de Montalembert, for valuable information about memories of the Hundred Years War in Normandy and Maine and for permission to reproduce the photograph of their château of Lassaye. I owe special thanks to Susan, Viscountess Mountgarret for help with research, for reading the typescript, for much photography, and for driving me to many sites in France associated with Henry V and his campaigns. I am also indebted to Peter Drummond-Murray of Mastrick for reading the proofs.

In addition I would like to thank the staffs of the British Library and the London Library for help and guidance on innumerable occasions, and also the honorary librarians of Brooks's, Mr Piers Dixon and Mr John Saumarez Smith.

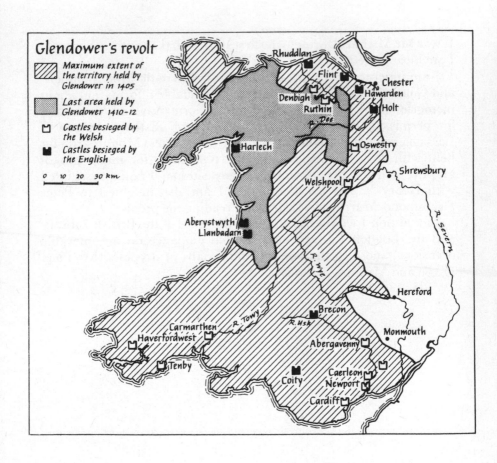

Glendower's revolt

Maximum extent of
the territory held by
Glendower in 1405

Last area held by
Glendower 1410-12

Castles besieged by
the Welsh

Castles besieged by
the English

0   10   20   30 km

Rhuddlan
Flint
Chester
Denbigh
Hawarden
Ruthin
Holt
R. Dee
Harlech
Oswestry
Shrewsbury
Welshpool
R. Severn
Aberystwyth
Llanbadarn
R. Wye
Hereford
Brecon
Carmarthen
R. Towy
R. Usk
Monmouth
Haverfordwest
Abergavenny
Tenby
Caerleon
Coity
Newport
Cardiff

North western France
1415-22

0 20 40 60 80 100 km

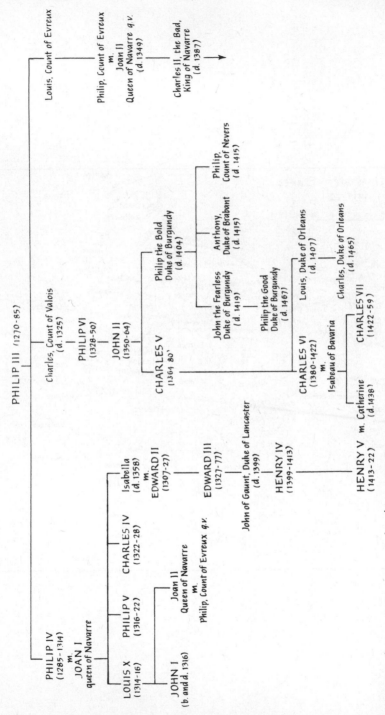

The claims of Henry V to the throne of France

EDWARD III (1327-77) m. Philippa of Hainault

Edward, Prince of Wales
(The Black Prince)
(1330-76)

RICHARD II
(1377-99)

Lionel,
Duke of Clarence
(1338-68)

Philippa
m.
Edmund Mortimer
Earl of March
→

Isabella
m.
Enguerrand de Coucy

John of Gaunt
Duke of Lancaster
(1340-97)

Blanche of Lancaster m. (1)

Catherine
m.
Henry III
of Castille

m. (3) Catherine Roelt (Swynford)

John Beaufort,
Earl of Somerset
(1371-1410)
→

Henry, Cardinal Beaufort
and Bishop of Winchester
(1374-1447)

Thomas, Duke of Exeter
(d. 1426)

Edmund,
Duke of York
(1342-1402)

Edward, Duke of York
(1373-1415)

Mary
m.
John IV
of Brittany

Richard, Earl of Cambridge
(1375-1415)
m.
Anne Mortimer

HOUSE OF YORK

Thomas, Earl of Buckingham
and Duke of Gloucester
(1355-97)

Elizabeth
m. (1)
John Hastings,
Earl of Pembroke
m. (2)
John Holland
Duke of Exeter
m. (3)
Sir John Cornwall,
Lord Fanhope

Philippa
m.
John I of Portugal

HENRY IV
(1399-1413)

HOUSE OF LANCASTER

The Children and Grand-children of Edward III

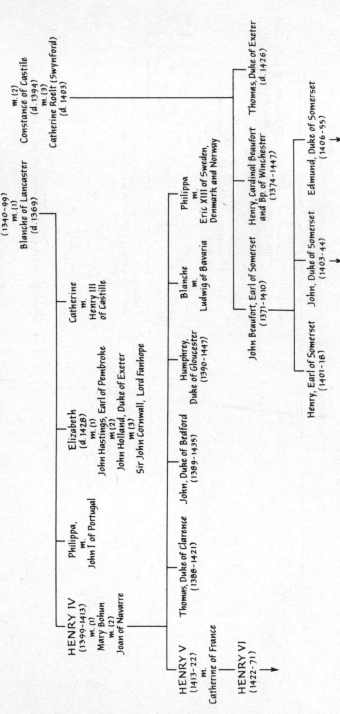

The Houses of Lancaster and Beaufort

Chronology

1387 Born at Monmouth on 16 September.

1394 Death of mother.

1398 His father, Bolingbroke, is banished.

1399 Accompanies Richard II to Ireland.
Bolingbroke deposes Richard II and ascends throne as Henry IV.
Becomes heir to throne and is created Prince of Wales.

1400 Richard II is murdered.
Campaigns with father in Scotland.
Owain Glyn Dŵr revolts and proclaims himself Prince of Wales.
Campaigns with father in Wales.

1402 He and Hotspur recapture Conwy in spring.
Campaigns with his father in Wales in autumn.

1403 Appointed King's Lieutenant on the Marches of Wales.
Campaigns in Wales in spring, burning Owain's houses.
Wounded in battle of Shrewsbury against Hotspur on 21 July.
Campaigns in Wales in autumn.

1405 Plot to place Earl of March on throne.
Archbishop Scrope's rising is crushed.
Franco-Welsh army invades England.
Campaigns in Wales in autumn.

1406 Appointed Lieutenant of Wales.
Campaigns in Wales in summer.
Besieges Aberystwyth.
Campaigns with father in Scotland in autumn.

1408 Earl of Northumberland defeated and killed at Bramham Moor.
Aberystwyth surrenders.

1409 Harlech surrenders.

1410 Becomes head of the King's Council during father's illness.

1411   Father recovers and dismisses him from the Council.
English expedition to France to help Burgundians.

1412   English expedition to France to help Armagnacs.
Suspected of plotting to depose his father.

1413   Henry IV dies in March and he becomes king.

1414   Lollard rising crushed in London.

1415   Southampton Plot to murder him and place March on throne.
Invades Normandy in August.
Harfleur surrenders to him in September.
Defeats French at Agincourt on 25 October.

1416   Emperor Sigismund visits Henry in England.

1417   Invades Normandy in August.
Takes Caen by storm in September.

1418   Captures Falaise in February.
Commences siege of Rouen in July.

1419   Rouen surrenders in January – English overrun all Normandy.
Negotiations with Duke of Burgundy and French queen in June.
Captures Pontoise in July.
Duke John of Burgundy murdered by Armagnacs in September.
Alliance between England and Burgundy in December.

1420   Treaty of Troyes with Charles VI and Philip of Burgundy –
recognised as 'Heir and Regent of France'.
Marries Charles VI's daughter, Catherine of Valois, in June.
Occupies Paris, installing English garrison.
Besieges Melun from July till its fall in November.

1421   Spends January in Normandy.
Returns to England with Catherine in February.
Duke of Clarence defeated and killed by French at Baugé.
Returns to France in June and relieves English at Paris.
Commences siege of Meaux in August.
Birth of his son, the future Henry VI.

1422   Continues siege of Meaux which surrenders in May.
Falls seriously ill in June.
Dies at Vincennes on 31 August.

Introduction

'I am the scourge of God'

Henry V

'I am an Englishman, and am thy foe'

Thomas Hoccleve, *The Regement of Princes*

On 19 October 1449 a cheering mob opened the gates of Rouen, the capital of Normandy, and Charles VII of France – once disinherited dauphin, now 'King Charles the very victorious' – rode in to wild rejoicing. Rouen had been occupied by the English for thirty years. Within less than a year they would be driven out of Normandy altogether. It was the end not only of an English Normandy but of an Anglo-French dual monarchy. In particular it was the end of one man's dream. The man was Henry V, who left an unhappy legacy when he died in 1422, a legacy that is still with us.

No one would deny the uneasy relationship between the French and the Anglo-Saxons. The former tend to distrust anyone who speaks English. Among the earliest and not the least reasons why this ingrained suspicion developed was the behaviour of English troops in France during the second half of the Hundred Years War, a war revived by Henry. No doubt French troops behaved as badly – but they were in France as Frenchmen, not as invaders who spoke a foreign tongue. The English had taken advantage of a civil war to conquer all north-western France. It was as if a French king had allied with the Yorkists during the Wars of the Roses, occupied south-eastern England, installed a French garrison at London and had himself declared heir to the throne, while at the same time turning Kent into a separate Anglo-French principality where he confiscated 500 estates and gave them to Frenchmen, besides settling 10,000 colonists at Dover. The humiliation and the atrocities would never have been forgotten. The French have long memories too.

Henry V is one of England's heroes. The victor of Agincourt was idolized during his lifetime, his memory inspired one of Shakespeare's most stirring (if scarcely greatest) plays, and the Victorians considered him a perfect Christian gentleman: 'He was religious, pure in life, temperate, liberal, careful and yet splendid,' says Bishop Stubbs, 'merciful, truthful, and honourable, discreet in word, provident in counsel, prudent in judgement, modest in look, magnanimous in act, a true Englishman.' In our own century Sir Winston Churchill could write of 'the gleaming King'.

That brilliant historian of the medieval English, the late K. B. McFarlane, thought Henry 'the greatest man that ever ruled England.' His achievements were remarkable. At home not only did he tame the Welsh, destroying Owain Glyn Dŵr, but he restored law and order to a hitherto strife-torn realm; across the Channel he conquered a third of France, married the French king's daughter and was recognized as heir and regent of France. So powerful is his spell that almost every English historian who studied him succumbs, bemused by his genius and dynamism, blind to any shortcomings. They attribute any criticism by French scholars to anglophobia.

Nevertheless his conquest of France was as much about loot as dynastic succession, accompanied by mass slaughter, arson and rape – French plunder was on sale all over England. It was very like the Norman conquest of England in reverse although lasting a mere thirty years. Just as William the Bastard had done, he seized the lands of the great nobles, and of many lesser nobles too, giving them to his soldiers. For three decades English interlopers, often sporting French titles, lorded it over hundreds of French estates – some great counties, others modest manors. They were, however, always in danger, dependent on English archers for survival. He not only evicted noblemen from castles but ordinary people from their homes. Countless Frenchmen of all classes emigrated from the territory conquered by him. When reproached with killing so many Christians in France, he answered, 'I am the scourge of God sent to punish the people of God for their sins.'[1]

The misery inflicted on the French by Henry's campaigns is indisputable. Any local historian in north-western France can point to a town, a château, an abbey or a church sacked by his men. Life in the countryside became a nightmare. When the English raided enemy territory they killed anything that moved, destroyed crops and food supplies and drove off livestock, in a calculated attempt to weaken their opponents by starving the civilian population. Occupied areas fared little better because of the *pâtis* or protection racket operated by English garrisons; villages had to pay extortionate dues in food and wine as well as money, failure to deliver sometimes incurred executions and burnings.

Yet Henry's ambition was inspired by something more complicated than mere desire for conquest. It was a need to prove that he really was King of England. His father had usurped the throne and, as the Yorkists would demonstrate during the Wars of the Roses, there were others with a better right to it in law. If he could make good his great-grandfather Edward III's claim to France he would show in trial by battle that God confirmed his right to the English crown.

During the nineteenth century French 'patriotic' historians reacted violently to the Hundred Years War, producing a portrait of Henry as distorted as the English icon. They saw fifteenth-century Anglo-Saxons as the first 'Boches'. English historians responded to this xenophobic outburst with equal chauvinism, together with a cool assumption of objectivity (although few writers can have taken less pains to hide their dislike of the French than the venerated Wylie and Waugh in their massive study of the king's reign). Even today English and French differ in their judgement. Harriss believes Henry had 'grasped' that the French crown 'could only be securely held by one whom the French people accepted as King in the same measure as Englishmen did . . . given the years, energy and luck, he might have reshaped the development of both nations just, as in brief space, he had restored the fortunes of England.'[2] By contrast Edouard Perroy thought that Henry's successes, 'his premature death at the height of unprecedented glory, have raised him very high, perhaps too high, in the estimation of posterity'. He refers to his 'hypocritical bigotry, his double dealing, his pretence of observing the law and redressing wrongs when he merely sought to gratify his own ambition'. It remains to strike a balance.[3]

English studies of the king tend to discount French chroniclers, save for tributes to him when he died. Admittedly some borrow from each other and several wrote years after his death. Nevertheless all were alive during his reign (Jean Juvénal des Ursins, the monk of St

Denis and Monstrelet being already in their thirties when he died), while all of them had spoken to people who had experienced the events of which they write. If they were prejudiced against him, then English chroniclers were biased in his favour. One prefers the testimony of the occupied to the occupiers – just as one accepts French rather than German versions of what happened in France between 1940 and 1944.

In England historians refuse to see the fifteenth-century phase of the Hundred Years War as a conflict between French and English. They argue that while the English had a sense of nationality no such people as Frenchmen existed, only inhabitants of regions of France with no common identity. Yet if France was not seen then as she is now, almost as a person, there was nevertheless a concept of a French realm symbolized by the phrase 'the honour of the fleur-de-lys'. By the fifteenth century the French had developed quite enough nationalism to consider their neighbours over the Channel hereditary enemies. If Henry did not think in national terms – for him France was 'my inheritance' – his subjects did and definitely tended to xenophobia. Many of France's miseries during this period were due to Frenchmen yet all French chroniclers unite in seeing the English as the worst of their foes. The French may have possessed only a vague sense of nationality when Henry invaded their country but they quickly developed one in fighting him. They took the king at his own word – 'I am the scourge of God' – save that to them he was the Devil's scourge rather than God's.

I

The Usurpers

'Heaven knows, my son,
By what by-paths, and indirect crook'd ways,
I met this crown; and I myself know well,
How troublesome it sat upon my head.'

Shakespeare, *King Henry IV*

'[Henry IV] in order to come into the honour and glory of the crown of the said realm of England had in time past by certain strange and dishonourable means deprived of that rank his first cousin Richard, king of England.'

Enguerrand de Monstrelet, *Les Chroniques*

There is a legend that in September 1387 Henry Bolingbroke, Earl of Hereford – the future Henry IV of England – hurried from Windsor to Wales to be present at the birth of his first child. When he crossed the River Wye near Walford the ferryman told him that his wife had borne a son. So delighted was the earl by the news that he at once gave the man the right to all the ferry's dues and tolls.

The boy was delivered in the gatehouse of Monmouth Castle in South Wales. (It is ironical that someone who was to inflict so much misery on the Welsh should have been born in Gwent.) His father was the son of John of Gaunt, Duke of Lancaster, who was himself the third son of King Edward III; in consequence Bolingbroke was first cousin to the king, Richard II, whose father had been the Black Prince. Edward's eldest son. Yet the child was not christened Edward or Richard but Henry, like Bolingbroke. Almost certainly this was because of Gaunt's marriage to the heiress of the earls of

1

Lancaster. They were a younger branch of the Plantagenets, descended from Henry III, who, so Gaunt claimed in private, were the rightful heirs to the throne of England.

Little Henry's mother, Mary Bohun, was one of the two immensely rich co-heiresses of the last Bohun earl of Hereford. Originally she had been destined for a convent but Gaunt would not let so rich a prize slip through his hands and obtained her hand in marriage for his son, who secured his late father-in-law's title. Mary gave Bolingbroke three more sons and two daughters before her death in 1394 aged only twenty-four.

She belonged to one of the most august of medieval England's noble families. The Bohuns were of Norman descent, having come with the Conqueror and originated from Bohon in Normandy. They intermarried with the Plantagenets on several occasions and Mary was descended from Edward I. Her father, hereditary High Constable (leader in battle) of England, besides being Earl of Hereford, had been Earl of Northampton and Earl of Essex. He had married a daughter of the Earl of Arundel and was closely related to every noble house in the land. Her sister and co-heiress had been married to Gaunt's younger brother, Thomas of Woodstock, Duke of Gloucester – her husband's uncle. The vast Bohun inheritance had been divided between the two girls, the Welsh estates going to Mary, which was why Bolingbroke was Earl of Hereford and why Henry was born at Monmouth. Her son's memories of her must have been slight but when he became king – perhaps in response to the magnificent effigy of his step-mother which lay beside that of his father in Canterbury Cathedral – he immediately commissioned a figure of her to be erected over her tomb at Leicester.

Apart from the king himself, the most important kinsfolk of the 'House of Lancaster' as it would soon be called, were the Beauforts. These were a left-handed branch of the family, Gaunt's children by his third wife Catherine Roelt (usually referred to as Catherine Swynford) who arrived in this world long before their parents' had been married and who took the name of 'Beaufort' from a castle of Gaunt's in France. They numbered three exceptionally able sons – John, Henry and Thomas – and a daughter, Joan, who married the rich, powerful and ambitious Earl of Westmorland.

Henry of Monmouth's life was tranquil enough during the 'Quiet Years' of King Richard's stormy reign. He shared a bedroom and a governess with his brothers, though later the boys usually lived apart from one another. He had a nurse to whom he was devoted; as soon

2

as he came to the throne he settled a generous pension on her. He visited his grandmother Joan, Countess of Hereford, who lived until 1419 and of whom he was clearly very fond; in the will he was to make in 1415 he twice describes her as 'our dearest grandmother'. It is reasonable to suppose that he was made miserable by the death of his mother when he was only seven. We know that he had at least one dangerous illness during childhood, being taken seriously ill at Leicester when he was eight. Otherwise we have very few details about his early years since no one saw him as a future king of England. The exception may perhaps have been Gaunt, that slightly sinister grandfather who despite careful marrying and constant scheming had failed to secure the throne which he coveted for himself in either Castile or Portugal.

No doubt Gaunt was visited fairly frequently by his grandson at his country palace in the Midlands, Kenilworth in Warwickshire. The duke had recently rebuilt this massive red sandstone castle out of his vast wealth. Although partly demolished during the Civil War enough of its once magnificent dining hall remains for one to obtain an idea of what it looked like in Henry's day. However, the timbered banqueting room known as 'The Plesaunce', next to a lake in the grounds, has long since vanished. During his reign he would frequently hold his court at Kenilworth which was clearly a favourite residence.

Henry's principal tutor was his formidably gifted young uncle, Henry Beaufort. However, there seems to be no justification for the claim that he was at Oxford when Beaufort was chancellor of the university. According to the Monk of Westminster's chronicle the boy enjoyed the usual amusements of the nobility of the period, especially hunting and falconry – for both of which he developed a passion which lasted all his life. Obviously he was taught the military arts. He learnt to play the harp – the duchy of Lancaster's accounts include an item of 8d for harp strings for him – and also the gittern, which may have begun his love of music. (He is known to have played the harp later in life, when campaigning in France.)[1] He learnt to read and write French and English, and also some Latin which he began to study when he was eight. One presumes that like most boys of his class he saw little of his father.

Then in October 1398 the eleven-year-old 'lord Henry of Monmouth' was summoned to court by his cousin Richard II. Although given £500 a year 'of the king's gift' the boy was in fact a hostage and in some peril. His father Bolingbroke had just been banished, in a long delayed settling of accounts, for his role in destroying Richard's favourites ten years before and also because he was the heir of John of Gaunt, the richest magnate in England. It was only a year since Richard had had another uncle, the Duke of Gloucester, murdered in his prison at Calais – smothered in a featherbed, despite the duke's pleas for mercy 'as lowly and meekly as a man may'. Young Henry was uncomfortably near to the throne.

His father, Henry Bolingbroke, Earl of Derby and Duke of Hereford, was handsome and well built, with curling moustaches and a small forked beard like the king's. Born in 1367 and three months younger than Richard he was doubly a Plantagenet as has been seen. Although self-indulgent and a womanizer, he was a keen and extremely able soldier, fond of fencing and jousting, who had been on crusade. He had visited the Knights of St John at Rhodes and the beleaguered kingdom of Cyprus and had fought at the side of the Teutonic Knights in Prussia and Lithuania against Europe's last pagans. Indeed he was the most travelled of all the Plantagenets, having journeyed to Venice and Milan, Vienna and Prague. Wherever he went he was accompanied by a household band of drummers, trumpeters and pipers, and was an accomplished musician himself. He was surprisingly well read in both French and English, French being his preferred language, and occasionally quoted Latin.

Despite these courtly qualities Bolingbroke had little in common with King Richard, who had never forgotten the earl's part in the rebellion against his authority in 1387, in routing his favourites' army at Radcote Bridge in 1388 and in bringing about their deaths; he may even have suspected Bolingbroke of plotting to depose him at the time. Although he promoted the earl to Duke of Hereford in 1398, Richard was determined that Bolingbroke should never succeed to Gaunt's enormous estates. Later that year, through Gaunt, Bolingbroke informed the king that the Duke of Norfolk had warned him that Richard had still not forgiven them for what had happened at Radcote; then, in the king's presence, he accused Norfolk of being a traitor. Norfolk denied the charges, whereupon Richard referred the dispute to a parliamentary committee. The committee – which everyone knew to be controlled by the king – ordered a trial by battle.

The duel was to take place at Coventry on St Lambert's Day (16 September) 1398 and would have been the social event of the year. Bolingbroke was the favourite because of his known strength and skill. On the appointed day he entered the lists in armour, his white war-horse barbed with blue and green velvet, sumptuously

4

embroidered with swans and antelopes of goldsmiths' work. His opponent's charger was caparisoned in crimson velvet embroidered with mulberry trees and lions of silver. But the king threw down a baton from his dais and stopped the fight. He banished Norfolk for life, Bolingbroke for ten years – he wanted neither to win, but to destroy both of them.

Any small boy would be thrilled at the prospect of his father fighting in such a combat. No doubt young Henry of Monmouth was disappointed that it did not take place. He must surely have been downcast by the sentence of banishment – which was also the reason for his summons to court.

King Richard was an alarming figure, neurotic and overbearing, untrusting and untrustworthy, prone to fits of furious rage. Besides having had his uncle, Gloucester, murdered he had had the Earl of Arundel beheaded at the Tower without trial in that same year of 1398. In addition he had recently sentenced the Archbishop of Canterbury (Arundel's brother) and the Earl of Warwick to perpetual banishment, the latter only just saving his life by grovelling for mercy. All of these had been involved in the rebellion of 1388 like Henry Bolingbroke, with whom the king was not yet finished. By this stage of his reign on some days Richard sat crowned on his throne from dinner, which was at 9.00 a.m., until dusk, every day, in total silence amid his courtiers; anyone who caught his eye had to kneel. Since the previous year he had been negotiating for his election as the Holy Roman Emperor (in place of Emperor Wenzel the Drunkard, soon to be deposed). An aesthete whose court was one of the most elegant in Europe, his fastidious mannerisms no doubt astonished his youthful hostage, such as his pioneer use of handkerchiefs – 'little pieces [of cloth] made for giving to the lord king for carrying in his hand to wipe and cleanse his nose'. But the King's delicate ways never inhibited him from shedding blood. Although Richard seems to have taken a liking to young Henry, it must have been unnerving for the boy to realize that this awe-inspiring figure, the realm's crowned and anointed sovereign who was always so aware of his own majesty, was the enemy of his – Henry of Monmouth's – banished father.

Although Richard was showing signs of megalomania he was far from stupid – in fact he was too intelligent for his own good. This was particularly evident in his attitude towards the Hundred Years War, in which both his father and his grandfather had won such glory. The conflict between France and England had arisen earlier in the

5

century because of the French monarchy's attempts to assert its authority over the English kings' duchy of Guyenne in south-western France whose capital was Bordeaux; and partly because of Edward III's claim to the French throne as the heir of his maternal grandfather, Philip IV. After some striking victories Edward had secured, by the Treaty of Brétigny in 1360, most of south-western France in full sovereignty, including not only Guyenne but Poitou and the Limousin together with many other districts. In return for this he agreed to abandon his claim to the French throne. Yet he had not succeeded in regaining all the lands in France which his ancestor Henry II had ruled in the twelfth century, a notable omission being the duchy of Normandy. What is more, the shrewdness of Charles V and the Constable du Guesclin quickly regained for France the territories ceded at Brétigny.

Richard realized that England simply could not afford to continue the war, that its expense was a grave source of weakness to the monarchy. On several occasions during the 1380s Parliament had refused to grant the taxes needed to pay for it, showing an obvious desire for more control of the central government. He admired French civilization and French luxury and was unusual for his age in being unmoved by considerations of military glory. He was correct in thinking that England, a comparatively poor and thinly populated land, should not embark on overseas conquest. However, he overestimated the strength of France, which was largely illusory despite the wealth and splendour of the Valois monarchy and of the French nobility; not only were the latter much too rich and independent but their king was afflicted by increasingly lengthy fits of insanity so that there was no national leadership. It has been argued that at this date France was not a nation but a collection of nations. Yet, although there was unquestionably great diversity in dialect and custom, this is an exaggeration. If semi-independent, the great nobles nonetheless regarded the king as the principal political figure in the country, as did the lesser nobility, even if there might not have been the close relationship which existed in England between Crown and Parliament. So determined was Richard to secure an Anglo-French peace that he seriously contemplated separating Guyenne from the English crown, with his uncle John of Gaunt as its duke and independent sovereign. The scheme came to nothing, but the English king compromised with a truce for twenty-eight years. He had already married the French king's daughter, Isabel, in token of his good faith. In addition he had gone so far as to try to make the Church in

England switch its allegiance from the Urbanist pope at Rome to the Clementist pope at Avignon since the latter was supported by the French.

Richard was unpopular with all classes, save in a very few parts of the country. His attempts to free the monarchy from the dictates of Lords and Commons, his high-handed treatment of great noblemen and of the City of London, his inefficient government and personal extravagance, above all his arbitrary taxation – of the sort which had provoked the Peasants' Revolt – were resented in particular. His pro-French policy was detested although it might have resulted in lighter taxation. His uncle, the murdered Duke of Gloucester, had led an anti-French lobby which rejoiced on hearing of the slaughter of 'those rare boasting Frenchmen' by the Turks at Nicopolis in 1396 although they had been on a crusade. The English remembered with pride the conquests of Edward III and the Black Prince, the victories of Crécy and Poitiers, a king of France being brought prisoner to London. They remembered too, with keen nostalgia, the loot and ransoms which had flooded back across the Channel; there was no longer the prospect, formerly open to all classes, of making one's fortune from plundering in France. Moreover one has only to read Chaucer (whose verse was extremely popular in court circles and who had been born half a century before Henry), to realize that French had ceased to be the language of the ruling class, even of intellectuals, although still used sometimes for formal or official purposes; as king, Henry's correspondence was always in English. Indeed there was a widespread feeling of hatred and disdain towards the French. In a poem of this period Eustache Deschamps has an English soldier shouting, 'Dog of a Frenchman [*Franche dague*], you do naught but drink wine all day long!'[2]

There was also an element of fear. French privateers were constantly harrying English shipping and raiding the South Coast. Froissart reports that the English said openly that their own king might be their ruin – 'His heart is so French that he cannot hide it, but a day will come to pay for all.'[3]

Richard's unsuccessful plan of creating Gaunt independent Duke of Guyenne, had been to some extent inspired by the hope that he would leave England and settle at Bordeaux. He was much too close to the succession. The king was childless and in 1398 his second wife Isabel of France was still only nine while the heir presumptive to the throne, Edmund Mortimer, Earl of March – heir by descent from Edward III's second son through the female line – was seven. There

7

was a rumour, recorded by the chronicler John Hardyng, that Gaunt had commissioned a forged chronicle containing a fable which purported to establish his son's right to the throne. Gaunt's wife, Blanche of Lancaster, had been the senior descendant of Edmund Crouchback, Earl of Lancaster, who was generally believed to have been the second son of Henry III and younger brother of Edward I. In reality (said the fable) Edmund had been Henry III's eldest son but had been set aside and made to appear the younger because of his deformity – in consequence all the English kings since then had reigned unlawfully and Henry Bolingbroke was the rightful sovereign. Hardyng says that Gaunt had copies of the forged chronicle placed in a number of influential monastery libraries. Whether Gaunt was responsible or not, the tale was certainly in circulation by 1399 even if it was nonsense.[4]

'Old John of Gaunt, time-honoured Lancaster', Henry's magnificent and semi-regal grandfather, died in February 1399 aged fifty-nine – a ripe old age by contemporary standards. England had never seen so rich and powerful a prince of the blood. He possessed thirty castles together with countless manors, mainly in the north, the Midlands and Wales, and was able to raise 1,000 men-at-arms and 3,000 archers in time of war. His duchy of Lancaster was an independent state in all but name, inside whose boundaries the king's writ was largely ignored. In London his palace of the Savoy was as splendid as any of his royal nephews'. In March Richard, despite previous assurances to Bolingbroke that he would allow him to inherit his father's estates, announced that the late Duke of Lancaster's lands and possessions were forfeit to the crown and that Bolingbroke's banishment was for life.

Now that he had added so substantially to his resources the king decided to take an expedition to Ireland where the Pale – the tiny area around Dublin and Kildare which was the only region directly controlled by the English – was in serious danger. In 1398 the Lord Lieutenant, the Earl of March (the heir presumptive to the throne) had been ambushed and killed near Kells by the O'Tooles and the O'Briens. The 'Wild Irish' led by Art MacMurrogh, King of Leinster, had swarmed into the Pale where they were still slaying, burning and looting. Richard and his army landed in January. He left his timid and inept uncle Edmund, Duke of York, behind as 'Keeper of England' while as hostages he took with him Henry of Monmouth, Bolingbroke's half-brother Henry Beaufort and Humphrey of Gloucester – son of the murdered duke. He had

8

intended to take the Earl of Arundel's son as well, but the young man escaped to France where he joined Bolingbroke. Richard also proclaimed March's son heir presumptive.

The English army marched up through Kilkenny and Wicklow to Dublin, losing many men. The Irish attacked their camps every night. During Henry's first campaign he must surely have agreed with Froissart that Ireland was a bad country in which to fight because of its dense forests, lakes and bogs. No doubt he marvelled at the wild-haired, long-moustached Irish chieftains, who went about half naked under yellow mantles. They rode ponies barefoot, using primitive saddles of padded cloth, and howled at their men in a strange, guttural language. While an important chief might employ as many as a hundred gallowglass mercenaries, who dismounted to fight on foot with huge axes (like the Lochaber axes of the Scots Highlanders), most of his men would be kern who carried only dirks and bundles of javelins. If no match for conventional troops, they were dreaded for more than their war whoops as they were skilled at ambushes and sudden attacks. (Even though they did not rip out and eat human hearts, as Froissart believed, they undoubtedly cut off heads for trophies.) Provisions ran out and Richard's men were starving when they reached Dublin. Art MacMurrogh demanded an unconditional peace, infuriating the king who set out on another wild-goose chase after him through bogs and forests until he found himself back at Waterford.

We know something of this inglorious campaign from a poem by a Frenchman in the royal service, Jean Creton. He tells us that Richard summoned the Duke of Lancaster's son whom he dubbed knight saying, 'My fair young cousin, henceforth be gallant and bold, for unless you conquer you will have little name for valour.'

Alarming news, delayed by bad weather, then reached the king. Bolingbroke had landed in England and was claiming the duchy of Lancaster. Richard wanted to return at once but the Duke of York's son, the Earl of Rutland, persuaded him to wait and concentrate his troops while sending the Earl of Salisbury to raise another army in Wales. The chronicler Thomas Otterbourne reports that the king told his young cousin, 'Henry, my boy, see what thy father hath done to me!' He added, 'through these unhappy doings thou wilt perchance lose thine inheritance.' Henry answered that he was not to blame for his father's actions. When Richard left for England Henry, with Humphrey of Gloucester, was confined at Trim Castle in County Meath.

9

The king had made himself thoroughly unpopular with all classes by his attempts to increase the power of the Crown. In all save a few regions everyone was alarmed by his arbitrary government, and by his murder of Gloucester and Arundel and the seizure of the duchy of Lancaster. He had quarrelled so bitterly with the people of London that he thought seriously of moving his capital to York. He had some supporters and to begin with not even his enemies contemplated deposing the realm's crowned and anointed monarch. But he had ruined himself by leaving England in the Duke of York's inept hands and by taking his henchmen with him.

Bolingbroke had landed at Ravenspur in Yorkshire on 4 July, kissing the earth, accompanied by Archbishop Arundel and the young Earl of Arundel. He was met by former officers of Gaunt's household with armed retainers, and quickly joined by his brother-in-law the Earl of Westmorland and the Earl of Northumberland – northern England's two most powerful men. Magnates from all over the country rallied to him. On 27 July the Duke of York came over, bringing many men. Next day Bolingbroke entered Bristol and Richard's most unpopular councillors – including his treasurer William Scrope, Earl of Wiltshire – were arrested there and immediately beheaded. The king only left Ireland that day and by the time he landed in South Wales his supporters had melted away. He fled to Conwy Castle, from where he was lured out by Northumberland who pretended he would keep his throne if he restored the duchy of Lancaster to Bolingbroke. As soon as he had left the castle Richard was ambushed and taken to Bolingbroke at Flint on 19 August. He was then brought to London, where he was greeted by a jeering mob who threw rubbish on him from the rooftops, and imprisoned in the Tower. Within fifty days Henry Bolingbroke had conquered both king and kingdom.

Bolingbroke was in effective control of the entire country. Originally he had merely hoped to recover his duchy. It is likely that when things began to go well he thought of making himself regent for Richard or for the heir presumptive, the young Earl of March and Ulster. He now decided to take the throne. On 29 September the king was bullied into abdicating. The following day an assembly of the Lords Spiritual and Temporal and of the Commons met in Westminster Hall in the presence of Henry Bolingbroke, who sat in the seat Gaunt had occupied as Duke of Lancaster. Articles of accusation against Richard were read, after which he was declared deposed. Bolingbroke then rose and, making the sign of the Cross, claimed the throne – in English: 'I that am descended by right line of the Blood coming from the good lord King Henry III.' Adam of Usk tells us a commission of lawyers and clerics had rejected the tale of Edmund Crouchback having been Henry III's first born son, but notwithstanding, Bolingbroke clung to the claim while also insisting that the kingdom was on the point of being destroyed by bad government and that he was the only man who could bring back law and order. No mention was made of the Earl of March. Archbishop Arundel then led Bolingbroke by the hand to the royal throne whereupon the assembly acclaimed him as King of England and France.

Henry IV, as he was now known, associated his sons in his usurpation by insisting on their right to succeed him. He had already sent a ship to bring his heir back from Ireland. After what seems to have been a stormy voyage – young Humphrey of Gloucester died from its effects – he landed at Chester and rode to London. Here on Sunday 12 October at the Tower he was knighted for a second time by his father together with his brothers and forty-five squires. At the coronation the next day he carried the sword 'Curtana'. On 15 October at Westminster, with the assent of parliament, he was given the titles once borne by Edward III's son, the Black Prince, being created Prince of Wales, Duke of Cornwall and Earl of Chester. He knelt before his father who placed a gold coronet studded with pearls on his head, a ring on his finger and a golden rod in his hand, after which the Duke of York led him by the hand to a lower throne next to the king's where he sat as heir apparent. A week later he was created Duke of Aquitaine, Parliament petitioning that since he was of tender years he might not go there just yet. Finally, on 10 November he was created Duke of Lancaster.

As for Richard II, he was kept in 'safe and secret ward'. On 28 October, disguised as a forester, he was removed discreetly from the Tower by boat and taken to Leeds Castle in Kent, then to Pontefract in Yorkshire. The unpitying Adam of Usk informs us that, 'The lord Richard, late king, after his deposition was carried away on the Thames in the silence of dark midnight, weeping and loudly lamenting he had ever been born.' The little Earl of March was also kept in safe and secret ward.

There were evil omens during the coronation. When he had been annointed Henry's head was found to be swarming with lice. Then, at the offertory, he dropped a gold noble which rolled away out of sight.[5]

11

After the coronation King Henry and his sons banqueted in public at Westminster Hall as was customary. He wore his crown and the princes their coronets. Halfway through the banquet the royal champion Sir Thomas Dymock – whose function was to defend the king's right to the crown in personal combat – rode into the hall in full armour, his golden-hilted sword sheathed in black; a herald proclaimed four times a challenge to anyone who denied that Henry was not rightful King of England. Henry IV said loudly, 'If need be, Sir Thomas, I will in mine own person ease thee of this office.' It was an open admission of the new Lancastrian dynasty's insecurity.

II

Prince Henry and Prince Owain

'. . . all this clamour of king Richard'

Henry IV

'Trembling even at the name of Mortimer'

Shakespeare, *King Henry IV*

Although he had won the crown of England, Henry IV was in a most unenviable position. His usurpation had weakened the monarchy dangerously while he faced many of the same problems as his predecessor. Moreover for the first six years of his reign he was on the verge of bankruptcy.

The customs on wool, the king's principal source of revenue, fell as low as £20,000 during 1402–7 compared with £46,000 during Richard II's reign. Henry's income averaged less than £90,000 a year – Richard's had averaged £116,000 – and he needed at least £140,000 even in peacetime. He could not pay the lavish rewards which he had promised during the march from Ravenspur, let alone redeem his pledge to cut taxes. He did nothing to improve the situation, merely borrowing from magnates, merchants or prelates with the result that the Crown's debts nearly became unmanageable.

Henry took away the dukedoms Richard had given his favourites – the Earls of Salisbury, Kent, Huntingdon and Rutland – but otherwise left them alone, hoping to play them off against other magnates. However in December 1399, at the invitation of the abbot, the earls met secretly with other supporters of Richard at Westminster Abbey whose monks were strongly for the ex-king. Among the conspirators was a former chaplain of Richard's household, one Maudelyn, who

13

bore a remarkable likeness to him. Henry was keeping the twelve days of Christmas at Windsor, which were to end with a tournament on the day of the Epiphany (6 January). The conspirators agreed to meet at Kingston-on-Thames on 4 January with a small armed force and ride by night to Windsor. Here other plotters who had got in on the pretext of having come for the jousting would overpower the guards and open the gates to them, whereupon Henry and his sons were to be killed out of hand. The earls would then proclaim Richard restored to his throne, and Maudelyn would impersonate him until he had been rescued from Pontefract.

Rutland, famed for unreliability and double dealing, had misgivings. He told his father the Duke of York who informed the king, almost at the last moment. Henry and his sons with only two attendants galloped to London, which the king knew to be loyal to him. Within two days he had raised an army of 20,000 men, mainly Londoners. When the earls and their troops, who had successfully seized Windsor a mere twelve hours after Henry's flight and proclaimed Richard, learnt that the king was advancing with a large army they retreated westward. After some skirmishing their troops deserted and they were lynched. Henry rode back to London in triumph having had sent before him their salted heads in baskets like fish being taken to market for display on London Bridge. The *Te Deum* was sung at St Paul's, Archbishop Arundel giving thanks to the Virgin Mary for 'rescuing the most Christian king from the fangs of wolves and the jaws of wild beasts, who had prepared above their backs a gallows mixed with gall and hated us with a bitter hate'.[1]

Richard's friends had signed his death warrant. Henry IV could not be safe while he was still alive. The ex-king was certainly dead by 17 February. Adam of Usk says that death came to him miserably as 'he lay in chains in the castle of Pontefract tormented by Sir [Thomas] Swynford with starving fare'.[2] A French source says that in his agony Richard ripped the flesh from his arms and hands and ate it. Other English sources claim implausibly that he starved himself to death. There is little doubt that he was murdered, either starved or smothered, probably in January 1400 within a few days of his friends' own deaths. His body lay at St Paul's for two days with only the face exposed – so that everyone could recognize it – and the rest of his corpse cased in lead, before being buried in the priory of the Black Friars at King's Langley in Herefordshire. Yet rumours he had escaped persisted well into the next reign. Many thought he was

14

in Scotland where the Scots kept a madman with a resemblance to him – the 'maumet of Scotland' – in custody until 1419.

In August 1400 Henry IV led a futile expedition into Scotland to force the King of Scots to pay homage. The Prince of Wales had command of seventeen men-at-arms and ninety-nine archers. As soon as they returned, unsuccessful, news came of trouble in Wales. Richard II's predilection for the North Welsh had made him more popular throughout the little country than any previous English monarch and the new régime was heartily disliked; not only was it foreign, it was not even legal. For some time there had been a dispute over land between Henry's good friend Lord Grey of Ruthin, an aggressive marcher lord, and Owain Glyn Dŵr of Glyndyfrdwy – the richest native landowner in Wales. Aged about forty, Owain was no mere hill chieftain but a cultivated nobleman who spoke French and English, and had read law at the Inns of Court in London. Through his father he was the representative of the old ruling princes of Powys Fadog, through his mother he was descended from the southern princes of Deheubarth. On 16 September 1400 Owain proclaimed himself Prince of Wales and sacked Ruthin, slaying and burning through the marches into Shropshire before being driven off and taking refuge in the hills.

Early in October the king and Prince Henry led a punitive expedition into Wales which lasted barely more than a week. The thirteen-year-old prince was left at Chester to govern his principality with a council headed by the Earl of Northumberland's son, Henry Percy, known as Harry Hotspur (whom Adam of Usk calls the flower and glory of the chivalry of Christendom), in real charge. No one yet realized just how serious the situation was in Wales. Welsh labourers, and even Welsh undergraduates from Oxford, were going home to fight for Owain, all bringing bows and swords.

Presumably the prince kept Christmas with his father in London. Here he would have seen the most exotic guest ever to spend the feast with the Plantagenets. The Emperor Manuel II Palaeologus of Constantinople had come to beg for help against the Turks, who threatened his pitiful remnant of an empire. He and his suite stayed with King Henry in his palace at Eltham just outside London, being entertained by jousts and games. Adam of Usk tells us; 'This emperor always walked with his men, dressed alike and in one colour, namely white, in long robes cut like tabards.' Adam was deeply moved to see a Roman emperor driven by unbelievers to try to find aid against them from the west. 'What dost thou, ancient glory

15

of Rome?'[3] The future Henry V's desire to go on crusade against the Turks may well have dated from his meeting with Manuel. His father could do nothing for the emperor, apart from giving him £2,000.

England had another problem besides the Welsh – heretics. John Wyclif's doctrines had begun to attract followers. As well as teaching the primacy of scripture and predestination, Wyclif, an Oxford don, had denied transubstantiation, the sacraments, and the authority of pope and cardinals. Archbishop Arundel persuaded the king to take action. In January 1401 Parliament passed the statute *De Heretico Comburendo*; henceforth bishops could hand stubborn heretics to the secular authorities for 'the burning death'. The first burning at the stake of a Lollard (the name given to Wyclif's disciples) took place in March.

In February 1401 the House of Commons warned that full-scale war threatened in Wales. Bards were spreading tales that Owain's coming had been foretold by Merlin. On Good Friday the Welsh seized Conwy Castle. When Hotspur and Prince Henry retook it at the end of May, nine Welshmen were immediately executed as traitors. They were hanged until half-dead, then castrated and disembowelled, their offal being burnt in front of them, before they were beheaded and quartered – presumably the boy prince was a spectator. We know from Adam of Usk that when King Henry led a punitive expedition into North Wales in October the prince witnessed similar butchery at Llandovery. Llywelyn ap Gruffydd Fychan of Caio was executed for deliberately guiding the English the wrong way. Adam also records how during this expedition 'the English invaded those parts [Powys] with a strong power, and utterly laying them waste and ravaging them with fire, famine and sword, left them a desert, not even sparing children or churches, nor the monastery of Strata Florida, wherein the king himself was being lodged, and the church of which and its choir, even up to the high altar, they used as a stable, and pillaged even the patens; and they carried away into England more than a thousand children of both sexes to be their servants'. Little was achieved and Prince Henry had the humiliation of having his horses and tents captured by Glyn Dŵr's men. Father and son withdrew at the end of the month.

On 2 November 1401 Owain Glyn Dŵr unfurled his banner of a golden dragon on a white field, before the walls of Caernarfon. He was accompanied by a great host of Welsh, but the garrison and townsmen sallied forth and drove them off. He nonetheless kept complete control of all the country round about. At the beginning of 1402 he burnt Ruthin and in April took prisoner his old enemy, Lord Grey. By now Owain was sending letters to the King of Scots and to the Wild Irish chieftains, asking them for help against the tyranny of their mortal foes, the Saxons.

The King tried to bolster up his position by impressive dynastic alliances with other royal families. In April 1402 he himself married Joan of Navarre, the widow of Duke John IV of Brittany and sister of King Charles III of Navarre. In July his daughter Blanche married Louis of Bavaria, the son of Rupert, Duke of Bavaria, who had just become King of the Romans. Negotiations were begun for the marriage of Henry's youngest daughter to the young King Eric of Denmark and Sweden, though the wedding did not take place until 1406.

In August 1402 the Scots crossed the border in strength but were routed by the Percies at Homildon Hill. Five earls were captured. In view of his own dismal military record such a victory was an embarrassment to King Henry. He gave orders that the prisoners must on no account be allowed to ransom themselves, depriving the Percies – to whom he owed the then vast sum of £10,000 – of a valuable windfall. They had thought him ungrateful enough before, after all they had done to help him win the crown. Hotspur refused to hand over the most important prisoner, the Earl of Douglas. Henry further angered them by his abandonment of Edmund Mortimer, Hotspur's brother-in-law. In the previous June, Mortimer, an important magnate in the Welsh marches, had been defeated at Pilleth near Knighton by Rhys Gethin, one of Glyn Dŵr's right-hand men, with the loss of 1,100 men. He was taken prisoner and sent back to Owain's lair in the mountains of Snowdonia. The King was far from displeased since it meant that the uncle of Richard II's heir was safely out of the way. (Sir Edmund's own claim to the throne was better than Henry's.) He forebade any attempt to ransom him. When Hotspur proposed doing so, the king shouted 'Traitor!', hit him and half-drew his dagger. There was a reconciliation of a sort – for the time being.

In the autumn of 1402 Owain struck in South Wales, attacking Abergavenny, Caerleon, Usk, Newport and Cardiff. Adam of Usk laments how 'like a second Assyrian, the rod of God's anger, he did deeds of unheard-of cruelty with fire and sword'. King Henry responded by assembling an unusually large force – 100,000 men and more if Adam can be believed – divided into three armies. One

17

was commanded by Prince Henry. Adam says that Glyn Dŵr and 'his poor wretches' hid in their caves and woods. But there was beating rain and hail, even snow. The English suspected that it was work of 'that great magician, damned Glendower'. They believed that he was a necromancer, that he called up an evil spirit and that he had a magic stone, spat up by a raven, which enabled him and his Welshmen to become invisible. On the night of 7 September there was suddenly so much wind and rain that the king's tent was blown down – had he not been sleeping in his armour he would have been killed.[4] The troops began to die from cold and exposure – 'his host was well nigh lost' records Friar Capgrave. By September Henry was back in London having failed for a third time to crush the Welsh. Apart from royal castles and those of the marcher lords, where tiny garrisons hung on grimly, Prince Owain was the effective ruler of Wales. Edmund Mortimer was so disgusted by the king's failure to ransom him that he married Glyn Dŵr's daughter, an alliance which had serious implications. In December he sent a letter to his tenants in Maelienydd announcing that he had joined Owain with 'the object that if King Richard should be alive, he be restored to his crown and, if not, that my honoured nephew who is rightful heir to the said crown shall be King of England, and that the said Owain will have his rights in Wales'.

In March 1403 Prince Henry was appointed the King's Lieutenant of the marches of Wales, making him, at sixteen, commander-in-chief in fact as well as name. On 15 May at Shrewsbury he dictated a report to the Royal Council. He had burnt Owain's houses at Sycharth and Glyndyfrdwy though 'we found not a soul'. Next day he had captured an important Welsh gentleman, one of Owain's chieftains, who offered £500 for his life. 'Howbeit this was not accepted but he had the death, as did divers of his companions.' He had devastated Meirionydd, a fair and well-inhabited land, while there was so little fodder in Powys that he made his men carry oats for their horses. A fortnight later he sent a report from Shrewsbury saying he was so short of money that he had had to sell his jewels. He warned that the Welsh were about to launch a serious offensive while he had had to divert troops to relieve and revictual the castles of Harlech and Aberystwyth. Although stressing that the situation was very grave, he also insisted that 'if the war could but be continued, the rebels were never so like to be destroyed as they are at this present'.

Early in July Owain struck again. Just how dangerous matters

18

were is shown by the postscript added to a letter dated 8 July from the Archdeacon of Hereford, Richard Kingston, to the king:

> And for God's love, my liege lord, thinketh on yourself and your estate or by my troth all is lost, else but ye come yourself with haste all other will follow after. And all on Friday last Caermarthen town is taken and burnt and the castle yolden by Richard Wigmore and the castle Emlyn is yolden and slain of town of Caermarthen more than fifty persons. Written in right great haste on Sunday; and I cry you mercy and put me in your high grace that I write so shortly; for by my troth that I owe to you, it is needful.[5]

However, four days later Glyn Dŵr was defeated seriously enough for him to postpone his invasion of England. This check saved the House of Lancaster from utter ruin. For the Welsh had planned to join forces with those of new, English, allies.

Henry IV's enemies, open and secret, had united against him: the Percies; the men of Cheshire and Shropshire who had always supported Richard II; and Owain and Mortimer. The principal architect of this alliance was Hotspur, abetted by his uncle, the Earl of Worcester, Steward of the Royal Household. Hotspur's first objective was Shrewsbury, where he hoped to capture Prince Henry and join forces with Owain. They would then proclaim that Richard II was still alive and still king, though once Henry IV had been defeated they would place the Earl of March on the throne.

The king first had definite news of the plot when he was at Nottingham on 12 July. Guessing that Hotspur and Worcester would make for Shrewsbury, he marched there at once, covering nearly sixty miles in three days. The prince must have been overjoyed to see him; many of his men had gone over to the enemy, including some from his own household. When Hotspur and Worcester arrived on 20 July they were thunderstruck at seeing the king's banner flying from the walls.

Undaunted, Hotspur chose his ground skilfully, on a hillside known as Hayteley Field; his right flank was protected by the River Severn, his rear by steep ground, his front by dense crops and small ponds. The position, two miles north of the town, was near a hamlet called Berwick where he and his men spent the night. A legend says that on calling for his sword the following morning, Hotspur was told it had been left at Berwick. Badly shaken, he cried, 'We have

19

ploughed our last furrow for a wizard in mine own country foretold that I should die at Berwick!' Yet Henry IV was uneasy too. He offered Worcester humiliatingly good terms, fearing the imminent arrival of the Welsh. 'You are not the rightful heir,' Worcester told him. 'We cannot trust you.'

The battle did not begin until midday. The royal army numbered perhaps 5,000 men, its right wing being commanded by Prince Henry while the vanguard was led by the Earl of Stafford. The king ordered two of his knights to wear royal surcoats so as to resemble him and confuse the enemy. Hotspur had about the same number of troops, among them being a particularly lethal contingent of crack Cheshire archers who wore King Richard's old badge of the White Hart. Henry IV sent his men uphill at his opponents on a dangerously narrow front. The Cheshire bowmen shot down into them at short range, wreaking murderous havoc – according to the chronicler Walsingham men fell on the king's side as fast as leaves fall in autumn after a hoar frost. The Earl of Stafford was killed and some of the royal troops ran for their lives. Prince Henry was himself badly wounded in the face by an arrow. He nevertheless refused to leave the field. The royal standard bearer fell and the king's banner went down. For a moment it looked as though the enemy must win. They had inflicted many casualties. Hotspur's prisoner the Earl of Douglas – who had become his friend and ally – slew both the knights in royal surcoats. Suddenly Hotspur fell, killed 'no man wist of whom'. His men fled, Worcester and Douglas being taken prisoner. At least 1,600 men were killed, many of the 3,000 wounded dying later. Next day, a Sunday, Worcester wept over his nephew's body, before being beheaded on the Monday. Hotspur's corpse was salted and placed in the pillory at Shrewsbury, propped up by two millstones – the head was then taken to York to be stuck up on Micklegate Bar, his quarters being displayed at other cities.

However, Owain was soon raiding again, concentrating on Hereford and Monmouth. The king simply did not have enough money to organize a proper offensive against the Welsh. In the autumn a French expedition arrived to help Owain and in November 1403 French ships attacked Kidwelly Castle from the sea. By the following January, the French were shipping cannon to the siege of Conwy. The Welsh captured Harlech and Aberystwyth in the spring of 1404. The former became Owain's residence, the latter his administrative headquarters. His men went on to take Cardiff, Caerphilly, Usk, Caerleon and Newport. He summoned a Welsh parliament to

Machynlleth. At the end of May ambassadors from '*Owynus, dei gratia, princeps Walliae*' were received at Paris by Charles VI, who presented them with a golden helmet – worn only by sovereigns – for his 'brother'. Next month the Welsh and the French signed a treaty of alliance against 'Henry of Lancaster'.

Prince Henry was given the Duke of York (Rutland) as his lieutenant in South Wales and the Earl of Arundel as his lieutenant in the north. His Welsh foes were heroic but scarcely formidable; although their great gentlemen went armed like English men-at-arms, most were bowmen or spearmen, even knifemen. The women perpetrated barbaric atrocities on the English dead and wounded. (After their victory at Pilleth in 1402, in the words of Friar Capgrave, 'full shamefully the Welshwomen cut off [English] men's members and put them in their mouths that were dead'.)[5] Henry's troops saw the 'Welch doggis' in the way their descendants would one day see Red Indians or Zulus.

Reporting to his father in June 1404 the prince says that the Welsh are preparing to attack Herefordshire and promises, 'I will do all that in me lies to withstand the rebels and preserve the English land.' The same day he wrote to the Council warning that if it cannot provide him with money; 'We must depart with shame and mischief and the country will be undone, which God forbid.' Winter postponed the threat. In the following March he reports how, hearing that 8,000 Welshmen were attacking Grosmont, he had sent Lord Talbot against them with a small force. 'Yet it is known that victory is not in the multitude of the people but in the power of God and well was this shown.' Talbot's men had slain between 800 and 1,000. In May at Pwll Melyn near Usk the English killed a further 1,500 including Glyn Dŵr's brother, Tudur, and took many prisoners, among them Owain's son, Gruffydd; the latter was sent to the Tower of London – 300 prisoners of lesser birth were beheaded on the spot. A fortnight later Prince Henry's men were again victorious, capturing the Welsh chancellor, Dr Gruffydd Yonge.

In February 1405 the governess of the Earl of March and his brother, Lady Despenser – whose husband had lost his life in the conspiracy of 1400 – suddenly fled from Windsor with the boys. She intended to join their uncle, Mortimer, and Owain, who were going to proclaim March as king. Henry IV pursued her in person, catching her at Cheltenham a week later. When questioned she accused her brother-in-law the Duke of York of plotting to kill Henry. York was sent to the Tower but nothing could be proved and

21

he had to be released. The two March boys were guarded more closely than ever.

Hotspur's father, Northumberland, old but still very dangerous, had contacted Glyn Dŵr and Mortimer. In February 1405 their envoys signed a triple indenture at Bangor to divide England among them. Northumberland would have England north of the Trent, the midland counties of Leicestershire, Northamptonshire and Warwickshire, and Norfolk; besides Wales, Owain was to have all lands west of the Severn and south of the Mersey; Mortimer would have southern England.

Northumberland's allies in the North were the Earl Marshal (Lord Mowbray), Lord Bardolf, Lord Clifford and Archbishop Scrope of York. A manifesto was posted all over York, complaining of burdens on the clergy, ruin facing the nobility and unbearable taxes on gentry and commons. The archbishop and his friends gathered a small force at Shipton Moor outside York. The Earl of Westmorland held them at bay and then tricked Scrope and Mowbray with a false parley, arresting them on 29 May. Despite protests from Archbishop Arundel and Lord Chief Justice Gascoigne, King Henry beheaded not only Mowbray but Scrope as well. Told that he would lose his head, the latter commented 'I shall die for the laws and good rule of England'. He was made to ride to his execution on a mare, his head facing the tail in token of ignominy. The *Brut* says that the king was immediately smitten by leprosy, while miracles began to be worked at the archbishop's tomb. Only the papal schism saved the king from excommunication. Northumberland and Bardolf fled to Scotland before joining Owain.

However, the rising had lost Henry IV his chance to crush the Welsh. In August 1405 Marshal Jean de Rieux with 800 men-at-arms, 600 crossbowmen, and 1,200 light horse landed at Milford Haven. A Franco-Welsh army then marched into England to within eight miles of Worcester. But the king was inside the city with a strong force and they withdrew. The French went home the following spring.

There was a crisis of confidence in King Henry throughout the entire country. He had failed to crush the Welsh, while over the sea Bordeaux was in constant danger. French and Castilian privateers put every English seaman in fear for his life. The king spent too much on his household, squandered Crown revenues and defaulted on loans. The Parliament of 1406, which sat for no less than 139 days between March and December (including the Commons' first all-

22

night sitting), forced him to appoint a council to oversee financial policy in general and royal household expenditure in particular. The prince, although absent in Wales, was its nominal head while the Speaker of the House of Commons, Sir John Tiptoft, MP for Huntingdonshire, was made Treasurer of the Royal Household.

Tiptoft, who became Treasurer of England the following year, was to play an important part in Prince Henry's life. He had joined Bolingbroke's household as a young man and was with him on the march from Ravenspur. He had become a Knight of the Royal Household by 1403, the year in which he entered Parliament. Against his will but much to the king's relief he was elected Speaker in 1406. He proved a consummate diplomat as well as an excellent administrator, retaining the confidence of both Henry and the Commons.[7]

Prince Henry returned home in April 1406 just before the Welsh received their heaviest defeat so far, losing several thousand men. In June Lord Powys defeated Northumberland and Bardolf, who fled to France. By the end of the year Owain was on the defensive. In a policy which combined conciliation and savagery, Prince Henry lured men away from Owain with offers of a pardon and concentrated on re-taking castles.

Aberystwyth had been Owain's headquarters since its capture in 1404. Prince Henry besieged the castle with 600 men-at-arms and 1,800 archers in June 1407. Six big cannon were shipped by sea from Bristol while others were brought by road – such as Henry IV's favourite, the 'Kinge's Gonne', weighing four-and-a-half tons. This was brought from Nottingham accompanied by 971 pounds of saltpetre, 303 pounds of sulphur and 538 pounds of made-up gunpowder. Vast amounts of gunstones, bow staves, bowstrings and arrows were assembled at Hereford. However, the castle was defended by the redoubtable Rhys the Black, Owain's ablest lieutenant, and the English made slow progress, two of their biggest guns blowing up. In September Rhys agreed to surrender if not relieved by All Saints' Day (1 November) but Owain, threatening to behead him, slipped briefly into Aberystwyth with reinforcements. The besiegers had to starve the castle into surrender. They were not helped by a dreadful winter, the worst in living memory, or by the dense woods.

Yet Anglesey, the granary of North Wales, had been subdued in 1406–7. In consequence not only was Aberystwyth doomed but Owain and his men were beginning to starve in their Snowdonian

23

fastness. Adam of Usk crowned his bizarre career (prebendary in Wales, successful lawyer in London, convicted horse-thief, banished man, papal chaplain in Rome, down-and-out in Flanders) by joining them as a double-agent. He gives us some idea of the life they led – 'sorely tormented with many and great perils of death and capture and false brethren, and hunger and thirst, and passing many nights without sleep for fear of the attacks of foes'.

Although by now in his late sixties Northumberland made a last attempt to raise England against the House of Lancaster. During the terrible winter of 1407–8 he and Lord Bardolf crossed the frozen Tweed but on 19 February their little army – mainly Percy tenants – was routed by the Sheriff of Yorkshire in the snow at Bramham Moor near Tadcaster. The Earl was killed and Bardolf died of his wounds the same night. It meant that Henry IV was at last secure on his throne. The supporters of Richard II and the Earl of March had been broken or driven underground, the Percies were destroyed and the tide was turning against the Welsh. The heir to the Scots throne, the future James I, had been intercepted on his way to France and would spend the next eighteen years in English captivity – King Henry joked that he himself could teach him French. And the French no longer had time to help the Welsh.

In France a duchy was not just a title as in England (save for Lancaster) but a huge concentration of rich estates whose dukes commanded large armies of vassals. The Dukes of Burgundy and Orleans had long disputed which of them was to control the poor mad king. Finally John of Burgundy had Louis of Orleans hacked to death one dark November evening in Paris, in the rue Vieille-du-Temp. The body was left lying in the gutter, its hands cut off to stop necromancers using it to raise the Devil. Louis's successor Charles (the poet duke) had married as his first wife Richard II's widow Isabel and wanted war with England; by contrast the Burgundians wanted peace since war would damage Flemish trade. When Isabel died in 1409 Charles married the daughter of Bernard, Count of Armagnac, who was a hardbitten southern nobleman of such forceful personality that the Orleanists were rechristened Armagnacs. John of Burgundy was a small, ugly man, cynical and treacherous. Besides his duchy he ruled the county of Flanders and held court at his two capitals of Dijon and Brussels with regal pomp. His two great blocks of territory (a vast area of eastern France and what is today Belgium and Holland) were separate; if he could secure the lands between, his power would enormously increase. The squabbles of Burgundians and Armagnacs grew bitterer and bloodier every day.

Meanwhile Prince Henry presided over Owain's final destruction. In the summer of 1408 Aberystwyth was at last starved into surrender, Rhys the Black marching forlornly into the hills. Early in 1409 Harlech too surrendered, Glyn Dŵr's entire family save for one son being taken prisoner; Sir Edmund Mortimer had 'brought his days of sorrow' to an end in the castle, dying during the siege. Henceforward Henry watched Welsh affairs from afar. Owain launched a last campaign in 1410 but his men were cut to pieces, his principal lieutenants including Rhys the Black being captured – to be hanged, drawn and quartered immediately. Glyn Dŵr roamed the mountains with an armed band for another three years. No one knows where or when he died.

Henry V's Welsh wars prepared him for the conquest of France. He had learnt siegecraft and gunnery (while agreeing with his father that it was cheaper to defend a castle than to capture one). He had also learnt how to control large areas of conquered territory by carefully sited small garrisons – using systematic terror, artificially induced famine and calculated conciliation to hold down the hostile population. He had employed Edward I's coastal fortresses as they had been during the thirteenth-century conquest of Wales; as strong-points reinforced and revictualled by ship, from whence to rush in fresh troops to isolated garrisons and launch surprise attacks. One day he would use France's inland waterways in the same fashion.

He now knew how to deploy very limited manpower to maximum effect. At Harlech five Englishmen and sixteen Welshmen had held the castle against Glyn Dŵr for several years while at one stage only twenty-eight men had defended the town and castle of Caernarfon. He understood how to combine the lethal fire-power of his bowmen in a defensive position with mobility, by giving them horses; carrying their own fodder, if necessary, they could cover long distances very fast, dismounting to shoot when in action.

There had been another crucial influence, Vegetius's *De Re Militari* which for medieval commanders was the equivalent of a modern staff manual. Because of its fourth-century author's preoccupation with infantry it had become especially popular in England after foot soldiers had learnt how to rout cavalry with arrow fire. There were several translations; some manuscripts which have survived were folded for carrying in the pocket on campaign. The section most read was the third, dealing with strategy and tactics, which we may be sure that Henry had studied closely. He noted Vegetius's advocacy of the use of hunger to destroy the enemy.

England had been horrified by the prospect of an independent Wales, and recognized that the war had been won by the prince. Here at last was the good governance promised by the king. Like so many gifted heirs, Henry was impatient for the power which he knew he was much better fitted to use than his ailing father.

III

'He Would Usurp the Crown'

'. . . the king suspected that he would usurp the crown, he being alive, which suspicious jealousy was occasion that he in part withdrew his affection and singular love from the prince.'

The First English Life of King Henry the Fifth

'Fair son, how can you have any right to it when I myself have none, as you know very well?'

Enguerrand de Monstrelet, *Les Chroniques*

Henry IV thought his malady a divine judgement on him for killing Archbishop Scrope (who had become known in Yorkshire as 'St Richard'). Many of his subjects thought the same. 'The king after that time lost the beauty of his face,' says Friar Capgrave. 'For as the common opinion went, from that time until his death he was a leper, and ever fouler and fouler.'[1] His face and hands were covered with huge pustules, 'great pushes like teats' and if the statue at York Minster (on a screen begun in 1425) is a true likeness, his nose spread horribly. The disease was conceivably venereal or perhaps tubercular gangrene, or it may have been some sort of embolism. His first attack, which made him scream that he was on fire, cleared up quickly enough, but the disease returned at intervals, accompanied by other afflictions. His mind was affected besides his body, making it impossible for him to govern. His court physician, Master Malvern, could do little for him so two Jewish specialists were brought from Italy, Messers Pietro di Alcobasse and Davido di Nigarello, but were no more effective. In 1408 he had a stroke and for some hours was thought to be dead.

27

When incapacitated by ill health, as he was to be sporadically for the rest of his reign, he tried to rule through his friend Archbishop Arundel. However, the archbishop was ousted at the end of 1409, resigning as chancellor. Prince Henry and the Beauforts – his old tutor, Bishop Beaufort, and Sir Thomas Beaufort, now Admiral of England, were undoubtedly responsible for Arundel's eclipse.

The Beauforts were an extraordinary phenomenon, as able and energetic as they were ambitious. Their mother, Catherine Roelt, had been employed as a governess by John of Gaunt's first duchess and they were all born when she was their father's mistress, while his second duchess was still alive. They were legitimized retrospectively by the pope and King Richard only after Gaunt made Catherine his third wife in 1396. When legitimization was bestowed on them by their half-brother, Henry IV, the words *'excepting the royal dignity'* were added to the patent on Arundel's advice. Their close relationship in blood to the king, combined with their disqualification from any claim to the crown, made them an obvious counterweight to the great territorial magnates and the princes of the House of York. John Beaufort, Earl of Somerset, was the eldest but died in 1410, his widow marrying Prince Thomas, the king's second son. Henry Beaufort, the next brother, had been born in 1375. A brilliant lawyer (both civil and canon), after studying at Aachen he became Bishop of Lincoln in 1398 and of Winchester in 1404. He was also a financier of genius, who quickly created a vast personal fortune out of his ecclesiastical revenues. His lifestyle was entirely secular, that of a great nobleman rather than a prelate, and he kept a mistress. Haughty and hot-tempered, he had a knack of making enemies, among them being Archbishop Arundel (who may well have disliked him for begetting a bastard on an Arundel niece). Thomas Beaufort, the third brother, who was made Earl of Dorset in 1412 – and later Duke of Exeter – was an unfailingly efficient and dependable soldier, in later years one of Henry's most valued commanders. He had first fought at his young cousin's side in Wales in 1405, a year during which he had played a key part in Archbishop Scrope's murder. His wife was one of the Nevilles of Hornby and a distant kinswoman of his powerful brother-in-law, the Earl of Westmorland, a firm ally of the Beauforts.

Prince Henry dominated the Council after Arundel's departure, packing it with his most trusted friends – the Beauforts, the Earls of Arundel and Warwick, Lords Burnell and Scrope. Of these the latter is especially interesting, as the only man whose measure was never taken by the prince.

Henry, third Lord Scrope of Masham, was a brilliant and attractive figure. Born in 1373 he was very rich and notably blue-blooded; in 1387 the Court of Chivalry had obsequiously described the Scropes as '*graundes gentilhommes et de noblez*' ever since the Norman Conquest. A kinsman of the archbishop, he had shrewdly disassociated himself from the rising of 1405, being rewarded with the manors of Thirsk and Hovingham. He and his brother-in-law, Lord Fitzhugh, were deeply interested in Christian mysticism and are known to have read jointly Richard Rolle of Hampole's *Fire of Love*. He spent great sums on his private chapel, whose vestments included over ninety copes, and owned eighty-three books, which was exceptional for a private secular library at that time. The prince was much impressed by 'my kind lord of Masham', sometimes inviting him to sleep in his bed. Scrope had escorted the Lady Philippa, Henry's sister, to Sweden in 1406 when she married King Eric XIII. The prince appointed this gifted, complex and enigmatic Yorkshireman from the Dales to be Treasurer of the Royal Household.[2] He was so successful that Archbishop Arundel was to retain him when he regained power.

Scrope soon informed the Council that running the country would not be easy. In consequence of perennial deficits the Crown's debts were huge. He estimated that the basic deficit for the year ahead was going to be over £16,000, without allowing for salaries. The prince had to extract more money from the Commons. After much decorous if heated wrangling he succeeded in convincing them that his priority really was 'good governance' and they granted it.

He must have personally approved the Council's decision to devalue the currency, providing extra revenue. At this date there was an endemic bullion crisis in Europe, a shortage of silver as well as gold. In 1410 the noble (the principal gold coin in circulation) was reduced in weight by twelve grains and the silver penny by three, other denominations being adjusted proportionately. The reform's effectiveness was demonstrated by the English coinage keeping these weights for over half a century. However, it can scarcely have been a popular measure.

The Commons were extremely nervous about the safety of the fortress and port of Calais, which since 1347 had been England's military and commercial bridgehead in northern France, dominated by English settlers. In 1410 Prince Henry appointed himself Captain of Calais. He found the garrison's pay chronically in arrears, the government owing over £9,000, and the men mutinous. Significantly, he nonetheless had estimates drawn up for the cost of maintaining Calais in time of war.

Henry showed both subtlety and rock-like self-confidence in his treatment of the man who was potentially the most dangerous in the realm, the Earl of March. So fearful had the king been of the very existence of Richard II's rightful heir that he always kept him in custody. Instead the prince freed the seventeen-year-old earl, attaching him to his own household in much the same way that he himself had once been attached to Richard II's – his father was too ill to demur. This ostensibly conciliatory approach, very carefully calculated, was to appear in Henry's dealings with other magnates when he ascended the throne.

By now the Duke of Burgundy was in full control of Paris where the lesser bourgeoisie and the academics, together with the mob, were his firm supporters. (His opponents were the wealthy bourgeois and high officials, together with the retainers and clients of the other princes of the Blood.) Duke John persuaded the Sorbonne to condemn posthumously the late Louis of Orleans as a tyrant, so that he could obtain a pardon from the king on the grounds that the assassination had been tyrannicide and not murder and that he was therefore guiltless. He endeared himself to the Parisians by lavishing gifts on the guilds (in particular that of the butchers who became his most bloodthirsty henchmen), by reducing taxes imposed by Armagnacs, and by executing several tax collectors. It was known that the Count of Armagnac was plotting to evict him from the capital at the point of the sword. Duke John now offered the hand of his daughter to Henry, together with four Flemish ports and future help in conquering Normandy, in return for immediate military assistance. In October 1411 the Earl of Arundel led 800 men-at-arms and 2,000 archers down from Calais to Paris, fighting side by side with the Burgundians to help them drive the blockading Armagnacs from their strong points at the bridge of St Cloud and St Denis. Such intervention did not please everyone in England.

It pleased even fewer people in France. Apart from the Duke of Burgundy, the French did not welcome the reappearance of the English in their midst. Crécy, Poitiers and the many raids during which 'the ancient enemy' from over the Channel had killed, raped, looted and burnt and which had ceased only a quarter of a century

30

before, were not forgotten. Moreover Arundel was a peculiarly aggressive and unpleasant figure. In his *Chronique de Charles VI* Jean Juvénal des Ursins, Bishop and Count of Beauvais, tells us that the English were so much disliked that it was difficult for them to find billets at Paris; decades later, in a letter of 1440, he cited with some bitterness the earl's expedition as the beginning of France's anarchy and devastation.[3] It was probably during this year of 1411 that one of King Charles's secretaries, Jean de Montreuil, wrote in his address *A tout la chevalerie de France*:

> When I see that they [the English] want to do nothing save lay waste and destroy this realm, from whom may God preserve it, and how they wage war to the death on all their neighbours, I hold them in such abomination and hatred that I love those who hate them and hate those who love them.[4]

Prince Henry's policies differed from his father's in many ways. He was opposed by what some historians have called a 'king's party' – which may well have been how contemporaries saw it. The opposition included not only old Archbishop Arundel and the king's brother-in-law, the Earl of Westmorland (despite his Beaufort loyalties), but Henry's younger brother, Thomas of Lancaster. Prince Thomas had quarrelled with the Beauforts over the inheritance of his wife, their brother's widow. A year younger than Henry, the future Duke of Clarence had been the king's Lieutenant in Ireland. Very much a soldier, with a passion for heraldry and a bastard son whom he cherished, he was a hot-tempered opponent. During conscious moments the king feared that the brothers might fall out after his death – he warned Henry, 'I fear that he, through his high mind, will make some high enterprise against thee.'

In November 1411 Henry IV recovered, dismissing Beaufort and reappointing Arundel as chancellor. Prince Thomas took his brother's place on the Council. The Prince of Wales and his friends had infuriated the king by suggesting that he might consider abdication.

There were further negotiations with the Burgundians and Armagnacs. Prince Henry realized that the former had most to offer. But in March 1412 the Armagnacs offered Aquitaine as it had been at its greatest extent under the Black Prince. In August Prince Thomas – recently created Duke of Clarence – together with his cousin, the Duke of York, led an expeditionary force of 800 men-at-

31

arms and 300 archers across the Channel to aid the Armagnacs. Landing in Normandy they marched down to Blois, killing, burning and looting. At Blois, however, they were informed that the Armagnacs had given in to the Burgundians and that their 'help' was no longer required – not even by the Duke of Burgundy. 'The Duke of Clarence and the English did innumerable evils, as many as any enemies could do, and said they would not leave the realm until they had received satisfaction and been paid their wages,' Jean Juvénal records. They extorted heavy compensation, amounting to £35,000 in all, of which a third was in jewellery. Clarence obtained 40,000 gold crowns and a jewelled cross worth 15,000 crowns; the Duke of York 5,000 crowns and a cross valued at 40,000 crowns. Lesser magnates shared in the booty, receiving similar pay-offs though on a smaller scale. They then marched down to Bordeaux, killing, burning and looting as before, and also kidnapping children whenever they could for sale as servants in England. Their exploits and their plunder aroused interest and admiration at home. Yet Prince Henry had been strongly opposed to the expedition because it meant abandoning the Burgundians, whose alliance he considered of far more strategic value than anything which the Armagnacs could offer.

The prince's opposition did not please his father, who suspected he was planning to depose him. He may have contemplated rebellion but he was far too sensible to give way to the temptation. Nevertheless he was deprived of any share in government for the rest of the reign. In June 1412 he came to London with a whole host of supporters to put his views, after which he went on a sort of progress through England. The king feared he was plotting a *coup d'état*. At Coventry on 17 June the prince publicly proclaimed his innocence of any such intention, announcing that he was assembling troops purely to help his father conquer Aquitaine. He then came down to London accompanied by his men. There was a formal reconciliation between Henry IV and his heir, which satisfied neither. In September, after being accused of stealing the Calais garrison's pay, he again came to London with a large armed following. He went straight to his father, unaccompanied, and after a tearful exchange they were reconciled for a second time.[5]

Henry IV had reason to fear for his crown. He had deposed Richard with the promise that he would save the country from inept government but by now he was incapacitated. Despite inadequate revenue and widespread disorder the prince was justifiably confident

32

that he could make the system work and give the country better administration and fairer justice.

Henry of Monmouth's precocious years of soldiering and politics had not prevented him from enjoying himself like other young men. Too many chroniclers speak of his dissipation for the traditional stories of a wild youth to be dismissed out of hand. The otherwise hagiographic *Gesta* admits that, 'Passing the bounds of modesty, he was the fervent soldier of Venus as well as of Mars; youthlike he was fired by her torches.'[6] The *First English Life* says 'he exercised meanly the feats of Venus' – using 'meanly' in the sense of 'moderately'.[7] Yet there is no record of any bastards. It may be relevant that his three brothers were curiously infertile in their marriages, only Thomas, the Duke of Clarence, begetting even a natural child.

Prince Henry is supposed to have had other amusements, including the odd pastime of disguising himself and then beating up and robbing his own household officials though there is no mention of this before the sixteenth century. He certainly spent a good deal of time in London where he had a great town house, once the Black Prince's – Coldharbour, near London Bridge, next to the church of All Hallows the Less. We know that his brothers, Thomas and Humphrey, were involved in a midnight brawl at a tavern in Eastcheap where they were drinking on 23 June 1410 and the uproar was such that the mayor and sheriffs had to be called to restore order; Thomas was involved in a similar disturbance the following year. Yet there is no evidence that Henry was ever Falstaff's 'good shallow young fellow'. And whatever vicious friends the prince may have had, Falstaff was not among them. (The real-life Falstaff, Sir John Fastolf, was a hardbitten and very professional soldier with no time for frivolity.) He may have enjoyed the company of Sir John Oldcastle, who on one occasion arranged a wrestling match for him, but Sir John was scarcely famed for vice. Nevertheless, so distinguished a historian as McFarlane accepts the tales of his wildness, commenting that when he became king the 'lawless and high-spirited youth became, as it were overnight, a bigot and a disciplinarian'.[8]

One may ask from where did Shakespeare derive his portrait of Henry. It has long been known that his principal source was Holinshed's *Chronicles*, which in turn was largely based on Edward Hall's *Union of the two noble and illustre families of Lancaster and York* of 1548 and, through a copy in the possession of John Stow the antiquary, on a translation of Tito Livio's official biography of 1437.

33

Henry's seal as Prince of Wales

(This translation, which includes details supplied by the family of the Earl of Ormonde who was with Henry in France, is *The First English Life*.) Shakespeare accepted much of the traditional portrait of a hero king yet his genius was too penetrating not to discern the megalomania and cruelty at which he hints once or twice.

There is evidence that Henry was a bigot even as Prince of Wales. Although it dates only from the sixteenth century it derives from an authentic Lollard tradition. We know from Foxe's *Booke of Martyrs* that the prince played an active role in suppressing heresy. In 1409 he personally superintended the burning of a Lollard tailor, John Badby, who had denied transubstantiation, saying that the consecrated Host was worse than a toad or a spider. When Badby began to scream, Henry had him pulled half-dead out of the flaming barrel in which he was being burnt and offered him a pension if he would recant. The man refused whereupon the prince had him put back in the barrel.[9]

King Henry IV died on 20 March 1413 in a room known as the 'Jerusalem Chamber' in the abbot's lodging at Westminster. The chronicler John Capgrave tells us that the royal confessor John Tille begged Henry to repent of his killing Archbishop Scrope and of his usurping the throne. The king answered that he had been absolved by the pope of the archbishop's murder, but that his son would never let him undo the usurpation. Even Tito Livio says that a few months before he died Henry IV admitted to his son 'I sore repent me that ever I charged myself with the crown of this realm'. Enguerrand de

34

Monstrelet relates how as the king lay on his deathbed the prince removed the crown from a table beside him but that he rallied and called for it. The dying man then asked his son what right he thought he had to it, since he himself had none. Prince Henry replied, 'As you have kept it by the sword, so will I keep it while my life lasts.'

IV

'No Lordship'

'. . . you have no lordship, not even to the kingdom of England, which belongs to the true heirs of the late king Richard.'

Archbishop Boisratier to Henry V

'John [Oldcastle] purposed to have slain the king and his lords at Eltham, that is to say, on Twelfth Night in the evening.'

A Chronicle of London

Henry V was such a successful king that it is hard to appreciate how at the start of his reign he was far from secure. Two months after his accession a poster nailed to the door of Westminster Abbey claimed that Richard II was alive in Scotland. It had been written by John Whitelock, a yeoman who had taken sanctuary in the abbey with three accomplices after spreading the story all over London. Richard II may have been safely dead but the Earl of March was unquestionably still alive and no longer a minor. Apart from its own household men, few people at this time felt a natural loyalty to the House of Lancaster.

He took no chances with Gruffydd ap Owain (Glyn Dŵr's son), Murdoch, Earl of Fife (the Regent of Scotland's son) and James, King of Scots. One of his first acts as king was to recommit these three to the custody of the Constable of the Tower of London. Although lodged comfortably enough at Windsor and Kenilworth as well as the Tower – then a royal palace besides being a fortress and often a scene of court life – it is clear they were under constant surveillance. Gruffydd was to disappear into obscurity while Murdoch was ransomed by his father for the vast sum of £16,000.

The King of Scots was not so lucky. He had already been a prisoner for seven years, since the age of eleven. He had no hope of release so long as Henry lived, even though the English might go through the motions of negotiating, and was not freed until 1423, a year after the king's death, having by then spent eighteen years as a prisoner of the English. Later he wrote poignantly how much he had envied birds and beasts, fishes of the sea, in their freedom during his 'deadly life full of pain and penance' and that he had been 'despairing of all joy and remedy'. When he did return to Scotland he proved a ruler of outstanding ability – and a strong Scotland was the last thing Henry wanted. The Scots were already traditional allies of the French in their 'auld alliance' and he was determined to use every means in his power to prevent them from going to the assistance of his prey across the Channel. He had no qualms about inflicting 'pain and penance' on King James.

Henry was crowned on Passion Sunday (9 April) by Archbishop Arundel, in the midst of a blizzard. 'On the same day,' records Adam of Usk, 'an exceeding fierce and unwonted storm fell upon the hill country of the realm, and smothered men and beasts and home-steads, and drowned out the valleys and the marshes in marvellous wise, with losses and perils to men beyond measure.' An eyewitness of the coronation told the Monk of St Denis that a large number of those present in the abbey thought that March should have been crowned instead, and that civil war seemed likely.[1] It was noticed that during the ceremony the king seemed oddly gloomy and that he ate nothing at the coronation banquet. It was rumoured that he did not eat for three days afterwards.[2] The inference is that he had an uneasy conscience, as someone who in his heart admitted to himself that he was an usurper.

These rumours are of vital importance for any understanding of Henry V's psychology and of his basic motives, of what really drove him. He must have been only too well aware that if March did not have supporters who were prepared to rise for him in armed revolt, and that if there was not much popular interest in the earl himself, there were nonetheless many who acknowledged privately that a glaring injustice had been done in depriving the rightful heir to the throne of his inheritance. During Richard II's reign the March claim to the succession had been recognized publicly not once but twice by Parliament, as vested in the person of the earl and, previously, of his father. And recognition by Parliament had played a key part in the House of Lancaster's usurpation. If ever Henry betrayed any hint of uneasiness, of self-questioning, it was now, during his coronation – and perhaps also on his deathbed. His insecurity has not received sufficient attention from historians.

Nevertheless from the very beginning of his reign Henry displayed extraordinary self-confidence in governing and at once began to apply the policy of carefully calculated conciliation which he had developed in Wales. The Earls of Huntingdon, Oxford and Salisbury – sons of the conspirators of 1400 – had their family estates restored, while steps were taken to persuade Hotspur's son to come home from Scotland and inherit his grandfather Northumberland's earldom. Lord Mowbray, brother of the rebel magnate who had perished with Archbishop Scrope in 1405, was invested as hereditary Earl Marshal of England, and permission was given to make votive offerings at the archbishop's shrine in York Minster. The brother and heir of the slippery Duke of York was created Earl of Cambridge. Richard II's body was brought from its obscure resting place and re-interred in the magnificent tomb he had had made for himself at Westminster Abbey. The gesture stressed that, whatever strange tales might come out of Scotland, Richard was dead.

Archbishop Arundel was replaced as chancellor by Bishop Beaufort. The old archbishop's nephew, the Earl of Arundel, became treasurer. Contrary to the late king's fears there was no trouble from the Duke of Clarence – now the heir to the throne – though to some extent the new monarch cut him down to size by creating their two younger brothers, John and Humphrey, Dukes of Bedford and of Gloucester.

By all accounts Henry V was already impressive at twenty-five – tall, well built and handsome. If the painting in the National Portrait Gallery (a sixteenth-century copy) is a true likeness, he had a florid, clean-shaven face with a high forehead, a long and commanding nose, full red lips, hazel eyes and auburn hair cut in a pudding basin crop – the fashionable military haircut of the day. This may well have been how he looked before ceaseless campaigning aged him prematurely and before he grew his beard. The contemporary sources also agree that he was unusually fit and muscular, wearing his armour 'like a light cloak' and, allegedly, able to run down a deer. However, according to the French astrologer Jean Fusoris, who was presented to him in the summer of 1415, despite a lordly manner and noble bearing he looked more like a prelate than a soldier. Complex, if dynamic and vital, reserved and secretive, icily cold, with complete self-control, he was someone very difficult to know and understand.

He said little and listened much. He both wrote and spoke Latin as well as French and English, and had probably acquired some knowledge of Welsh. He possessed a large library to which he was always adding, reading avidly; his books included histories of the Crusades, treatises on hunting, devotional treatises and such contemporary works as Chaucer's *Troilus and Criseyde*, Lydgate's *Life of Our Lady* and Hoccleve's *De Regimine Principum* – the last two dedicated to him as the patron of both authors. According to Tito Livio, 'he delighted in songs and musical instruments.'[3]

Henry was almost obsessively conventional and orthodox. 'Every age has its own mentality', if Jung is to be believed, and the king's seems to have been wholly in tune with that of the first half of the fifteenth century. There was nothing eccentric about him save for his dynamism. He appears to have subscribed wholeheartedly to the fashionable cult of pessimism. 'At the close of the Middle Ages, a sombre melancholy weighs on people's souls,' says Johan Huizinga. 'All that we know of the moral state of the nobles points to a sentimental need of enrobing their souls with the garb of woe.' Huizinga emphasises that 'all aristocratic life in the latter Middle Ages is a wholesale attempt to act the vision of a dream', explaining that 'the passionate and violent soul of the age, always vacillating between tearful piety and frigid cruelty . . . could not dispense with the severest rules and the strictest formalism'. Such attitudes were displayed by the king throughout his reign. When he lay dying and claimed that, had he lived, he would have gone on to recapture Jerusalem he was not indulging in a personal flight of fancy but doing no more than express a duty acknowledged by every contemporary western monarch.[4] On every formal occasion he made use of the language and forms of chivalry, enlisting symbolism to enhance their dignity. Commenting on his death the dauphinist Jean Juvénal des Ursins, who was often hostile towards him, noted that Henry dispensed the same justice to poor folk as to great. The king's justice for humble people (to whom he and his campaigns had brought so much misery) derived from a chivalrous belief, at that time much in vogue, that it was a knight's duty to protect the weak. This, rather than all the wearisome exhortations in Lydgate's and Hoccleve's doggerel, also reinforced his genuine conviction that a ruler must provide 'good governaunce'. But when all is said and done, Henry must remain as much of an enigma to historians as he was to contemporaries. The most one can say with confidence about him is that friends and foes admired and feared him, and that they did not love him. The sole qualities with which the chroniclers credit him are military skill, strict and indeed harsh justice, and ostentatious piety.[5]

His religious experience seems to have been conventional in the extreme. He possessed the fashionable respect for Carthusian monks, though he did not share Lord Scrope's taste for mystical literature. He was constantly going on pilgrimage to the shrines of wonder-working saints and had the 'mechanistic' religion of his period to a very uncomplicated degree. He heard several Masses a day, recited the psalms of the little office, and made a point of not allowing himself to be interrupted when at prayer. As soon as his father died and he was king, the *First Life* informs us that Henry:

> called to him a virtuous monk of holy conversation, to whom he confessed himself of all his offences, trespasses and insolencies of times past. And in all things at that time he reformed and amended his life and manners. So after the decease of his father was never no youth nor wildness that might have any place in him, but all his acts were suddenly changed into gravity and discretion.[6]

The same admiring source also says that 'from the death of the Kinge his Father until the marriage of himself he neuer had knowledge carnally of weomen'.

Indeed what struck observers most about Henry was his piety. Chroniclers are unanimous in agreeing that he had some sort of religious conversion on ascending the throne, as a result of which he dismissed his former boon companions. Some historians (like Edouard Perroy) may consider him a hypocrite yet his God was clearly very real to him. Nevertheless his beliefs must seem very strange and alien, even to the most traditionally minded twentieth-century Catholic. He had a fervent devotion for the undeniably eccentric St John of Bridlington – the canonization was purely local – a wonder-working Yorkshire holy man who had died as recently as 1379 and possessed a reputation for curing physical deformities besides casting out evil spirits; he was also said to have walked on the water. Henry's spiritual life had some faintly sinister undertones, what the late E. F. Jacob terms 'his dark superstitious vein'.[7] No doubt the king was normal enough in refusing to let even the greatest in the land interrupt him when he was hearing Mass, in his constant visits to shrines, and in consulting hermits. Yet he also had a strong and well-attested belief in demons and in witchcraft.

It may be that Henry's dark side was evident in his choice of confessors. He apparently favoured a combination of distinguished intellect and fanatical orthodoxy. John of Gaunt had begun a Lancastrian tradition of taking Carmelite friars instead of Dominicans as confessors and ambassadors, roles which they performed for the House of Lancaster for over a century. The first spiritual adviser whom the king appointed after his accession was the learned provincial of the 'white friars', Steven Patrington, who had been one of Wyclif's original opponents at Oxford. However, he was seldom available after 1415 when he was made Bishop of St David's.

Patrington was succeeded as Henry's confessor by the next Carmelite provincial, Thomas Netter, who in some ways seems to have stepped from the pages of a Gothick novel. Netter (sometimes called Walden, from having been born at Saffron Walden) was obsessed by hatred of Lollardy; his own order called him 'the hammer of heretics', 'the swiftest fire that ever smote the trunk of heresy'. He had co-operated with Friar Patrington in writing *Fasciculi zizaniorum Magistri Joannis Wyclif,* in its day considered to be a mighty work of refutation, and he later produced a mammoth compilation which defended the Catholic faith against proto-Protestant heresies. Almost as soon as the king had ascended the throne Friar Netter preached a sermon at Paul's Cross accusing him of being lukewarm in persecuting Lollardy. Perhaps revealingly, his rebuke inspired the reverse of resentment. Shortly after, Henry announced that he was raising the standard of the church, as heir of 'Duke Moses, who slew the Egyptian that he might deliver Israel', since it was well known that certain priests were profaning the word of God, sowing discord with the pestilential seed of Lollardy. He quickly came to esteem Friar Netter.

This earlier, English, Torquemada had been at Badby's trial and burning in 1410. He claimed that he had seen a spider running across the heretic's face as he burnt, trying to get into his mouth, a creature so large and horrible that several men were needed to beat it off.[8] That the king had such confidence in Netter tells us a good deal about him.

Henry's piety was given concrete expression in the two monasteries which he founded during the very first year of his reign. Both were for orders much in fashion at the time. The Carthusians, for whom he endowed a charterhouse at Sheen near London, were respected far and wide for their holiness, cherished for the power of their prayers to save men from the consequences of sin. They were much more active and outward-looking than modern Carthusians, having a profound and widespread influence on popular devotion. They took retreatants into their charterhouses and gave spiritual council to the serious laity. The Bridgettine monastery of Syon at Twickenham nearby (later removed to Brentford), which he began building in the same year, was for an order of women and men founded by St Bridget, Queen of Sweden, less than a quarter of a century before. The king also contemplated establishing a house of Celestines, an order of monks with a strict interpretation of the rule of St Benedict, at Sheen, but they had too many French associations and he reluctantly abandoned the scheme.[9]

His piety was certainly far too conventional for the Lollards who, if the tradition recorded by Foxe is to be credited, referred bitterly to him as 'the prince of priests'. The Lollards or 'Bible Men' insisted that true religion could only be learnt from the Scriptures. (Which was why, alone in Western Europe, England had in 1408 banned translations of the bible.) They considered that among priests the pope was anti-Christ and that bishops, canons, monks and friars all transgressed the Ten Commandments. The friars in particular were children of Cain, according to Wyclif (the Lollards' founder); apostates and idolaters who practised murder, robbery and seduction. The Carmelites – the order to which Patrington and Netter belonged – were said to bear a strong resemblance to the fourth of the beasts of Daniel in the Apocalypse, with its iron teeth and claws and ten horns. All organized bodies within the Church were contrary to Christ's teaching, the principal duty of a priest being to preach the Gospel. Lollard beliefs were summed up in the *Twelve Conclusions* which had been nailed to the door of St Paul's in 1395. These rejected transubstantiation, auricular confession, praying to the saints, pilgrimages, indulgences, celibacy (which, they claimed, led to unnatural lust and child murder), and the wealth of the Church. In addition the *Conclusions* attacked the goldsmiths' and armourers' trades as luxurious and sinful. Such opinions contained the seeds of social as well as religious revolution, which might just conceivably have plunged England into the same bloody millenarian wars which convulsed Bohemia. One of the reasons for the sect's failure was its inability to attract followers from among the ruling class save for a handful of knights and small landowners, most of whom were anti-clericals rather than religious reformers.[10] There were exceptions, however.

The leader of these 'cursid caitifs, heires of dirknesse', was Sir

John Oldcastle, from Herefordshire, who had done good service during the Welsh wars. The *Gesta* says of him that 'slaughtering and pillaging the Welsh secured his promotion to knighthood'. He was a valued friend of the king, even if he had gone on Clarence's expedition to France. During the Parliament of 1410 he had led a group of like-minded anti-clerical knights of the shire, most of whom had served with him against Glyn Dŵr; a modern historian has compared them to 'Cromwellian Ironsides'. Nevertheless, however violent John Oldcastle's career may have been, he possessed a considerable intellect, and corresponded with the Bohemian heresiarch Huss. Suddenly, in March 1413, just after the king's accession to the throne, Archbishop Arundel informed Henry that a heretical book found in London, in the shop of a limner (illuminator) in Paternoster Row, belonged to Sir John. The King did not realize how serious his trusted friend was in his curious views – he had just sent twenty-six wrestlers to amuse Henry at Windsor – and tried to persuade so useful a servant to deny them. Oldcastle prevaricated, ignoring a citation to appear before Arundel. Eventually the king had him arrested and sent to the Tower in chains. During his trial Sir John insisted that the Host remained plain bread at the consecration and that there was no need for auricular confession, finally shouting at the tribunal that pope, prelates and friars 'will drag you down to hell'. He was excommunicated and sent back to the Tower. He escaped shortly after, with the help of fellow Lollards, in October 1413.

Oldcastle went underground at safe-houses in London to organize a Lollard rising. Posters stuck on church doors claimed that '100,000 men' were ready to fight for the new opinions. In almost every English county his agents summoned the people to rise, as the artisans and labourers had done in the Peasants' Revolt of 1381. The Lollard programme attracted considerable support, as much because of economic misery as from religious feeling. Sir John was to be regent, while the king, nobility and clergy were to be placed under restraint, and the abbeys dissolved and their riches shared out. Many Lollards anticipated the Taborites of Bohemia in dreaming of a new Jerusalem. Oldcastle and his friends – Sir Roger Acton, Sir Thomas Talbot, Sir Thomas Cheyne – were more than mere anti-clericals who wished to purify the Church.[11]

Sir John modelled his *coup d'état* on that of Richard II's would-be restorers in 1400. He planned to smuggle armed Lollards disguised as mummers into Eltham Palace where Henry was keeping

Christmas and seize him and his brothers on Twelfth Night (6 January) 1414. Some sources say he meant to kill them. The second stage would be the arrival of a Lollard army in London; men from all over England were to assemble at Fickett's Field, just outside Temple Bar in St Giles Fields, on Wednesday 10 January. However, one Thomas Burton (later rewarded with 100 shillings as a 'king's spy') kept Henry fully informed throughout. At 10 o'clock on the evening of Twelfth Night the mayor and his men-at-arms raided a carpenter's shop at the Sign of the Axe near Bishopsgate. They found the carpenter and seven other Lollards dressed as mummers, among them a squire of Oldcastle's, about to set off for Eltham. Despite the failure of the plot's first stage Sir John did not call off the assembly at Fickett's Field of – in the words of the *Gesta* – 'this same raven of treachery with those of his crows who, as arranged, were to flock to him from almost every part of England'.[12] The King was waiting for them with his troops. As they arrived in the grey hours before dawn they were arrested. For all the boasts of '100,000 men' only 300 came to the field, of whom eighty were captured – the rest, including Oldcastle, fled into the gloom. Three days later, on 13 January, seven of the prisoners who were proven Lollards suffered the 'burning death' – fires lit beneath them as they hung in chains from gibbets. During the next fortnight another twenty-five were hanged in batches; four new pairs of gallows, popularly named 'The Lollers' Gallows', were erected in St Giles Fields for the purpose. Henry felt more secure by the end of January and the remaining prisoners were eventually freed on payment of heavy fines. Sir Roger Acton, Oldcastle's principal lieutenant, was among those executed, who 'for the space of a month was swinging on the gibbet' records Adam of Usk. However, the chief organizer of this pitiful little conspiracy was not caught until 1417. Writing at the end of 1416 the author of the *Gesta* says that Sir John 'lurked in holes and corners out of the sight of men, and indeed still does, like another Cain, a vagabond and a fugitive on the face of the earth'.[13]

Strangely enough Oldcastle had been smuggled out of London by the Archdeacon of Westminster and was later sheltered by the Abbot of Shrewsbury and the Prior of Wenlock – all three Benedictine monks. The monastic community at Westminster had long been known for stubborn fidelity to King Richard and it seems hostility to the Lancastrian usurpers was still so strong that orthodox Catholics were ready to ally with heretics against the regime. It is also known that when he was on the run Sir John was in contact with Glyn Dŵr's son, Maredudd, who had not yet submitted to Henry V and continued to roam the Welsh hills.

During the Parliament which met at Leicester in April 1414 a savage statute was enacted against Lollards. Every secular official, including mayors, was required to take an oath to root out heresy in his district, being empowered to arrest, question and imprison suspects. Even if those accused were acquitted, they were to be kept under observation for years afterwards. There were more burnings, such as that of the London furrier John Claydon in 1415. The Lollards were broken and driven underground.

As Jeremy Catto has written, 'from the Leicester Parliament of 1414 until the triumph of toleration in the eighteenth century, religion was established and enforced by public authority, and dissentient voices were subjected to the rigour of statutory felony. By contrast, before 1400 religion was outside the competence of the secular power.'[14] In clerical matters the king was in many respects the precursor of Henry VIII, and began to institutionalize the concept of a national church. In part his attitude stemmed from formalist piety, in part from dislike of any challenge to his authority. Over a century before the title was actually used Henry V would act as though he were 'supreme governor of the church of England'.[15]

The new king proved no less effective in secular matters. One of his most impressive achievements was his swift restoration of law and order. Throughout his father's reign, despite the promises of 'good governance' of 1399, England had been convulsed by banditry and rioting, cowed by bribery and intimidation. Henry V's policy was a characteristic blend of neatly gauged conciliation and merciless punishment. His campaign against disorder began at the Leicester Parliament; in the words of Chancellor Beaufort it was 'for the chastisement and punishment of the rioters, murderers and malefactors who more than ever abound in many parts of the kingdom'. This was followed by a frenzy of judicial activity. Since murder and robbery had been particularly prevalent in the north west Midlands, the Court of King's Bench sat at Lichfield and Shrewsbury for over a month, issuing 1600 summons. There were commissions of inquiry in Derbyshire, Devon, Nottinghamshire, Yorkshire, and in North and South Wales. These were regions where treasons, felonies and trespasses had been especially widespread. By the autumn of 1414, King's Bench had a huge backlog of cases. The king, who watched the court closely and sometimes intervened, cleared the backlog by declaring a general pardon extending even to murderers and rapists

– charters of pardon were purchased by nearly 5,000 persons. Fines were used in other cases in preference to prison sentences, with the hint that military service was a sure way of regaining royal favour. Henry read personally all petitions addressed to him, a practice which he continued when campaigning abroad. His success is shown by the fact that disorder did not return during his reign, not even in the long periods when he was away in France.[16]

His priority was plainly law and order, not the punishment of crime. This has to be seen in the context of his preparations for war and need to recruit an army. Under strict discipline criminals can make excellent fighting men, as their aggressive instincts are directed at enemies abroad and away from the population at home. It has been estimated that as many as twelve per cent of Edward III's troops were outlaws serving in hope of a pardon and although no similar analysis exists for his great-grandson's soldiers the percentage was no doubt very similar.

Henry was only able to achieve as much as he did during the fifteen months before his invasion fleet sailed for France because he had an unusually gifted team of administrators, men with whom he had worked in 1409–12. These included all the key members of his council; Bishop Beaufort (Chancellor), the Earl of Arundel (Treasurer) and John Prophet (Privy Seal), together with Langley, Bishop of Durham, and Chichele, Bishop of St David's, who have been described, not inaptly, as ministers without portfolio.[17] They attended the rather larger meetings of the Royal Household which was soon widened to admit the Dukes of Bedford and Gloucester, the Earl of March, Lord Fitzhugh, Sir Thomas Erpingham, and Richard Courtenay, Bishop of Norwich. Council and Household both met regularly for discussions whose minutes sometimes read like those of any modern board meeting. On Sunday 27 May 1415, for example, the Council met to nominate individuals for specific duties and specialized committees: Chichele, Lord Scrope, Sir John Mortimer and two clerical diplomats were to brief envoys to the Duke of Burgundy; Bedford and Bishop Beaufort were to consider the redemption of pawned crown jewels; Bishop Beaufort was to pressure the bishops to take more steps against Lollards; other committees were nominated to deal with such matters as policy for the seneschal of Guyenne, appointing commissions of array in every county, supplies for the invasion fleet and sailors' pay. The council could be ruthless enough, especially where money was concerned; on the previous Friday it had summoned ten Italian merchants before it, ordering them to furnish a war loan of £2,000 – when this was refused the Italians were promptly sent under guard to the Fleet prison.

The king tried to enlist the sympathy of all Europe by stressing his moderation. He declared that he was ready to forego his own claim to the throne of France if the French would give him Aquitaine as it had been in 1360, after the Treaty of Brétigny. His envoys travelled everywhere, putting their master's case and complaining of French injustice towards him. Meanwhile, inexorably, he made his preparations for war. He was too busy to be on his guard against danger at home.

In some quarters the new dynasty was still resented. As late as the summer of 1415, when Henry was on the point of launching his invasion of France, another extremely serious anti-Lancastrian plot very nearly succeeded. On 1 August the Earl of March came suddenly to Porchester Castle from where the king was directing the embarkation. He demanded an audience and revealed that his brother-in-law, the Earl of Cambridge, had tried to enlist him in a plot to overthrow Henry. He was to be denounced in a proclamation as 'Henry of Lancaster, usurper of England'. As Cambridge later explained in a confession, 'I purposed to have had the aforesaid earl [of March] into the land of Wales without your consent, to confer upon the earl the sovereignty of this land if that man whom they call King Richard had not been alive, as I know very well he is not.' (This was in reference to the pseudo-Richard in Scotland.)[18] Henry Percy, Hotspur's son, not yet restored to his grandfather's earldom, was to cross the border into England with a Scots army and raise the North, while a Davy Howell was to hand over the royal castles in Wales, where Owain's old followers were waiting to rise. Howell, a distinguished commander, seems to have known nothing of the plot. In addition Sir John Oldcastle and his Lollards would raise the Welsh border and the West Country. It was the old alliance of Percy, Mortimer and Glyn Dŵr.

There had been long discussions between March, Lord Clifford – who refused to be drawn into the conspiracy – and the two other ring-leaders, Sir Thomas Grey and Lord Scrope at the Itchen ferry, under the very walls of Southampton, and also at supper parties at March's manor of Cranbury near Winchester. A plan to fire the invasion fleet was rejected. Finally it had been decided to assassinate King Henry on the very day that March had his audience.

Henry struck at once. Cambridge, Scrope and Grey were arrested

47

without delay and a jury was impanelled the same day. The following day they were found guilty and a commission presided over by Clarence sentenced them to death. Grey was executed at once but, as was their right as lords, Cambridge and Scrope demanded to be tried by their peers. Many of these were at Southampton waiting to go over to France and twenty soon met, under Clarence's presidency, confirming the sentences. Henry commuted these to beheading, the privilege of lords, though he had Scrope dragged ignominiously on a hurdle through the streets of Southampton – no doubt to be pelted with filth and stones – to the place of execution outside the north gate, where 'their heads were smit off'.

The plot has not been taken seriously enough by historians (even if Wylie calls it a 'really formidable shock'), because it failed. Yet the conspirators included a member of the royal family, a magnate who was a former Treasurer of the Household, and a redoubtable and extremely influential soldier. Cambridge and Scrope were genuine powers in the land, both Knights of the Garter, with many friends, allies and clients. Walsingham says that the tender-hearted king wept at their fate. He is more likely to have shed tears because of their denial of his right to the throne.

Richard of Coninsburgh, Earl of Cambridge, was the younger brother of that arch-intriguer, the Duke of York, who was, however, not implicated in the plot. As well as being March's brother-in-law, Cambridge had been Richard II's godson. No doubt Henry thought he had secured his loyalty by creating him an earl. His daughter was married to the eldest son of Sir Thomas Grey of Heton Castle (and of the Towers of Wark-on-Tyne and Nesbit) in Northumberland, constable of Bamborough and Norham Castles in the same county – both key strongholds. Grey was also a son-in-law of the Earl of Westmorland while his wife's brother-in-law was the Earl of Northumberland. He was therefore very well connected and very much respected throughout the North Country. The *Gesta* admits that he was 'a knight famous and noble if only he had not been dishonoured by this stain of treason'.[19]

It was the defection of Scrope which shook Henry, the enmity of someone so brilliant, who had been one of his closest friends. Presumably he would have endorsed Friar Capgrave's verdict; 'Sober was the man in word and cheer and under that hypocrisy had he a full venomous heart.' Indeed the attempted coup has earned Lord Scrope the contempt of history. Shakespeare makes Henry rebuke him with an extremely plausible speech:

Ingrateful, savage and inhuman creature!
Thou, that didst bear the key of all my counsels,
That knewst the very bottom of my soul

Yet Scrope's real motives have never been identified. The contemporary rumour that he had been bought by the French for 'a million of gold' was without foundation. He himself said that the conspirators had invited him to join them because he was the nephew of the murdered archbishop, which seems the most likely explanation; his piety verged on mysticism, and he cannot have been unmoved by the cult of 'St Richard' at York Minster. The person who knew Henry best, outside his family, was not prepared to have him as his king.

The 'Southampton Plot' was inept and ill conceived. The devout Lord Scrope could never have brought himself to join forces with the Lollard heretics, whom he detested, and at one point he appears to have tried to talk his fellow plotters out of going ahead with it. Nonetheless Henry had only been saved at the last moment because March lost his nerve. If Cambridge's confession is to be believed, the earl's chaplain had urged him 'to claim what he called his right' and his household had been convinced that he meant to do so. March undoubtedly feared that the king intended to 'undo' him, and had recently been shattered by Henry forcing him to pay 10,000 marks (nearly £7,000) as a marriage fine to ensure he remained subservient and did not meddle in politics. During the final French attempt to avoid war the astrologer Jean Fusoris, who accompanied the embassy to England, heard that many people would have preferred March to be their king. But he possessed either too little ambition or too little self-confidence. He seems to have been an unusually amiable and kindly young man, moderately gifted, with a healthy sense of self-preservation. He was understandably reserved and somewhat suspicious, and above all very much in awe of the cousin who had stolen his crown. Investigating his personal accounts McFarlane discovered that he had a weakness for gambling – losing £157 between the autumn of 1413 and the spring of 1414 at cards, tables, raffles and dice, and betting on cockfighting. 'There are also some suspiciously large payments to a certain Alice at Poplar and some other signs of a fondness for low as well as high company.'[20]

Later March served Henry well enough during the campaigns in France, though he was to fall under suspicion at least once again. He died childless in 1425 when his claims passed to his sister, the Countess of Cambridge (the widow of the earl who had perished in

49

the Southampton Plot). Her son Richard, Duke of York, was to claim the throne in 1460 – on being asked why he had not done so before, he replied, 'Though right for a time rest and be put to silence, yet it rotteth not nor shall it perish.'

Henry V believed that there was only one way to end 'all this clamour of King Richard', as his father put it. He had to prove to the world that God's blessing was on the new dynasty. The sole method of doing so was trial by battle.

V

The English Armada

'We exhort you in the bowels of Jesus Christ to execute and do that
thing that the Evangelist teacheth, saying "Friend, pay that that thou
owest and restore that that thou wrongfully detainest." And to the
end that the blood of innocence be not spilt, we require due resti-
tution of our rightful inheritance by you wrongfully witholden from
Us.'

Henry V to the Dauphin, 1415

'Nor with you can our sovereign lord safely treat.'

The Archbishop of Bourges to Henry V, 1415

Henry's preparations for his grand design, the invasion and
conquest of France, are further evidence of the many-sided
genius he had displayed in Wales and in ruling England during his
father's illness. He solved with ease countless problems of logistics
and organization. He also showed himself to be a skilled and ruthless
diplomat.

Almost from the moment he succeeded to the crown, he was
making ready for war with France. As early as May 1413 he had
ordered that no bows or guns were to be sold to the Scots or to other
foreigners. Throughout 1413–14 he was buying bows, bow strings
and arrows, while guns were being founded at the Tower and at
Bristol, and gun powder and gunstones manufactured in large
quantities. He also purchased, or had manufactured, siege towers,
scaling ladders, battering rams and other tools for demolishing and
breaching walls, and collapsible pontoon bridges. Timber, rope,
mattocks, picks and shovels were stockpiled, together with every

51

other conceivable necessity for siege warfare – from calthrops to iron chains, from sea-coal to wood-ash. In October 1414, 10,000 gun-stones costing £66 13s 4d were delivered to the Tower.[1]

Yet at the same time the king was negotiating with the French. Full-scale civil war had broken out between the Burgundians and the Armagnacs. The Duke of Burgundy sought military assistance from England – understandably the Armagnacs tried to outbid the duke at the English court.

Although the king wanted war, he was careful to give every appearance of taking seriously the negotiations which took place in 1413–15. At this stage his aims were probably limited to recovering Aquitaine as it had been under the Black Prince, after the Treaty of Brétigny in 1360. This included not just Guyenne, Poitou and the Limousin but almost all France between the Loire and the Pyrenees west of the Massif Central – amounting to a third of the realm. Had he obtained it through diplomacy there is little doubt that he would have demanded more territory, which would inevitably have led to conflict.

The first thing Henry needed for an invasion was money. He made every effort to improve the collection of revenue and see that it was spent to maximum effect. He increased the yield from Crown lands and such dues as marriage fees and wardships. The excellent relations he had established with the Commons when Prince of Wales stood him in good stead – they were impressed by his businesslike ways and trusted him. They approved his right to regain his 'inheritance' in France in the Parliament of November 1414, while urging him to exhaust every diplomatic possibility before going to war. One reason for their co-operation was satisfaction with his proclamation of a general pardon. Even so he had to borrow. He did not possess the enormous credit facilities extended to his great-grandfather Edward III by the Florentine banking houses. His only source of credit was his revenue and his personal valuables – and only the revenue of the year in hand, since he refused to anticipate future revenue.

Commissioners were sent all over England to raise loans from prelates and religious orders, from noblemen and country gentlemen, from city corporations and from merchants great and small – Dick Whittington, the London merchant (and sometime mayor) advanced some £2,000, while large numbers of tradesmen lent sums as small as 10d. The biggest creditor was Bishop Beaufort who contributed not less than £35,630 in the course of his nephew's reign.

Nevertheless the king still had to pledge all his jewellery and not just his 'little jewels' as in the past but the very vestments from the Chapel Royal, even his crowns: of the 'Harry Crown' Sir John Colvyl held a fleur-de-lys with rubies, sapphires and pearls; John Pudsey, esquire, a pinnacle with sapphires, a square ruby and six pearls; Maurice Brune a pinnacle similarly ornamented; and John Staundish another pinnacle likewise ornamented. He was to go on borrowing throughout his reign, though most loans would be paid back in full.

In August 1414, after having manoeuvred the Duke of Burgundy into offering neutrality should he attempt to make himself King of France, Henry sent an embassy to Paris led by Richard Courtenay, Bishop of Norwich. First the embassy demanded the French crown and kingdom for its master, then it lowered its terms to Normandy, Anjou, Maine, Touraine, Poitou and the lands between Flanders and the Somme, and Aquitaine as it had been in 1360. This amounted to all western France. They also demanded the still unpaid ransom of King John II (who had been taken prisoner at Poitiers in 1356), most of Provence, and the hand of Charles VI's daughter, Catherine, with a dowry of two million crowns. In response, the Armagnac Duke of Berry – effectively Regent of France since Charles had gone off his head again – offered most, though not all, of Aquitaine and a dowry of 600,000 crowns. His terms were rejected. The following month the Armagnacs again made peace with the Burgundians, and Henry had to reassess his bargaining position.[2]

In February 1415 Bishop Courtenay led another embassy to Paris, asking this time merely for Aquitaine in full sovereignty and a dowry of only a million crowns. The French refused to improve their previous offer apart from raising the dowry to 800,000 crowns. These were generous terms yet they were rejected once more. The original version of Shakespeare's story of the tennis balls probably dates from the embassy's return, that the haughty French 'said foolishly to them that as Henry was but a young man they would send to him little balls to play with and soft cushions to rest on until he should have grown to a man's strength'.[3] (This is from the almost contemporary chronicle of Canon John Strecche, who had many informed friends at Court.) The tale may well have been a piece of propaganda, invented and put about by Henry's agents.

By June the king was at Winchester, ready to receive one final despairing embassy from the French before launching his invasion. He received the envoys at the bishop's palace on the 30 June, giving every appearance of taking them seriously. He was in cloth of gold from top to toe and leant against a table – flanked by the royal dukes on one side, by the Chancellor, Beaufort, and various prelates on the other. During the ensuing negotiations the French offered to add the Limousin to their previous offer, to no avail. Their leader Guillaume Boisratier, Archbishop of Bourges, lost his temper when Henry said that if Charles VI did not meet his 'just' demands he would be responsible for a 'deluge of Christian blood'. 'Sire,' retorted the prelate, 'the King of France our sovereign lord is true King of France, and regarding those things to which you say you have a right you have no lordship, not even to the kingdom of England which belongs to the true heirs of King Richard. Nor with you can our sovereign lord safely treat.' At this Henry stormed out of the conference chamber.

The Chancellor, Beaufort, then read out a prepared document. The gist was that if Charles VI refused to hand over the Angevin empire immediately, Henry would come and take it by the sword, and the crown of France with it, that he had been driven to this course by Charles's delays and refusal to do him 'justice'. The archbishop answered that the English were mistaken if they thought that the French had offered concessions out of fear and the English king might come when he liked to be defeated, killed or taken prisoner.

On 6 July 1415 Henry declared war formally, a war for which he had been preparing for over two years. He called on God to witness that it was the fault of Charles VI, for refusing to do him 'justice'. The author of the *Gesta* tells us the king had copies made of 'pacts and covenants entered into between the most serene prince the King of England Henry IV, his father, and certain of the great princes of France on the subject of his divine right and claim to the duchy of Aquitaine' and sent transcripts to the Council of the Church at Constance, to the Holy Roman Emperor Sigismund and to other monarchs, 'that all Christendom might know what great acts of injustice the French in their duplicity had inflicted on him, and that, as it were reluctantly and against his will, he was being compelled to raise his standard against rebels.'[4]

An army of over 10,000 men assembled at Southampton. It consisted of 2,000 men-at-arms and nearly 8,000 archers, with a few un-armoured lancers and knifemen. They were supported by armourers, smiths, farriers, surgeons, cooks, chaplains, engineers, carpenters and masons. There was a team of miners – to tunnel beneath the enemy's walls – and sixty-five gunners under four Dutch master-gunners. There were bowyers and fletchers to make and replace bows and arrows. There was even a royal band, consisting of trumpeters, fiddlers and pipers, led by the king's master-minstrel, Mr John Stiff.

Just as later English armies included colonial contingents, many of Henry's troops were Welshmen though we do not know the exact number. The most notable were Davy Gam Daffyd ap Llewellyn of Brecon, who had served under him against Glyn Dŵr and who was later killed at Agincourt, and Davy Howell – probably the man mentioned in Cambridge's confession – whom Henry was later to appoint captain of the castle of Pont d'Ouve, near Carentan. Another who distinguished himself was Gruffydd Dŵn who would also fight at Agincourt, and stay on in France after the king's death. (Gruffydd had no less than seventy-seven Welshmen under his command when he was captain of Tancarville in 1438).[5] Having fought against the Welsh for years and having employed them to crush their fellow countrymen Henry – who probably understood a little of their language – knew all about their courage, their ferocity and their propensity to commit atrocities. Wales contained all too many penniless minor gentry with ancient pedigrees and fiendish pride, who had no hope of finding gainful employment. Military service in France solved their financial problems while deflecting them from rising against the English again. Those who could afford it fought as men-at-arms though most served as archers, bringing their great knives with them (they wore these behind their backs, dangling from the base of the spine, which gave rise to the legend that the 'English had tails'). A few Welsh gentlemen, Owain's irreconcilable veterans, were to fight by the side of the French at Agincourt.

All troops, whether English or Welsh, had been recruited by the indenture system, captains being commissioned to hire specified numbers of men at a stipulated rate. Normally the captain advanced the first pay-packets, after which he was refunded by the Exchequer which from then on supplied the cash for future pay. The Duke of Clarence brought 240 men-at-arms and 720 archers, the Duke of York and the Earl of Dorset, 100 men-at-arms and 300 archers each, the Earl of Salisbury forty men-at-arms and eighty archers. Lesser men brought smaller retinues, John Fastolf bringing ten men-at-arms and thirty archers, while two of the royal surgeons had only six archers between them. A duke was obliged to bring fifty horses, a knight six, and a man-at-arms four. Every horse was to have a groom, though generally grooms came from among the archers. A duke was

55

paid 13*s* 4*d* a day, an earl 6*s* 8*d*, a baron 4*s*, a knight 2*s*, a man-at-arms 1*s* and an archer 6*d*. Save for the very great – who often ended up out of pocket – this was good money. (We know from the income tax returns of 1436 that the average income of a great nobleman was £865, of a well-to-do knight £208, of a minor gentleman or merchant from £15 to £19, and a ploughman might earn perhaps £4 a year.) There was also the prospect of ransoms and loot – men of all classes must have remembered how their grandfathers had made fortunes during Edward III's campaigns in France. The king was mercilessly strict in his insistence on a full complement at the muster; when the Duke of Gloucester was found to be two men-at-arms short, he was punished by receiving no pay for a year and having in consequence to find his troops' pay from his own resources. For in Wales Henry had begun to develop an efficient system of 'muster and review', and was determined that he was not going to be charged for non-existent soldiers, known as 'dead souls'.

The king was fortunate in possessing a ready-made reservoir of corps commanders in his nobility. G. L. Harriss has calculated that 'of the seventeen members of the upper nobility in 1413, eleven were within the age-bracket eighteen to thirty-two, the age when the fighting man was at his peak. Henry himself was twenty-six – exactly in the middle'.[6] Many had already served with him in Wales against Glyn Dŵr, including Lord Salisbury and Lord Warwick and Sir John Holland (not yet restored to his father's earldom of Huntingdon) and such greybeards as the Duke of York who was over forty. The latter had a good name as a soldier. So did the Duke of Clarence, who had earned it in Ireland and during his French expedition of 1412. Furthermore the king was clearly an excellent trainer of good officers.

For his rank and file, Henry had a substantial nucleus of veterans who had fought for him – or against him – in Wales. The captains, and in consequence their men too, came from all over the kingdom. McFarlane believed that all those who fought in the wars in France were 'gentlemen by birth and their servants' but this was not invariably the case. (Even if of gentle blood, many of those who were later promoted captains had joined as penniless adventurers.) The 'servants' were often tenants rather than house or estate staff, while there is evidence that a fair number of tradesmen – butchers, fishmongers, barbers, dyers – left their shops and went and fought in France.

One may ask what was their motive. The answer can only be loot.

56

McFarlane has produced countless examples of Englishmen from all classes who did well out of 'spoils won in France'. Admittedly M. M. Postan, after equally extensive research, was able to cite almost as many instances of Englishmen who were impoverished as a result of campaigning in France. This was usually through arrears to pay or from being captured and having to pay a heavy ransom.[7] Yet one may guess with some certainty that, however it turned out in the end, most of the troops who took part hoped – indeed expected – to win rather than lose and that French plunder was the prospect which drew them like a magnet to serve in the war across the Channel.

The vast majority of men-at-arms, the front-line close-combat troops, came from the lesser gentry as their equipment was so expensive. They wore plate-armour from top to toe, over a thick felt suit to prevent bruising. Since the jupon (a form of surcoat) was going out of fashion, in action they looked like mobile statues of burnished steel. The conical bassinet with a snout-like visor pierced by breathing holes was being replaced by the round-topped close-helmet with a simpler visor, or else by the sallet – a cross between a *Wehrmacht* tin hat and a metal sou'wester which could be pulled down over the face. Hands and feet were protected by articulated steel gauntlets and sollerets. Such armour weighed as much as sixty-six pounds but it was distributed all over the body (British troops 'yomped' for many miles across rough ground in the Falklands with over eighty pounds on their backs). Whether on horseback or on foot, its wearers had an enviable sense of invulnerability, and were able to discard their shields. Nevertheless, while a costly armour from Nuremberg or Milan – cunningly ridged and fluted to deflect blows – could stand up to almost any weapon, cheaper armours could be smashed in. The worst drawback, however, was heat; on a sunny day, despite air holes in his felt suit, a man-at-arms boiled in his own sweat and quickly became exhausted.

The man-at-arms rode a special weight-carrying horse like a modern heavy-weight hunter. (Other similar breeds are the Irish draught-horse and the Norman Percheron.) When mounted, his primary weapon was a massive lance, twelve feet long, designed to knock an opponent out of the saddle. However, whenever possible, English men-at-arms preferred fighting on foot; indeed in France this was termed 'the English method'. Although a long, straight sword hung at his left side, balanced by a bollocks-hilted 'misericord' dagger – so called from being used to dispatch the mortally wounded – on the ground he employed a short steel-shafted battleaxe, a

57

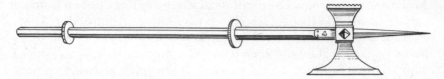

The poleaxe Carried by men-at-arms, and often by archers, it was part axe, part hammer and part pike. Its steel-plated shaft was virtually indestructible.

battle-hammer, a mace or a flail. (The latter, often called a morning-star, was a spiked ball and chain swung by a short handle.) Above all he had the pole-axe, designed to rip open or smash an enemy's armour, inflicting terrible lacerations and bruises. This was basically a half-pike, five feet long, its steel shaft ending in a spike. The head was half axe and half hammer. This was perhaps the most lethal weapon evolved during the entire Middle Ages – significantly, the instrument wielded by butchers in abattoirs was also known as a pole-axe.

As long as they were able to shoot from a defensive position little could stand before Henry's archers, although they could be routed easily enough by enemy horse if unprotected by men-at-arms. Yew was the wood most favoured for longbows, whose length averaged six feet. Arrows were usually made of ash. They were thirty inches long, flighted with goose-wing feathers and they had a four-sided 'bodkin' point – a case-hardened steel spike. The best longbowmen could shoot as many as twelve arrows a minute and had a plate armour piercing range of up to sixty yards, only the most expensive armours were protection against them. Mounted archers carried a lance, a strong spear rather than the battering-ram type used by men-at-arms. The archers' side-arms were sword and misericord, supplemented by either a pole-axe, a billhook or a 'maul' (a leaden mallet with a five foot long wooden handle). Head covering varied from a sallet to a wickerwork cap banded with iron, while in addition to metal or leather gauntlets – together with a leather bracer on his drawing arm to save it from the bow string – the archer's body was protected by a 'jack'. The jack was something like a modern flak-jacket; made of as many as twenty-five layers of deerskin, often studded with metal and stuffed with tow, it reached half-way down the wearer's thighs.

The invading army included twice as many mounted archers as

those who marched on foot, no doubt reflecting the King's experience in Wales. Remounts would have to be obtained locally in France. Mobility was essential. The archers operated in much the same way that the Boers did against the British in South Africa, or Teddy Roosevelt's 'roughriders' did against the Spanish in Cuba – as mounted infantry, dismounting to shoot. Since they were also equipped with lances they could, if necessary, remain on horseback and reinforce a charge by the men-at-arms, riding with them.

It is also probable that, in the interests of mobility, men-at-arms wore half-armour or jacks when raiding or skirmishing. Usually at the close of an engagement archers and men-at-arms, on foot together, would charge the enemy, using pole-axes as rifle and bayonet were to be used in the twentieth century. The French were always at a disadvantage because of their predilection for the higher velocity crossbows with which they equipped their own archers. These weapons, which in any case were much heavier to carry, had such a slow rate of fire that going into action with them against bowmen must have been like facing repeaters with single-shot rifles.

There was an artillery train of bombards and culverins. The former were heavy bronze or iron guns, often of huge bore, on fixed wooden platforms, which travelled in ox-wains. Although primitive, they were far from being ineffectual, as is often suggested. They were generally founded at the Tower of London or in Bristol by bell-founders, who frequently operated them on the battlefield. Their greatest defect was sub-standard gunpowder which often disintegrated into its component parts; sulphur, saltpetre and charcoal. Nevertheless, since the 1370s founding had improved steadily, especially in bronze, while an art in mixing powder had developed, elm-wood tampons being placed between the charge and the gun-stone. No doubt their rate of fire was very slow, since they had to be swabbed out with vinegar and water after each discharge. They were set off by a red-hot iron firing-piece kept in a charcoal brazier and a shot every five minutes was considered a remarkable performance. Yet such cannon could fire gunstones weighing several hundred-weight up to 2,500 paces and were increasingly effective against city or castle walls. Stone shot constituted an early form of shrapnel, disintegrating on impact into razor-sharp splinters.

To some extent artillery reflected weaponry from the days before gunpowder. If bombards were the heirs of trebuchets (the stone-throwing catapults once siege-warfare's principal tool), culverins were successors to the mangonels (huge mechanical bows whose enormous arrows had hitherto been the most formidable missile weapons available). These culverins were surprisingly sophisticated. Although not yet able to cast reliable bombards, even the iron founders could produce adequate if cumbersome guns of small calibre which fired metal bullets weighing as little as twenty-one pounds. Those in bronze or brass were still better. A bronze example in the cathedral museum at Meaux, found in the river Marne in 1896, is thought to have been lost by the English during the siege of 1421–2. It is a thick octagonal tube five feet long, with a round bore and a crude but effective breech-block hammered in during casting. It was mounted on a wooden tripod and transported in a cart. Although slow to reload and inaccurate, it was every effective at short range; at Castillon in 1453 an enfilading shot from a culverin went through six men. It was the ancestor of the handgun and the arquebus.

Munitions and provisions required organization on a truly massive scale. The king's experience of planning such sieges as that of Aberystwyth must have been invaluable. He spent many weeks during the summer of 1415 at Porchester Castle, on the coast near the embarkation point of Southampton, directing operations. The munitions included siege engines (towers, scaling ladders and battering-rams), gunpowder and its ingredients, stone shot, bow staves packed in canvas, arrows in tuns, bow strings, collapsible boats of wood and greased leather, mining tools, masons, armourers and all the other craftsmen. Provisions included bread, dried fish, salted meat, flour, beans, cheese and ale, which came into the depots from all over England. To ensure that they had as much fresh meat as possible, cattle, sheep and pigs were driven from as far away as Yorkshire and the West Country. Clothing and shoes were also collected at the depots. All this had to be loaded onto the ships. In addition there were vast numbers of horses to feed and water.[8]

Some sources say that the invasion fleet was as large as 1,500 vessels, though no doubt many were very small craft indeed. The transports were either hired – including 700 from the Low Countries – or requisitioned with their masters by the royal admirals. They also press-ganged men to crew them. Some of the vessels were adapted for carrying horses, with doors cut in their sides and stalls constructed by using hurdles as partitions. The ships were also fitted for combat, having large bridges or 'castles' built fore and aft from which the archers could shoot down on attackers. Their unfortunate owners lost a great deal of money, having their cargoes unloaded compulsorily and being paid only a small sum for each quarter year that their vessels were in the king's service. They came from the West Country, from the Cinque Ports, from East Anglia, from the North Sea ports. It took three days to assemble such an armada, filling Southampton Water and every small bay and inlet down the coast as far as Gosport.

The cog This clinker-built cog is a small example of the ships which carried Henry V's troops. A few were as large as 1000 tons and had doors cut in their hulls to facilitate the transport of horses.

61

Ships were also needed to patrol and guard the sea, so that the French would be unable to intercept the invasion. These were the 'King's Ships' – Henry's navy, which was one of his most remarkable achievements. When he came to the throne there were seven King's Ships; by 1415 there were fifteen and by 1417 there would be thirty-four. William Catton was appointed Keeper of the King's Ships in July 1413. Early in the following year a wealthy South-ampton merchant, William Soper, was engaged to assist him. A programme of buying and building vessels began at once. Soper built a dock and a store house at Southampton, and at nearby Hamble he constructed other storehouses, together with fortified moorings where the ships could shelter from enemy raiders. As well as building ships he refitted them. Under his direction the port grew into a full-scale naval base. War at sea was basically an extension of war on land and warships were no more than fighting troop carriers. Those which carried the largest complement of archers and men-at-arms were considered the most formidable. Accordingly, Soper's priority was to provide the king with vessels of between 500 and 1000 tons – a vast size at the time – with two masts.

Even so, most of Henry's warships in 1415 were those long-forgotten craft, ballingers. The French, and to a lesser extent the English, had tried using galleys in the Channel but being designed for the Mediterranean they were ill-suited to such choppy water. The ballinger was apparently developed by the English during the late fourteenth century as an answer to the galley. It was a big clinker-built sailing barge of around fifty tons, perfectly at home in English waters, while being additionally equipped with up to fifty oars. Shallow draughted, it could penetrate into the narrowest anchorages or up rivers without difficulty. It was also ideal for cross-Channel raids or privateering – becalmed French merchantmen were at its mercy. It was manned by forty sailors, ten men-at-arms and ten archers. By 1415 the king possessed ten of these versatile craft. They and his big sailing ships ensured that his invasion was untroubled by enemy warships.[9]

For all his confidence in his 'right', Henry was far from sure that he would return from his adventure, that God would give judgement in his favour. He had a will drafted, in which he trusts that he will be received into Abraham's bosom through the prayers of the Virgin, the saints and his special patron, John of Bridlington. It contains directions for his burial in Westminster Abbey and many bequests – though interestingly Clarence is left nothing. He signed it at

Winchester on 24 July, writing on it in English; 'This is my last will, subscribed with my own hand, R.H. Jesu Mercy and Gramercy Ladie Marie help.'

The armada to recover the king's 'right' set sail on the fine and sunny afternoon of Sunday 11 August. Henry had been on board the *Trinity Royal* since the day before, but the fleet was delayed by three ships catching fire and burning down to the water line – which was widely regarded as a sinister omen. However, the chaplain who wrote the *Gesta* and was on board with the king remembers that, 'As we were leaving the coast of the Isle of Wight behind, swans were seen swimming about among the fleet, and they were spoken of as a happy augury'.[10] No one except Henry and his principal commanders knew the armada's destination save that it was somewhere in France – some of his troops may well have thought they were bound for Guyenne. His security was almost modern in its thoroughness.

Henry V had never had any intention of securing his inheritance across the Channel by peaceful means. He had employed diplomacy purely to discredit French sincerity in the eyes of the world. Whatever the cost, he wanted war – a war which would justify the House of Lancaster's deposition of Richard II and disinheritance of the Earl of March. If his 'right' in France should be confirmed by God giving him the victory in battle, such a victory would simultaneously establish his right to the throne of England beyond all dispute. As the *Gesta* makes clear, he was hastening 'to seek a ruling from the supreme judge'.

VI

'Our Town of Harfleur'

'We have many times, and in many ways, sought peace . . . And well considering that the effect of Our wars are the deaths of men, destruction of countries, lamentations of women and children, and so many general evils . . . We are induced to seek diligently for all possible means to avoid the above-mentioned evils, and to acquire the approbation of God, and the praise of the world.'

Henry V's challenge to the dauphin

'They put out alle the French people both man woman and chylde and stuffed the town with English men.'

The Brut of England

At five o'clock in the afternoon of Tuesday 13 August the English fleet sailed into the Seine estuary. They anchored off the chalk headland of the Chef de Caux, three miles from Henry's objective – the port of Harfleur. He forbade his troops to land before him under 'pain of death,' going ashore at a spot where Le Havre now stands, between six and seven o'clock in a beautiful dawn. On landing the king fell on his knees and prayed God to give him 'justice'. By Saturday the disembarkation was completed. He issued orders, again under 'pain of death', that there must be no arson, that churches and church plate were to be left alone and that women and priests must go unmolested. No harlots might come within three miles of the camp; after a first warning any harlot who did so would have her left arm broken. Nor must there be any swearing. In the words of the late Professor E. F. Jacob, Henry meted out 'that mixture of firmness and humanity which has always been the mark of the good English regimental officer'.[1] He established his camp on a hill about a mile north-west of the unfortunate little town, and 'when all the tents and pavilions and halls [marquees] were erected and set up, they seemed a right great and mighty city'.

Clarence established a second English camp under his command on a hill on the other side of the town, to the east in the direction of Rouen. When 'at dawn in clear sunlight' he and his men suddenly appeared over the brow of the hill, the sight caused 'real fear and dread' among the besieged. In addition, the English fleet blockaded the harbour. By 19 August the English had surrounded Harfleur and had enclosed it with a stockade, so that no one could get in or out.

Nevertheless, the beleaguered town had formidable defences. Its wall was unusually strong – polygonal, two-and-a-half miles in circumference and with twenty-six towers. Its three gates could only be reached across drawbridges from barbicans on the other side of a wide moat. Each barbican was strengthened by a circular bastion or 'bulwark' built around it, consisting of tree-trunks bound together by iron chains, reinforced by baulks of timber and covered by turf, with embrasures for guns and crossbows to fire through. In addition, an earth rampart had been thrown up between the wall and the moat. To the north the town was protected by the flooded valley of the river Lézarde, 'a quarter as wide again as is the Thames at London', to the south by the Lézarde itself and to the east by marshes. To seaward the harbour was guarded by two tall towers, by chain booms and by huge stakes on the seabed. It had an extremely competent commander in Jean d'Estouteville. Admittedly the garrison was under-strength though Raoul de Gaucourt, a redoubtable fighting man who lived near by, slipped into the town with 300 men-at-arms just before it was sealed off from the world outside.

Henry was determined to have Harfleur. The 'key of the sea of all Normandy' (the *First Tudor Life*'s description), it was also an ideal bridgehead from which to overrun Normandy and threaten Paris. The king saw it as another Calais, but better placed strategically. No doubt his spies had reported to him that the town contained few troops and the arrival of Gaucourt's force at the last moment may well have thrown his plans out. It certainly put fresh heart into the defenders. When Henry summoned them to surrender 'his' town to the rightful Duke of Normandy, Estouteville sent a sardonic refusal; 'You left us nothing to look after, and we've nothing to give you back.'

The English first attempted to tunnel underneath the moat to mine the walls. However, the French dug counter-tunnels and attacked the miners underground. The moat made it impossible to get close enough to use battering rams. Henry had recourse to his artillery which included cannon he had had in Wales, such as the 'Messenger' and the 'King's Daughter'. In all he possessed twelve heavy guns, but it took time to move them into position beneath the walls as they were impeded by the garrison firing at them from the ramparts, where they had mounted cannon of their own. The enormous English siege guns slowly trundled forward on vast wooden platforms until they were within range, then began to fire from behind protective wooden screens which tilted up; the gunners were also shielded by trenches and earthworks. The barrage continued day and night.

Henry's cannon, of a size they had never seen before, terrified the French. Stone shot as big as millstones knocked wide holes in the walls while, so the *Gesta* informs us, 'really fine buildings almost as far as the middle of the town were totally demolished or threatened imminent collapse.'[2] The king supervised the bombardment tirelessly, spending whole nights in loading and laying his guns. Although the French managed to fill the breaches with palisades and tubs of earth, Henry was optimistic. On 3 September, writing to Bordeaux to order 600 casks of wine, he says that it will take only another eight days to reduce Harfleur, after which he intends to march towards Paris by way of Montivilliers, Dieppe and Rouen before going south to Guyenne. But at the end of eight days the town was still holding out.

Disease struck the English camp. 'In this siege many men died of cold in nights and fruit eating; eke of stink of carrions,' records Friar Capgrave.[3] They were killed by the bloody flux, dysentery, induced by unripe fruit, sour new wine and local shellfish; a consignment of food contaminated by the sea may have been partly responsible. According to Monstrelet not less than 2,000 Englishmen perished, and another 2,000 were so ill that they had to be shipped home. Casualties included the Earls of Arundel and Suffolk and also Bishop Courtenay of Norwich, the king's valued servant and close personal friend, who died in his arms; among those invalided back to England were the Duke of Clarence and the Earl of March. There were also many deserters. Yet nothing could deflect Henry.

The English cannon bombarded remorselessly the south-western bastion, which was the key to the siege. At the same time the English miners tunnelled forwards to undermine the walls, setting fire to the props which they placed beneath the foundations. By 16 September the bastion and the barbican which it had defended were in ruins, the moat on either side being filled in. The garrison made a sortie, setting fire to the English stockade. A second sortie ended in disaster. The English shot gunstones covered with flaming tow into the bastion where the tree-trunks and timber baulks caught fire, burning for two days. The French abandoned both the bastion and barbican to the besiegers.

By now the garrison was starving and there was no sign of any attempt to relieve it. Like the besiegers it had been stricken by the bloody flux. Nevertheless it refused the severe terms offered by Henry, though it could see the English pushing bridges across the moat, wheeling siege towers towards the walls and bringing up scaling ladders. On 17 September the king gave orders for a general assault on the following day and launched an even more intensive bombardment – including volleys of fire arrows. On 18 September the weary, sleepless defenders despaired and sent envoys to treat with Henry; they agreed to surrender if relief had not come by 22 September. No relief came. Accordingly on the day specified, a Sunday, the garrison's leaders and sixty-six hostages walked out between rows of armed English to where the English king was waiting for them. By his orders they wore only shirts and had halters round their necks; they were forced to remain for several hours on their knees before being admitted to the royal presence. He was in a great silken pavilion, clad in cloth of gold and seated on a throne, while at his right stood Sir Gilbert Umfraville bearing his helmet with its crown, and his pole-axe. Even then it was some time before Henry deigned to look at them. He then upbraided them for withholding *his* town of Harfleur, 'a noble portion of his inheritance', from him 'against God and all justice'.[4]

Then the Cross of St George was hoisted over the town gates, together with the leopards and lilies of the royal standard. Next day the king went barefoot to the half-destroyed parish church of Harfleur to offer up thanksgiving for his victory. His terms were that Gaucourt, together with sixty knights and 200 gentlemen in the garrison, were paroled and ordered to present themselves as 'faithful captives' at Calais at Martinmas (11 November) when they would be taken into custody for ransoming. The richer bourgeois were immediately sent to England to await ransoming. Some 2,000 of the 'poorer sort' were expelled 'amid much lamentation, grief and tears for the loss of their customary although unlawful habitations'. As

Henry explained, none of them, rich or poor, had any right to their houses, for they belonged to him 'by right'. Only a few of Harfleur's inhabitants were allowed to stay, on condition they took an oath of allegiance. Any goods or money found in the city were shared out among the troops, while a certain Richard Bokelond was granted 'the inn called the Peacock' as a reward for bringing two provision ships to the siege. On 5 October the king ordered a proclamation to be made in London and the greater English cities, offering houses in Harfleur, with cash subsidies, to all merchants and artisans who would come over and settle. Eventually, over a period of several years at least 10,000 English colonists arrived in Harfleur. Henry had the former townsmen's title deeds publicly burnt in the market square. He was determined to turn Harfleur into a second Calais, another English town on the French littoral. However, the king received much praise from earlier English historians for not sacking the place, in accordance with the letter of the law, and for providing the poor whom he expelled with five sous a head to help them on their way.[5]

With his almost modern instinct for public relations, on 22 September Henry wrote to the mayor and aldermen of London announcing Harfleur's capture – and also asking them to send him news of themselves from time to time. This was a correspondence he kept up throughout his campaigns in France.

Harfleur was a valuable acquisition, which would prove its worth in later years. Yet the fact remains that the siege was a disastrous start to Henry's campaign; he had lost over a third of his troops. In a carefully composed letter to the mayor of London he says that he has won a great victory, even though his counsellors were begging him to go home as quickly as possible and not to march into France lest the French hem them all in 'like sheep in pens'. Nonetheless, although he abandoned his original plan of advancing on Paris, the king insisted on marching up to Calais with his sadly depleted troops, many of them still suffering from dysentery.

Much ink has been wasted on trying to explain this foolhardy adventure. There was seemingly little to be gained by it, in terms of reconnaissance, plunder or reputation, while it was obviously a considerable gamble since the French were known to be gathering in great strength. Why did so coolly objective a soldier take so unprofitable a risk? He hints why in words to his Council: 'Even if our enemies enlist the greatest armies, my trust is in God, and they shall not hurt my army nor myself. I will not allow them, puffed up with pride, to rejoice in misdeeds, nor, *unjustly against God, to possess my goods*. It cannot be too much emphasized that, for all his use of the latest military technology, Henry's mind was fundamentally medieval. During the siege he had sent a challenge to the Dauphin Louis to a single combat which would decide who was to inherit Charles VI's throne – 'to place our quarrel at the will of God between Our person and yours'. Louis, a fat and sluggish nineteen-year-old, wisely declined. The march up to Calais was intended to be a divinely protected military promenade which would demonstrate that God not only recognized his claim to the crown of France but, far more important, to the crown of England.

VII

'That Dreadful Day of Agincourt'

'Starkly the left arm hold with the bow
Draw with the right, and smite and overthrow'

A fifteenth-century translation
of Vegetius's *De Re Militari*

'Agincourt is . . . a school outing to the Old Vic, Shakespeare is fun,
son-et-lumière, blank verse, Laurence Olivier in battle armour; it is
an episode to quicken the interest of any schoolboy ever bored by a
history lesson, a set-piece demonstration of English moral superiority
and a cherished ingredient of a fading national myth. It is also a story
of slaughter-yard behaviour and of outright atrocity.'

John Keegan, *The Face of Battle*

On 6 October Henry V marched out from Harfleur. Calais was
160 miles away and he expected to reach it in eight days' time.
He had approximately 900 men-at-arms and 5,000 archers, grouped
in three 'battles' with skirmishers on the wings. The king and the
Duke of Gloucester led the main army, Sir John Cornwall the
advance guard, and the Duke of York and the Earl of Oxford the
rearguard. Henry was plainly anxious to make all speed possible,
travelling without artillery or baggage wagons, his troops bringing
only what they could carry on pack-horses – mostly the men-at-arms
'harness' and provisions for the eight days. He intended to march
north to the River Somme, then south-east along its bank until he
reached the ford of Blanche-Taque and then go straight on to Calais.
To ensure a safe crossing he had sent orders for a force from Calais to
seize the ford. (It had been used by his great-grandfather Edward II
in 1346 on his way to Crécy.) No doubt he hoped for a minor

70

engagement en route from which he could extract some semblance of a victorious trial by battle.

As was customary, the English slew and looted as they went, their passage announced by columns of black smoke from burning farm-houses. The abbey of Fécamp also went up in flames, women who had taken refuge in its church being dragged out and raped. Most of the archers were mounted so that the English were able to average nearly twenty miles a day, though such a pace must have been gruelling for those on foot with quivers holding fifty arrows. When fired on by the garrison at the castle of Arques as they were about to cross the River Béthune, Henry threatened to burn the town, extracting supplies of bread and wine for not doing so – it was the same story at Eu when crossing the Bresle. The army looked forward to an easy road over the Somme, which the king expected to reach by midday on 13 October.

Only six miles from the river a prisoner captured by English scouts reported that the tidal ford at Blanche-Taque was blocked by sharp stakes, and that Marshal Boucicault was waiting on the other side with 6,000 troops. (The force from Calais had been intercepted and driven off.) Henry personally interrogated the prisoner, telling him he would lose his head if he did not tell the truth but the man stuck to his story. In the meantime the tide came in and made the ford impassable. The king marched on eastward along the southern bank of the Somme to look for another ford. An eye-witness, the author of the *Gesta*, records the dejection of the army:

> Expecting to have no alternative but to go into parts of France higher up and at the head of the river (which was said to be over sixty miles away) . . . at that time we thought of nothing else but this: that, after the eight days assigned for the march had expired and our provisions had run out, the enemy, craftily hastening on ahead, would impose on us, hungry as we should be, a really dire need of food and at the head of the river if God did not provide otherwise, would with their great and countless host and the engines of war and devices available to them, overwhelm us, so very few we were and made faint by great weariness and weak from lack of food.[1]

Every ford appeared to be held by the French, who kept pace with the English from the other bank. There was a real danger of discipline breaking down. At Boves they drank so much wine, extorted from the castellan by the usual threats, that Henry forbade them to drink any more – when an indulgent commander told the

71

king that they were simply filling their bottles, Henry snapped, 'Their bottles indeed! They're making big bottles of their bellies and getting very drunk.' By now they had eaten their rations apart from a little dried meat, which they supplemented with nuts and what vegetables they could dig up in the fields.

The king took advantage of a loop in the river to make a short cut and outdistance the enemy who had to go the long way round. He still managed to enforce discipline, hanging in full view of the army a man caught sacrilegiously stealing a cheap copper gilt pyx from a church. (During later campaigns he would not be so particular.) Then on 19 October two unguarded fords were found at Voyennes and Béthencourt near Nesle. They could only be reached through the marshes over causeways which had been destroyed by the French ; 200 archers, bows on backs, struggled through a quagmire at Béthencourt to wade waist deep across the river and establish a bridgehead on the far bank; a similar operation at Voyennes was also successful. Henry was not disposed to be merciful to the local peasants who had hung red clothes and blankets out of their windows, as a symbol of the *Oriflamme* (the sacred battle banner of the kings of France) and of defiance; he ordered every house whose occupants were unhelpful to be burnt to the ground. The causeways were repaired with window-frames, doors, roof-timbers and stair-cases from their hamlets as well as with hurdles, tree-trunks and straw. As soon as the causeway at Béthune could support a horse, Sir Gilbert Umfraville and Sir John Cornwall crossed at the head of 500 men-at-arms, just in time to drive off an attack on the archers' bridgehead. By an hour after nightfall the entire English army was over the Somme and in much better spirits. They did not yet know that the main body of the French was only six miles away at Péronne.

Estimates of the number of French troops vary considerably but they almost certainly outnumbered the English by four to one and may have been as many as 30,000, of whom 15,000 were men-at-arms. Their leaders, Marshal Boucicault and the Constable d'Albret – Constable of France – were cautious veterans who wanted to leave Henry alone and let him go back to England while they concentrated on recovering Harfleur. They were overruled by more pugnacious, less experienced spirits. Among the latter were not only the Armagnac Dukes of Orleans and Bourbon but Burgundian magnates like the Duke of Brabant and the Count of Nevers, who were the brothers of Duke John. Although he himself still vacillated, his son, the future Duke Philip, regretted for the rest of his life that he had not fought in the campaign. Even Burgundians could not stomach an English invasion. However, Charles VI, momentarily sane, and the Dauphin Louis stayed away; they did not wish to be taken prisoner, as Charles's grandfather, John II, had been at Poitiers.

On 20 October, a Sunday, three French heralds arrived at Henry's camp. They remained on their knees, keeping silence until given permission to speak. 'Right puissant prince, great and noble is thy kingly power,' began their spokesman. 'Our lords have heard how you intend with your army to conquer the towns, castles and cities of the realm of France and to depopulate French cities. And because of this, and for the sake of their country and their oaths, many of our lords are assembled to defend their rights; and they inform you by us that before you come to Calais they will meet with you to fight with you and be revenged of your conduct.' Henry replied calmly, 'Be all things according to the will of God.' Yet there was a hint of uneasiness in his answer to the heralds' enquiry as to what road he would take. 'Straight to Calais, and if our enemies try to disturb us in our journey, it will not be without the utmost peril. We do not intend to seek them out, but neither shall we go in fear of them either more slowly or more quickly than we wish to do. We advise them again not to interrupt our journey, nor to seek what would be in consequence a great shedding of Christian blood.'[2] Then he sent the heralds back to their masters, each with a hundred gold crowns. He realized that he had been outmanoeuvred and expected to be attacked the next day. He ordered his men to take up positions, anticipating an onslaught from the direction of Péronne where the enemy had their camp. But it became clear that the French were not going to attack, so he gave orders for everyone to get a good night's rest before continuing the march.

They awoke to a morning of drenching rain, beneath which they set out. For some days there were no serious incidents though ominous signs were not lacking, such as the road being churned up as if by the feet of 'an unimaginable host'. The rain was unrelenting, driven into their eyes by the wind; they had to sleep in it. Many of them were weakened by dysentery and kept their breeches down. They were all famished. Morale sank very low indeed.

On 24 October a terrified scout reported to the Duke of York that he had sighted the enemy through the drizzle. The English had just forded the 'river of swords', the little River Ternoise. The chaplain tells us that 'as we reached the crest of the hill on the other side, we

73

saw emerging from further up the valley, about half a mile away from us, hateful swarms of Frenchmen'. They were marching in three great 'battles' or columns, 'like a countless swarm of locusts',[3] towards the English to intercept them. For the French commanders had decided to make Henry stand and fight, and there was no hope of escape. He had been out-generalled. The English trudged on through the mud and the wet to the hamlet of Maisoncelles, where they bivouacked, preparing to spend yet another night under torrential rain. Even the king was shaken, releasing his prisoners and sending some of them into the French camp with a message that, in return for a safe passage to Calais, he was ready to surrender Harfleur and pay for any damage he had done. The offer was rejected. A Somerset knight, Sir Walter Hungerford, told Henry that they could do with 10,000 more archers, at which the king rounded on him, retorting that he was a fool since the troops they had 'are God's people'. He added, again with a hint of uneasiness, that no misfortune could befall a man with faith in God so sublime as his own.

A set-piece confrontation was the last thing he wanted. He had only seen one before, at Shrewsbury, where he had very nearly been on the defeated side and had almost lost his life. He shared Vegetius's opinion: 'a battle is commonly decided in two or three hours, after which no further hopes are left for the worsted army . . . a conjuncture full of uncertainty and fatal to kingdoms.' In any case he was more of a gunner, a sapper or a staff officer, than an infantry commander, and this was going to be an infantry battle. It was clearly with the utmost misgivings that he prepared for a general engagement.

According to English sources the French passed the night dicing for the English lords they expected to capture and for the rich ransoms they would demand. Later it was said that they were so confident that they had brought a painted cart with them in which to bring Henry back to Paris as a prisoner. They had plenty of wine and provisions and the sound of their feasting could be heard in the English camp. The Picard squire, Monstrelet, (born in 1390 and a contemporary) tells us, however, that the French passed a depressing night during which not even their horses neighed. He also says that, 'The English played their trumpets and other musical instruments, so that the whole neighbourhood resounded with their music while they made their peace with God.'[4] For, as all sources agree, the English were understandably terrified, confessing their sins to each

74

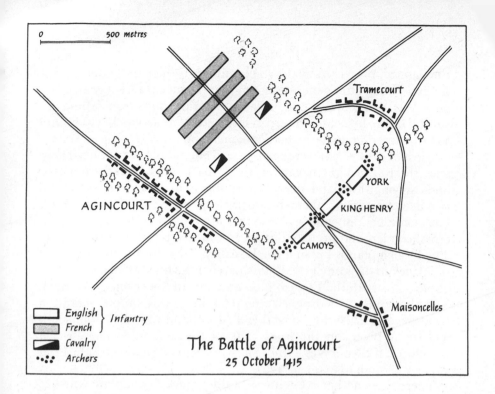

The Battle of Agincourt
25 October 1415

English ⎫ Infantry
French ⎭
Cavalry
Archers

Tramecourt

YORK

KING HENRY

AGINCOURT

CAMOYS

Maisoncelles

0   500 metres

other if the queues for priests were too long. The king ordered them
to keep silent during the night, under pain of forfeiture of horse and
armour for a gentleman, and of the right ear for a yeoman and
anyone of inferior rank. (The reality behind Shakespeare's 'touch of
Harry in the night'.) Armourers were kept very busy servicing
weapons, as were the fletchers and bowyers. All were exhausted after
their gruelling eighteen-day trek, all were sodden and starving, and
all must have dreaded the next morning. Henry had got his trial by
battle with a vengeance.

The chaplain, a fearful eyewitness, records how 'in the early dawn
the French arrayed themselves in battle-lines, columns and platoons
and took up position in that field called the field of Agincourt, across
which lay our road towards Calais, and the number of them was
really terrifying'. It was a vast open field sown with young corn, two
miles long and a mile wide but narrowing in the middle to about a
thousand yards, where a small wood hid the village of Agincourt to
the west and another small wood hid that of Tramecourt to the east.
The King had spent the night in the village of Maisoncelles to the
south, the French in and around that of Ruisseauville to the north.
The site, off the road from Hesdin to Arras, remains miraculously

75

unchanged, preserved by the re-planting of trees in the same clumps for generation after generation. On that particular day, because the corn was newly sown and because the rain had been falling for several days, the field had turned into a sea of mud which was bound to be churned up by large bodies of men and horses.

Most of the French were men-at-arms in full plate armour. There were three lines of them, each six deep, the first two lines dismounted and carrying sawn-off lances. A third line remained mounted, as did two detachments of 500 men-at-arms who were on the wings. They had some cannon and even some catapults together with a few crossbowmen and archers but there was no room to deploy them. The French plan – if plan it can be called – was for the horsemen on the wings to dispose of the English archers, while their men on foot got to grips with the English men-at-arms and overwhelmed them. They hoped that the English would facilitate this simple operation by attacking. Even the Constable d'Albret and Marshal Boucicault took their places in the front rank of the first line. The French therefore left themselves without any proper command structure, let alone any room to manoeuvre.

There was another eye-witness besides Henry's chaplain who has left an account. This was 'Messire Jehan, bastard de Waurin, sieur du Forestal', a Picard nobleman born in 1394 who fought on the French side and whose father and younger brother were killed in the ensuing combat. Waurin recalls what it was like for the French nobles to prepare for battle:

> And the said Frenchmen were so heavy laden with armour that they could not support the weight nor easily go forward; firstly they were armed in long steel coats of plate down to the knee or even lower and very heavy, with armour on their legs below, and underneath that white harness [felt], while most of them had on basinets with chain-mail; the which weight of armour, what with the softness of the trampled ground . . . made it hard for them to move or go forward, so that it was only with great difficulty that they might raise their weapons, since even before all these mischiefs many had been much weakened by hunger and lack of sleep. Indeed it was a marvel how it was possible to set in place the banners under which they fell in. And the said Frenchmen had each one shortened his lance that it might do more execution when it came to fighting and dealing blows. They had archers and crossbowmen enough but would not let them shoot, since so narrow was the field that there was room only for men-at-arms.[5]

The English also took up their positions at dawn. They were by now down to 800 men-at-arms at most and probably slightly under 5,000 archers. The former, dismounted and carrying sawn-off lances like the French, were grouped four deep in three 'battles', each one flanked by a projecting wedge of archers four or five deep; on both wings there was a horn-shaped formation of archers curving gently forward so that they could shoot in towards the centre. By the king's orders every archer stuck an eleven foot long stake, sharpened at both ends, into the ground in front of himself as protection against enemy cavalry. There were not enough troops for a reserve, so great was the disparity in numbers, the baggage train behind being guarded by ten men-at-arms and thirty archers. However, the English front did at least cover the entire centre while the flanks were protected by the woods.

Descriptions of Agincourt omit to comment on the relatively advanced age of the men whom the twenty-six-year-old monarch chose as his key commanders for this critical confrontation. The right was under his cousin, Edward, Duke of York, who at forty-two was the senior member of the royal family; fat and extremely cunning, once a favourite of Richard II, he was a natural survivor and by medieval standards in advanced middle age. The left wing was under Lord Camoys, married to Hotspur's widow, who had seen service against the French as long ago as the 1370s. A still more reassuring figure was 'old Sir Thomas Erpingham', Knight of the Garter, who had charge of the archers. Born in 1357 he had been a household man of both John of Gaunt and Bolingbroke, accompanying the latter into exile in 1397 and on his march from Ravenspur to seize the crown. He had become Steward of the Royal Household in 1404 and was someone whom the king had known for most of his life. Henry, as overall commander, took the centre himself. It is significant that he did not entrust one of the main commands to his brother Humphrey – he was plainly anxious to have the coolest and most reliable heads available.

The author of the *Gesta* was among the other chaplains, the sick and the supernumaries who stayed near the baggage. He says that he and his fellow English priests were so frightened that he believed the French to be thirty times larger than the English army, and that he and his companions prayed throughout 'in fear and trembling'. Nonetheless, he kept his head sufficiently to watch the battle and gives the best eye-witness account of it.[6]

Henry heard three Masses and took Communion before donning a burnished armour, over which he wore a velvet and satin surcoat, embroidered in gold with the leopards and lilies; on his helmet was a coronet, 'marvellous rich', studded with rubies, sapphires and many pearls. Then, riding a small grey pony – a page leading a great war-horse behind him – he rode up and down the line in front of his troops. His eve-of-battle speech struck a familiar note – he 'was come into France to recover his lawful inheritance and that he had good and just cause to claim it'. He warned the archers that the French had sworn to cut three fingers off the right hand of every English bowman captured. 'Sirs and fellows,' he promised his army, 'as I am true king and knight, for me this day shall never England ransom pay.' When he had finished they shouted back, 'Sir, we pray God give you a good life and the victory over your enemies!'

In the justified belief that it would be best for the English to open the battle, the French remained motionless, some 700 yards away. After waiting for four hours Henry decided that his cold, wet, hungry and weary men had stood there quite long enough and resolved to make the French attack. He ordered Erpingham to take the archers forward just within range of the enemy. When Sir Thomas signalled that he had done so, by throwing his wand of office into the air, the king gave the command, 'Banners advance! In the name of Jesus, Mary and St George!' His men therefore, as was their custom, first knelt and kissed the earth on which they made the sign of the cross, placing a morsel of soil in their mouths in token of desire for communion. Then, trumpets and tabors sounding ('which greatly encouraged the heart of every man'), they marched forward as steadily as the soggy ground permitted, shouting in unison at intervals, 'St George!' The little army was now within 300 yards of the vast host of the enemy, many of its men bedraggled and lacking equipment, especially the archers who went barefoot because of the mud. The latter replanted their stakes, a horse's breast high and angled so as to impale, and began to shoot. Volley after volley hissed up into the air for a hundred feet before descending noisily onto the Frenchmen who kept their heads down beneath the arrow storm – even if few arrows penetrated their expensive plate armour the clatter must have been unnerving.

Now the first line of the enemy, 8,000 strong, began to advance, roaring hollowly from inside their close helmets their traditional war cry of '*Montjoie! Saint Denis!*' At the same time 500 mounted French men-at-arms, led by the Sieurs Guillaume de Saveuse and Clignet de Brébant, charged the English on each flank. The archers repulsed them with ease. Three horses were impaled on the stakes and their riders killed, among them Saveuse. What drove the enemy horse off, however, was arrow fire under which their poor mounts became unmanageable, screaming and bolting back through those advancing on foot. They knocked many over, throwing the line into confusion. They also galloped over their gunners and catapult men, besides trampling down the sparse contingent of French archers and crossbowmen. Their example was contagious – after only one discharge the entire enemy artillery withdrew rather than face English arrows.

The first line of the dismounted French men-at-arms trudged grimly on, often sinking knee-deep into the mud on account of their weight, an exhausting business for a heavily-armoured man. Their ranks included the greatest names of France, royal as well as noble, for among them were the Dukes of Bourbon and Orleans. The English archers shot point-blank at their flanks – armour-piercing range. To avoid the murderous hail the French flinched away towards the centre, bunching up, so that the line turned into a dense scrum. Nevertheless they came doggedly on, though trying to keep away from the wedges of archers between the English battles who were also shooting at them. At last three tightly packed columns of French infantry crashed into the English men-at-arms, with such an impact that the latter were flung two or three yards back.

But the French were packed so close together that they could not raise their arms to use their weapons, while those in front were pushed over by those behind. Once down it was almost impossible for them to regain their feet. The fallen were soon pressed further down by more and more men falling on top of them in ever growing heaps; many drowned in mud or were suffocated by the bodies above. (John Hardyng, a former squire of Hotspur's who was present, says specifically that 'more were dead through press than our men might have killed'.) As soon as their arrows were exhausted, the English archers seized 'swords, hatchets, mallets, axes, falcon-beaks and other weapons' – even stakes according to the *Gesta* – and rushed at their enemies. Lightly clad, they jumped on top of the prostrate men-at-arms, frequently three deep, to get at their companions. Yet more Frenchmen were pushed off their feet and lost their balance as the second line came up behind.

The English men-at-arms were saved from being similarly pushed over because there were so few of them. An exception was the fat Duke of York, who was trampled under foot and suffocated. They were able to use their own weapons, at close quarters and to maximum effect. Tito Livio, who had met many who had been in the battle, says that Henry fought 'like a maned lion seeking his prey'. Some Frenchmen fought back ferociously and Tito's patron, the Duke of Gloucester, 'sore wounded in the hams with a sword', fell half-dead, with his feet towards the enemy. The king stood over him, fighting off assailants until his brother could be picked up and carried to the rear.[7]

The Duke of Alençon, a prince of the Blood, who had led the second French line, was one of those in the mêlée round Gloucester. He had left the scrum for a moment, mounting a horse to go back and rally the growing number of deserters. Failing, he returned and, together with a handful of French men-at-arms, attacked Gloucester's party. One source says he hacked a fleuret from Henry's helmet. At last, beaten to his knees, Alençon surrendered to the king and removed his helmet, whereupon a berserk English knight cut him down with an axe.

The French were everywhere lying in heaps, sometimes higher than a man on his feet. Many were alive, prevented by their armour from rising. The English finished some off as they lay like stranded turtles, thrusting a dagger through their visors, but the majority – perhaps as many as 3,000 – were pulled out and sent to the rear as prisoners for ransom.

Suddenly a shout went up that the third, mounted, French line was about to attack. The Duke of Brabant, a younger brother of the Duke of Burgundy, and another prince of the Blood, had arrived late. Being without a surcoat he borrowed a tabard from his herald and then tried to persuade the French reserve to go into action. In the event he charged almost alone and was eventually unhorsed; because of his tabard he was unrecognized and had his throat cut. It is possible that this happened at a slightly earlier stage in the battle. What is certain is that after the rout of the second line two brave French noblemen, the Counts of Marle and Fauquembergues, swore to kill Henry or perish and prepared to launch a final despairing charge with a mere 600 men.

The king was already uneasy enough about the prisoners at the rear. Just before the start of the battle local peasants had raided his baggage but had been driven off. It was possible they might try to raid it again. When it looked as though he might expect a serious attack from the third line and that it was possible the captured men-at-arms might break free and join their comrades, he ordered their liquidation. His men were horrified, not from compassion but at the prospect of losing such valuable ransoms. Henry promised to hang anyone who refused to obey. He detailed 200 archers to slaughter the prisoners; in the words of a Tudor chronicler, they were 'sticked with daggers, brained with pole-axes, slain with mauls', and finished off by being 'paunched in fell and cruel wise'.[8] We know from a survivor, Gilbert de Lannoy, that one batch were burnt to death in the hut where they were confined. Those spared were worth great sums, such as princes of the Blood like the Duke of Orleans. The king stopped the slaughter when he realized that he was not threatened by a serious attack from the French third line and was throwing money away.

This massacre of prisoners in 1415 is Henry V's one generally acknowledged peccadillo. Almost every one of his English biographers and historians tries to absolve him of guilt, referring to the lack of condemnation by contemporary English chroniclers, or to 'the standards of the time'. In reality, by fifteenth-century standards, to massacre captive, unarmed noblemen who, according to the universally recognized international laws of chivalry, had every reason to expect to be ransomed if they surrendered formally, was a peculiarly nasty crime – especially by someone who constantly claimed to be a 'true knight'. The chronicler Waurin notes with horror that it was done 'in cold blood' (*'de froit sang'*).

The charge by Marle and Fauquembergues had been routed without difficulty, since by then the English not only outnumbered them but were protected by ramparts of French corpses. Both Marle and Fauquembergues lost their lives. The remainder of the French third line, its nerve broken, rode off the field. In under four hours the English king and his tiny army had routed a force many times larger. For a loss of 500 men at most they had slain nearly 10,000 of their opponents, if one includes the prisoners they had put to death. Besides York, the English notables killed numbered only one peer, the young Earl of Suffolk (whose father had perished of fever at Harfleur), and a handful of knights – among them that redoubtable Welsh veteran Davy Gam with his two son-in-laws, Walter Lloyd and Roger Vaughan. The French had lost the Dukes of Alençon, Bar and Brabant, the Count of Nevers (another brother of the Duke of Burgundy) with eight other counts, ninety-two barons, 1,500 knights and countless gentlemen. Among the prisoners who had survived the massacre were the Dukes of Bourbon and Orleans, the Counts of Eu, Richemont and Vendôme, with 1,500 gentlemen.

81

The rest of the day was spent searching for overlooked prisoners and cutting the throats of the disabled or worthless. The bodies of the English dead were taken to a big barn at Maisoncelles which was piled high with faggots and then set alight to burn throughout the night as a funeral pyre. That evening Henry's most distinguished captives served him at supper on bended knee. God had spoken, giving his verdict on the trial by battle – now he knew that he was in truth King of England, and of France too. He named his victory 'Agincourt' after the nearby castle.

It began to rain again. Next morning, wearier than ever, the English army resumed their march to Calais through the downpour. The troops were weighed down with expensive armours looted from the dead and from their prisoners. Still seriously short of rations, they now had to feed the prisoners as well. When the army reached Calais on 29 October its welcome left much to be desired. Many men were refused entry, while those admitted had to sell their armours and their prisoners to pay for the extortionate prices they were charged for provisions.

The king lodged at his castle of Guisnes outside Calais, where he imprisoned his own extremely valuable captives. Understandably, he was in an excellent mood, telling the Duke of Orleans that his victory was scarcely to be wondered at 'for never were there greater disorders, sensuality and vices than now prevail in France, which it is horrible to hear described'. It would be many years before some of these prisoners came home; Marshal Boucicault would die in captivity at Methley in Yorkshire in 1421 while Orleans was not released from the Tower of London until 1440. Even so, they were luckier than many humbler fellow captives later sold as servants in England by the Calais merchants (who had bought them from the troops) when it was found that they could not pay their ransoms.

So certain was Henry of God's favour that he proposed to his commanders that the army should attack some neighbouring French town. They listened with incredulity, pointing out he had very few troops, many of them badly wounded while others were still suffering from the bloody flux and that everyone wanted to go home. He had to agree to return to England.

The Sieurs d'Estouteville and de Gaucourt, with others paroled at Harfleur, came, as 'faithful captives', to Calais and surrendered to the king. Now he was ready to depart, sailing on Saturday 16 November during a raging storm. Two ships sank and the French prisoners on board the royal ship found the voyage worse than their worst moments at Agincourt – they were deeply impressed by their captor's seemingly cast-iron stomach.[9]

VIII

'To Teach the Frenchmen Courtesy'

'So great was the love that they had to the king in every way; and so much the desire of his return, that a right great number of them went into the water upon their feet until they came unto the king's ships, purposing to bear him to the land in their arms.'

The First English Life of King Henry the Fifth

*'A giant that was full grim of sight,
To teach the Frenchmen courtesy.'*

Inscription on a statue welcoming Henry home to London

At home, England had been deeply concerned about the fate of the king and his army. There was no news for three weeks, during which alarming rumours had circulated. At last, on the day that Henry marched into Calais, triumphant letters from him reached the Chancellor, Bishop Beaufort and the Mayor of London, Nicholas Wolton (popularly known as 'Witless Nick'). The Chancellor read the glorious tidings from the steps of St Paul's and then the bells of all the City's churches pealed until sunset. The news swiftly travelled throughout the entire country, which rejoiced, relief heightening everyone's joy.

The king and his battered fleet sailed into Dover, just as night was falling, on 16 November. They had been running before the wind to survive the storm, which was why they had made so fast a crossing. They were greeted by a frantically cheering crowd, some of whom rushed waist-high into the waves to carry Henry ashore on their shoulders. He spent Sunday quietly at Dover, and then rode to Canterbury where he spent two days, offering thanks at the shrine of

St Thomas, before going up to Eltham the following Friday. He entered his capital on Saturday 23 November.

First he was welcomed at Blackheath by several Londoners, who had been waiting for him since dawn. They were headed by Witless Nick and the twenty-four aldermen in their scarlet robes, while everyone else who could afford it wore red robes in token of rejoicing. Having congratulated the king, the citizens hurried back before him to London to see the pageant which had been prepared. When he came to London Bridge at about 10.00 a.m. he was greeted at the Surrey side by huge effigies of a giant and giantess erected on top of the bridge tower, and by trumpets. The giant was armed with a battle-axe and held out great keys as though offering them to Henry. A xenophobic inscription on it declaimed:

> *A* gyaunt *that was full grym of syght,*
> *To teche the Frensshmen curtesye.*[1]

An inscription on the tower read 'THE CITY OF THE KING OF JUSTICE'. In the middle of the bridge were two tall pillars of simulated marble and jasper, one with a golden antelope bearing a shield displaying the royal arms, the other with a golden lion grasping a staff from which floated the royal standard. Above the tower at the far end stood a beautiful statue of St George in armour, his left hand holding a scroll which hung down over the battlements and was inscribed 'TO GOD ALONE BE HONOUR AND GLORY'. In a house next to the bridge choristers dressed as angels, with gilt wings and gilded faces, sang 'Blessed is He who cometh in the name of the Lord.'

The tower of the conduit at the Tun in Cornhill was covered in crimson and flanked by white-haired prophets in golden copes, who released a flock of sparrows and sang a psalm when Henry rode by. The tower of the conduit at the beginning of Cheapside – London's richest street – had a green canopy emblazoned with the City's arms; next to it stood more patriarchs representing the twelve apostles and twelve English kings who likewise sang a psalm of jubilation when the king drew near. These offered him loaves wrapped in silver leaves and wine from the conduit, just as Melchizedek offered bread and wine to Abraham when he returned from his victory over the four kings. An entire wooden castle had been built round the cross in Cheapside, with elaborate towers and ramparts. Beautiful maidens came forth from it to welcome Henry, singing and dancing before

85

him with timbrels – 'as though to another David coming from the slaying of Goliath, who might very suitably represent the arrogant French', comments the *Gesta* smugly. The maidens sang, in English, '*Welcome, Henry ye fifte, Kynge of Englond and of Fraunce*', showering the monarch with laurel leaves and gold coins, and then singing *Te Deum*. The tower of the final conduit before St Paul's was decorated with niches in which stood 'exquisite young maidens' holding gold cups from which they gently blew golden leaves down on the king as he went forward to dismount and enter the cathedral for a Mass of thanksgiving presided over by eighteen vested prelates.

'The City was decked in all the raiment of gladness, and rightfully there was great joy among the people,' says Adam of Usk. The author of the *Gesta*, who was an eyewitness, and to whom we owe most of this account, gives eloquent testimony to the enthusiasm of spectators of all classes:

> apart from the dense crowd of men standing still or hurrying along the streets and the great number of those, men and women together, gazing from windows and openings, however small, along the route from the bridge, so great was the throng of people in Cheapside, from one end to the other, that the horsemen were only just able, although not without difficulty, to ride through. And the upper rooms and windows on both sides were packed with some of the noblest ladies and womenfolk of the kingdom and men of honour and renown, who had assembled for this pleasing spectacle, and who were so very becomingly and elegantly decked out in cloth of gold, fine linen and scarlet, and other rich apparel of various kinds, that no one could recall there ever having previously been in London a greater assemblage or a more noble array.[2]

What gave particular pleasure was the sight of the captured French noblemen being paraded behind the king.

A famous carol, or song of rejoicing, was written to celebrate this wonderful day:

> Owre Kynge went forth to Normandy,
> With grace and myght of chivalry;
> The God for hym wrought
>   marvelously,
> Wherefore Englonde may calle, and cry
>   Deo gratias:
> Deo gratias Anglia redde pro victoria.

The carol goes on to glory in his having

> made a fray
> That Fraunce shall rywe tyl domes day

and to exult in the humiliation of the traditional enemy:

> Ther dukys, and erlys, lorde and barone,
> Were take, and slayne, and that wel done,
> And some were ledde into Lundone
> With joye, and merthe and grete renone.

There is an unmistakeable note of xenophobia.

Amidst all the gaiety of this triumph, the author of the *Gesta* was struck by Henry's odd expression. He looked strangely sober and pensive, and he was dressed in purple – the colour which English monarchs normally wore when in mourning. He may well have been contemplating his plans for the conquest of France and for seizing its crown. However most spectators who watched him seem to have attributed his restrained bearing to his known piety and humility.

Henry's delighted subjects did more than simply welcome him with a pageant. On 24 November, 200 prominent Londoners, Witless Nick at their head, presented him with £1,000 in gold coin at a special ceremony; the gift came in two gold basins worth another £1,000. Even before he had returned to the capital, at a Parliament presided over by the Duke of Bedford, the Commons had granted the king for life a subsidy of 4 marks (£2 13s 4d) on wool-sacks, of 3s on wine-tuns and poundage of 1s on other goods. The clergy in convocation had agreed that he should levy two extra 'tenths'. The Agincourt carol was speaking for the entire nation in saying that England ought to thank God for so marvellous a victory.

Henry's reputation now stood very high indeed, and not just in his own country. England had acquired an important role in European diplomacy, one which its ruler knew how to exploit to the full. His principal object was to ensure the Duke of Burgundy's neutrality during any future invasion of France and he was well aware that the Duke's nightmare was an anti-Burgundian alliance between the Kings of England and France and the Holy Roman Emperor Sigismund. At the same time Henry was anxious to impress world opinion of both the justice of his claim to France and his moderation

87

– world opinion being embodied by the council of the Church then meeting at Constance. The emperor was the most promising instrument for his purpose.

Sigismund of Bohemia was a brother of the deposed Emperor Wenzel the Drunkard, and therefore an uncle of Richard II's first wife. Elected King of the Romans in 1410, proclaiming himself emperor in the following year, formerly King-Consort of Hungary, he was now King of Bohemia in his own right and, from his capital of Prague, eager to enhance his prestige as titular overlord of western Christendom. He was a cruel and violent-tempered man, primarily a soldier – although a disastrous commander – and a lover of pleasure whose time was spent in womanizing and jousting. He nonetheless had a good intellect and was a fine Latinist and patron of letters. His plan was simple and not ignoble; to heal the schism in the Church by ending the scandal of a disputed papacy, and then to unite Christendom in a revived Crusade. However, his debauchery and dishonesty undermined his credibility.

Henry had considerable sympathy with Sigismund's plan, which appealed to his own pious ideals. For over thirty years there had been two popes, one at Rome and the other at Avignon. This number increased to three in 1410 – Benedict XIII at Avignon, Gregory XII at Rome and John XXIII at Pisa. The council which met at Constance from 1414–17 was determined to end a situation in which some countries recognized one pope and others another, by making all three resign. Bishop Hallum of Salisbury told Pope John – the former Baldassare Cossa, a professional *condottiere* – that he disgraced his office. John had been deposed in 1415. In Gibbon's words, 'the most scandalous charges were suppressed; the vicar of Christ was only accused of piracy, murder, rape, sodomy, and incest.' Eventually the council secured the removal of all three pontiffs (pausing only to burn Oldcastle's correspondent, the Bohemian heresiarch Huss) and the election of a universally acceptable pope, Martin V (Colonna). Sigismund enjoyed great prestige since it was he who had forced Pope John to summon the council. Where the English king differed from the emperor was on how to achieve the next stage of the plan – securing peace between European rulers – even if he was as enthusiastic an advocate of a new crusade.

Sigismund had been urging an alliance between himself, England and France since 1414, an alliance against the rising power of Burgundy which was encroaching on imperial territory. In pursuit of his aim the emperor travelled all over Europe. He arrived in Paris early in 1416 with the avowed intention of making peace between France and England. The Armagnac faction, which still controlled Charles VI, regarded Agincourt as a temporary setback and expected the fall of Harfleur any day. They were irritated by the emperor's pretentions, disgusted by his dirtiness, his heavy drinking and his even heavier whoring; on one occasion he invited 600 'ladies' to dinner. (A sixteenth-century legend claims that in hell the Holy Roman Emperor was endlessly bathed in a red-hot bath and put to bed in a red-hot bed by ladies whom he had led astray during this life.) They did not relish paying his bills.

After several weeks at Paris, Sigismund decided to further his mission in England. The French encouraged him, hoping he might secure the release of the magnates who had been taken prisoner at Agincourt. Accompanied by 1,500 knights he crossed the Channel in 300 ships provided by Henry. As his fleet sailed into Dover on May Day 1416 he was met by the Duke of Gloucester and a large entourage who all rode into the waves with drawn swords, refusing to let him land until he had formally denied any claims to jurisdiction over the realm. As he journeyed towards London he was greeted at each halting place with increasing splendour until finally, a mile outside the capital, he was met by the king and 5,000 persons of quality. After a splendid progress through the City the 'most Christian and most superillustrious [*superillustrissimus*] prince' was given the royal palace of Westminster as a residence during his stay in England. This lasted four months, in which time he received every honour in Henry's power. The emperor was formally welcomed by Parliament in the name of the English people. (This was less empty a gesture than it sounds since in theory Sigismund was the sword temporal of Christendom and the ultimate monarch. Until 1964 Catholic missals contained a prayer for the Holy Roman Emperor with, however, the proviso that it was no longer said; 'the empire being vacant'.) The king presented him with his own collar of gold 'S's, something worn by all English magnates, and invested him as a Knight of the Garter at Windsor. It was particularly gratifying that Sigismund gave the Order's chapel the actual heart of St George which he had brought with him. He was entertained in the most lavish way possible – his normally frugal host putting the French to shame. Sigismund succumbed to these blandishments, signing a treaty of offence and defence at Canterbury which recognized the English king's right to the French throne.

During September and October Henry, the emperor and the Duke of Burgundy met at Calais to conclude a mutual alliance. Sigismund's role was largely ceremonial, since the English monarch had extracted every public gesture he required of him. Burgundy was a different matter. After elaborate ceremonies – and the surrender of the Duke of Gloucester as a hostage – Burgundy was 'engaged with the king alone, until the dusk of the evening in secret consulation', later followed by an official banquet. The author of the *Gesta* writes of Duke John that 'in the end, like all Frenchmen, he would be found a double-dealer [*duplex*], one person in public and another in private'.[3] John agreed in a secret treaty to recognize all Henry's claims, promising that as soon as the English had conquered enough French territory he would pay homage to Henry as his sovereign. Whether the treaty represented Duke John's real intentions or not, it certainly demonstrated the English king's skill as a diplomat, convincing the Burgundians that Henry had to be taken very seriously indeed and not just as a soldier.

There was still a thoroughly hawkish war party in France, led by Bernard, Count of Armagnac, newly appointed as constable and leader of the realm's military forces. The constable-count, a ferocious Gascon, out-manoeuvred the Dukes of Anjou and Berry – who cravenly favoured peace – and secured control of the pitiful King Charles who had slipped into madness yet again. He had very little opposition. The Dauphin Louis died in December 1415 and his brother John who succeeded him was a prisoner of his father-in-law the Duke of Burgundy. Armagnac was strong enough to keep Burgundy at bay while the other leaders of his own faction, the Dukes of Bourbon and Orleans, were prisoners in England. Their ransoming had been forbidden by King Henry. He concentrated on recapturing Harfleur. The garrison commander there, the Earl of Dorset (the former Sir Thomas Beaufort), had been feeding his men by raiding deep into the countryside round about, almost to the gates of Rouen, and doing considerable damage. In March 1416 – alerted by the flames from plundered farmhouses which were an infallible sign of the presence of English troops – Armagnac intercepted Dorset and his army, taking him by surprise at Valmont with a charge and riding down his men-at-arms and his archers. Although the English extricated themselves, eventually routing their pursuers, it was only with great difficulty and after suffering many casualties. Dorset did not dare continue his raids and Harfleur began to starve. Armagnac besieged the town, hiring nine carracks and eight galleys from Genoa to blockade it. The Genoese did more than blockade, they devastated

Portland Bill, raided the Isle of Wight and threatened both Portsmouth and Southampton – though an attempt to fire the King's Ships in Southampton Water was beaten off. No English merchantman dared to put to sea since the Genoese made the Channel too dangerous. A single vessel laden with provisions managed to slip into Harfleur by flying the fleur-de-lys, relieving its beleaguered defenders but only for the moment. The French had every reason to hope that they would soon starve it into surrender. It became a focus of English national pride – the Commons 'groused full sore' at the mere suggestion that it might be used as a bargaining counter.

In August 1416 the Duke of Bedford sailed with the King's Ships to succour the famished garrison. He was joined by a fleet from the Cinque Ports. On 16 August the duke engaged the Franco-Genoese warships in the mouth of the Seine, opposite Harfleur. A notably bloody hand-to-hand combat ensued, vessels lashed gunwale to gunwale, during which Bedford was severely – though not fatally – wounded. The English were disadvantaged by the superior height of the carracks' fighting castles fore and aft, from which the enemy shot down at them with crossbows, and hurled flaming tow to set their ships alight. They also threw quicklime into their eyes. The English replied with bows and small cannon. After five hours of carnage the enemy were routed and the English sailed triumphantly into Harfleur. When they sallied out from the walls next morning they found the French had abandoned the siege.

Henry believed that the French enemy and its Genoese carracks were nonetheless still a danger, and steadily increased his own fleet.[4] By the summer of 1417 he had eight square-rigged, two-masted carracks, the best fighting ships of the day (among them being those captured by Bedford from the Genoese), six smaller square-rigged cogs, nine of the indispensable ballingers and a large sailing barge. He also possessed three square-rigged nefs or 'great ships', which he had had specially built; the *Jesus*, the *Trinity Royal* and the *Holigost*. Most were surprisingly big: the carracks were 500 tons each, the *Trinity Royal* and the *Holigost* 750 tons, and the *Jesus* (recently laid down for the King at Smallhythe in Kent) was 1,000 tons. Eventually there would be as many as thirty King's Ships, some even larger than the *Jesus*, such as the *Grace Dieu*. An account has been left of her by a Florentine seaman who saw her at Southampton in 1430. He says, 'truly I have never seen so large and magnificent a construction, I had the mast measured on the first deck and it was about twenty-one

91

feet in circumference and 195½ feet high. From the gallery of the prow to the water was about fifty feet and they say that when she is at sea another corridor is raised above this. She was about 176½ feet long and about ninety-six feet in the beam.' As has been seen, the advantage of such height in medieval sea battles was that it enabled archers to fire down on the enemy; such vessels could carry a crew of eighty and up to 250 fighting men. Skippers were not particularly well paid, the master of the *Jesus* receiving ten marks (£6 13*s* 4*d*) a year while the master of a ballinger got only five marks. The King's Ships were to prove their worth again and again. In June 1417 the Earl of Huntingdon engaged a Franco-Genoese fleet commanded by the Bastard of Bourbon off La Hogue at the end of the Cherbourg peninsula in a battle which lasted all day. He was victorious, capturing four carracks and the Bastard himself – who had with him his men's pay for an entire quarter – while the remaining five enemy carracks ran for shelter in the Breton harbours. Henry's ships continued to patrol the Channel but met with no more opposition. Not only was the sea free from privateers (whether French, Genoese, Castilian or Scots) so that English merchantmen could trade in safety, but the king now commanded the sea routes which he needed for his invasion.

When Parliament met in March 1416 the Chancellor, Beaufort, preached what can only be called an invasion sermon. After complaining of the 'unjust' French refusal to recognize Henry's claim to be their ruler – 'Why do not these miserable and hardhearted men see by these terrible divine sentences that they are bound to obey'? – he exhorted the assembled Lords and Commons to help the king with money. Many contributed, no doubt not just from indignation at the spectacle of Henry being deprived of his 'rights' but out of sheer national pride.

The king was tireless in his attention to finance, obtaining £136,000 from taxes, a remarkable achievement. He also raised loans wherever he could. He borrowed 21,000 marks (£14,000) from Beaufort on the security of his best crown, and another large sum from the City on a jewelled collar. Lesser sums, some very small, were secured from prelates and abbots, from magnates and squires, from city corporations and merchants, on the security of anything precious in the royal coffers, whether crowns, jewels, relics or altar plate. He had learnt this technique during the Welsh war. There were the usual problems of provisions, munitions and logistics. Early in 1417 the sheriffs were instructed to have six wing feathers plucked from every goose in their county and sent to depots, while bow staves and arrows were ordered by the barrel.

During the king's absence England had remained astonishingly peaceful under the regency of John, Duke of Bedford. Henry's restoration of law and order had held up very well, and after Agincourt his reputation ensured its survival. Such a hero no longer had anything to fear from Ricardians or Lollards, even though a pseudo-Richard was still alive in Scotland and though John Oldcastle still roamed the Welsh border. The Scots regent was not going to give trouble when his king was a prisoner in England while Wales was a cowed and broken land. Henry felt sufficiently secure to restore the Earl of Northumberland to all his honours and estates. He had no cause to worry about leaving his realm for a second time in the hands of so capable a regent as Bedford.

Nevertheless there was an incident in 1416 which, if scarcely dangerous, must have been extremely distasteful to the king. In April in the Court of King's Bench a canon of Wells Cathedral, Richard Bruton, was charged with treasonable talk. He had told one of his tenants that Henry was not the real King of England and that his father had had no right to the crown. Bruton had also said that he thoroughly approved of what Scrope and his friends had tried to do, and that he himself was ready to contribute £6,000 towards deposing Henry. Admittedly this conversation had taken place on 14 October 1415, before Agincourt, but it was an uncomfortable reminder that many Englishmen had reservations about the right of the House of Lancaster to rule over them.[5]

Henry's brothers ranked first in his team of commanders though their capabilities varied considerably. Aggressive and impetuous, Thomas of Clarence was the team's Murat – essentially a dashing cavalryman who was ideal for the attack or spearheading unexpected thrusts into enemy territory, but whose grasp of strategy and tactics was faulty. His only interest other than soldiering and the tournament was heraldry for which he had a passion. The Duke of Bedford, a big fleshy man with a huge hook nose, very unlike the handsome Clarence, was a far more gifted, if less enthusiastic, soldier; his attention to detail and steadiness won major battles on both land and sea. He was also a remarkably effective administrator, of such high calibre that the king never hesitated in entrusting him with the regency, the 'home front'. Jean Favier emphasizes the extraordinary co-operation and support he gave to his royal brother.[6] The most striking quality of this unusually good-natured man, one which Henry did not share, was that he understood and liked the French, a liking they reciprocated. Gloucester, youngest of the brothers and the family intellectual, was least useful – vain, opinionated and headstrong, adequate if given limited tasks under strict supervision. The other member of the family to belong to the team was Henry's uncle, the Duke of Exeter (Thomas Beaufort, formerly Earl of Dorset, created a duke for life in 1416). He was a superb fighting soldier as he had showed by his defence of Harfleur and by snatching victory from defeat at Valmont. A thoroughly dependable workhorse, he was often given immense responsibility.

'The wars in France turned the higher nobility into professional soldiers,' says G. L. Harriss.[7] Foremost among these soldier noblemen were the Earls of Salisbury, Warwick and Huntingdon, and Lord Talbot. Thomas Montacute, Earl of Salisbury, a year younger than the king and the son of Richard II's favourite, was the most brilliant commander of the entire Hundred Years War after Henry himself. Henry had total trust in him – although to begin with he may have had reservations because of his parentage. A complete professional, he was a daring raider into enemy territory who could extricate his men from the most dangerous situations; at the same time he was a skilled artilleryman and expert in siegecraft, like the king, and no less sound on staffwork or in finding supplies. Above all, he had a shrewd grasp of strategy and tactics. Although a ferocious disciplinarian he was popular with the troops. He was dreaded by the enemy. Shakespeare probably conveys accurately enough what the French thought about him:

> *Salisbury is a desperate homicide;*
> *He fighteth as one weary of his life.*

His ways with prisoners did not endear him to the French – after capturing the château of Orsay in 1423 he brought the garrison back to Paris with ropes round their necks.

Richard Beauchamp, Earl of Warwick, was five years older than Henry and had campaigned with him against Glyn Dŵr. He was an avaricious knight errant with a taste for the spectacular; in 1408 he had performed a long, roundabout pilgrimage to Jerusalem, a species of grand tour during which he stayed with Charles VI at Paris, with the Doge of Venice and with the Grand Master of the Teutonic Knights in Prussia, fighting in tournaments whenever possible – most notably a ferocious duel on foot against Pandolfo

Malatesta. At the same time he was a steady and resourceful commander in the field and an excellent administrator. The king had so much respect for Warwick that he appointed him a governor and tutor of his son. There was, however, an extremely unpleasant side to the earl, who was basically a hard, cold and ruthless politician-soldier; one day he would burn Joan of Arc.

Another well-tried commander, four years older than Henry, who had also done good service in Wales, was Gilbert, Lord Talbot. The youngest of the team was John Holland, the son of Richard II's step-brother, to whom the king only restored his father's earldom in 1417. From a military point of view he was undeniably precocious; born in 1396, he had distinguished himself during the 1415 campaign, leading the first landing at Harfleur and fighting with outstanding gallantry at Agincourt.

Almost as useful as these four were Sir John Cornwall (the future Lord Fanhope), Sir Gilbert Umfraville (styled 'Earl of Kyme'), Sir John Grey (soon to become Count of Tancarville), Sir Walter Hungerford (the first Lord Hungerford) and Lord Willoughby d'Eresby. Cornwall was a 'left-handed' Plantagenet, being descended through a bastard line from Richard, Earl of Cornwall and King of the Romans – Henry III's brother – and having married as his third wife Henry IV's sister, Elisabeth, who fell in love with him after a dazzling performance at a tournament. (He was also Huntingdon's stepfather, by his second marriage.) A specialist in the assault, with Huntingdon he had been the first to land at Harfleur, and he was the first to force his way over the Somme on the march to Agincourt, where he had fought magnificently. Although by now well into his forties he was to prove one of the most aggressive of all the king's soldiers. Umfraville, a Northumbrian from Redesdale, was another extremely able commander – a young man who was popular with the men and whose attractive personality can be sensed over the centuries. Sir John Grey of Heton (brother of Sir Thomas of the Southampton Plot) was another dashing Northumbrian who was a natural soldier. Sir Walter Hungerford of Farleigh Hungerford in Somerset, who became Steward of the Royal Household, was a former MP for Wiltshire and Somerset and a former Speaker of the House of Commons. Despite his legendary loss of nerve at Agincourt he was a sound fighting man who made a fortune out of ransoms and loot during the war. Willoughby d'Eresby who, although thirty-two by 1417 had not been at Agincourt, spent the rest of his long life fighting in France and was yet another dedicated commander.

There was a host of lesser talent from outside the ranks of the upper nobility. Like Hungerford, some had profited from ransoms won at Agincourt, and all hoped for opportunities for fresh plunder in France. Even though unattracted by the prospect of arduous and dangerous campaigning, every prominent landowner must have been aware that he risked Henry's displeasure if he failed to obey the royal summons to serve abroad. The king also wanted men to administer the territories he was going to conquer; gentlemen such as Sir John Assheton (a former MP for Lancashire), Sir Thomas Rempston (Knight of the Garter and a former MP for Nottinghamshire), Sir Rowland Lenthall from Herefordshire, Sir John Radcliffe from Westmorland, and many others. They came to fight, however advanced in years, bringing their own men-at-arms and archers with them, though, as will be seen, more often than not other duties awaited them. Not just the peerage but the entire landed gentry of England, including thirty MPs, were to be mobilized for conquest across the Channel. Most would serve as simple men-at-arms.[8] They have been called the most bellicose squirearchy in Europe.

Henry did more than prepare to mobilize. He secured the Duke of Brittany's neutrality. Brittany stood in relation to France rather as Scotland did to England. Even though the French king was technically the duke's overlord, there was an ancient, long-established sense of a separate identity which verged on separate nationality. Breton lawyers claimed that 'the country (*pais*) of Brittany is a country separate and distinct from others'. Not only were its dukes consecrated in a coronation ceremony at the Breton capital of Rennes, but they possessed their own order of chivalry, the Knights of the Ermine (named after the ermine fur which was the ducal coat of arms and the banner of Brittany).

The duke at that time, John V (1399–1442), a cunning and faithless politician, had little cause to favour Henry, who had taken his brother prisoner at Agincourt. The king disliked him intensely and had neither forgotten nor forgiven the ferocious activities of Breton privateers in the recent past. Nevertheless the duke was invited to England and apparently visited Southampton in April 1417. Henceforth the English and the Bretons signed a series of truces pledging themselves to refrain from acts of war against each other. John V did so most unwillingly and many Breton contingents served unofficially with the French armies. However, the duke was a realist. Although he far preferred the Valois to the Plantagenets he was determined to be on the winning side and was obviously impressed by the English king. It was vital for Henry that Brittany should stay out of the conflict and he somehow succeeded in maintaining peace. It was a considerable diplomatic achievement.

In November 1416 the author of the *Gesta* recorded 'the king's unbreakable resolve to go overseas in the following summer to subdue the stubborn and more than adamantine obduracy of the French, which neither the tender milk of goats nor the consuming wine of vengeance, nor yet the most thoroughgoing negotiations, could soften'. He adds that Henry's aim was that 'the two swords, the sword of the French and the sword of England, may return to the rightful government of a single ruler'.[9] He may well have been echoing the king's own words, since Henry frequently put his case in similar terms.

IX

The Fall of Caen

'*Down goeth the wall; in and upon them then!*'

A fifteenth-century translation
of Vegetius's *De Re Militari*

'This storm of war raised up against us by the people of England'

Jean Chartier, *Chronique de Charles VII*

By March 1417 the king was gathering ships and troops. As before, many vessels were hired from the Low Countries; in addition a number of Venetian merchantmen were commandeered and, despite having lost so many carracks to the English, the Genoese also supplied some boats. Henry left London for Southampton at the end of April. There were the same massive preparations as in 1415. The assembly of men, livestock, food, tools, and weaponry, was, if anything, on a larger scale than before. The *Brut of England* speaks of 'guns, trebuchets, engines, sows, bastilles, bridges of leather, scaling ladders, mauls, spades, shovels, picks, pavises, bows and arrows, bowstrings, shafts and pipes full of arrows' and that 'thither come to him ships laden with gunpowder'.[1] (Trebuchets were rock-throwing catapults, sows and bastilles were armoured shelters for attacking walls and siege-towers, while pavises were standing shields for protecting archers as they shot.) Probably as many as 12,000 men-at-arms and bowmen mustered, with perhaps 30,000 supernumaries – miners, engineers, armourers, farriers, gunners, masons (to make gunstones) etc. The fleet in which they were to embark numbered not less than 1,500 sail. The invasion was delayed until the late summer, till Lord Huntingdon had eliminated any danger from the Genoese carracks in France's service; even then, the Earl of March was ordered to 'skim the sea' and guard against any further naval threat, though none would be forthcoming. The king had a healthy respect for warships. The embarkation began on 23 July. On 30 July his second armada set out for France. His own ship was distinguished by a mainsail of purple silk which bore the royal arms.

Henry intended not just to invade but to conquer Normandy – a full-scale Norman Conquest in reverse. The duchy was to be another Guyenne. Territory would be held by occupying strongholds – cities, towns or châteaux – at strategic key points. It was essential to reduce every one of these in the areas invaded since even a small enemy garrison behind the lines could, if led by a skilled commander, disrupt communications and supplies. The king must have had maps of a sort, although none have survived – otherwise he could never have planned the forthcoming campaigns with such brilliant precision.

As a soldier Henry V is generally thought of as the victor of Agincourt, who used archers to mow down the French chivalry. Yet he was first and foremost an artilleryman whose campaigns in France were spent in siege warfare as they had been in Wales. The impact of his cannon on the French was comparable to that of Guderian's tanks in 1940. After the ravages of Edward III and the Black Prince, cities and towns throughout northern France – hitherto often largely unwalled, as at Caen – had fortified themselves massively, though only against stone-throwing catapults, sappers and scaling ladders. Just at the moment when the tide turned against the English in France during the 1370s the revolution in gunnery began. Previously cannon had only been able to fire stone or metal balls which weighed three pounds at most and were of negligible importance in siegecraft – suddenly it became possible to discharge missiles of up to 800 pounds. The English had employed the new weaponry to devastating effect in Wales. A treatise on war, dedicated to Lord Berkeley in 1408, speaks of 'great guns that nowadays shoot stones of so great piece that no wall may withstand them as hath been well showed both in the north country and in the wars of Wales.' The use of such artillery for sieges had not yet been experienced in France – as Henry was almost certainly aware. English bows might be evaded successfully, as the great French leader Bertrand du Guesclin had shown when fighting the Black Prince in Aquitaine, but not English siege guns.

If his victory at Agincourt had settled nothing with regard to his claim to the French throne, it at least meant that Henry could be sure the French would never again dare face him in a head-on battle. On this certainty he based his plan for conquest. Essentially a strategist, he knew the importance of time and timing, how to make the most use of very limited manpower; it has been estimated that during his reign England's *total* effective fighting force was no more than 15,000 men. His method was to capture as quickly as possible a line of strongholds facing the direction from which the French counter-attack would come. He would then overrun the territory behind the line by taking every enemy town and fortress which it contained. Since the French would not dare to penetrate his line of strongholds to relieve them, he could bombard, mine, and blockade them into surrender at his leisure – there was no need for costly assaults. The process was completed by installing small English garrisons in the captured towns and castles, often only a bare handful of men. He could then extend the area of conquered territory by seizing another line of French strongholds further forward. A network of spies, operating at first apparently from Calais, seems to have been sent out to discover enemy troop movements and objectives. All this was accompanied by a ceaseless diplomatic offensive. In Jean Chartier's words, Henry was truly a '*subtil conquérant*'.[2]

The French must have been aware of the military build up across the Channel, and the imminent arrival of an armada. They were deeply apprehensive, just as the English would be when awaiting the Spanish armada in 1588, but since their defeats by Bedford and Huntingdon they had no ships left to intercept the invasion fleet. Understandably, they expected the English to land at Harfleur, though a few thought they might land somewhere in the vicinity of Boulogne. Again as before, Henry kept his destination secret until the very last minute. Instead of Harfleur and the north bank of the Seine, it was the mouth of the little river Touques (between the modern resorts of Deauville and Trouville), landing on the south bank. A small enemy force of 500 horses was quickly brushed aside. After disembarking the king had Mass said in thanksgiving, dubbed forty-six new knights and appointed Clarence the army's official commander-in-chief. He then set up camp and dispatched Huntingdon and Salisbury to capture the castles of Bonneville and Auvillers – the two nearest strongpoints, both of which surrendered almost at once – and sent a scouting party up the Touques to reconnoitre. His overall strategy was to overrun Lower Normandy (Normandy south of the Seine) and his first objective was its capital, Caen, the duchy's second city. Within three days of landing Clarence had advanced up the Touques and taken the town of Lisieux, inspiring such terror that its entire population fled, leaving only two aged cripples behind. By 14 August Clarence had occupied the suburbs of Caen.

Thomas Basin is a particularly useful source of information about the English invasion. A Norman, born at Caudebec in 1412, he studied in Paris during the English occupation and was appointed Bishop of Lisieux in 1442, being nearly forty before he became a subject of the French king and having worked as an English official. He wrote a history of Charles VII and of his son and successor, Louis XI, being commissioned by the latter to report on the poverty in the provinces devastated by the war and to suggest ways of relieving it. He records of 1417:

> It is not easy to convey what terror was inspired among the inhabitants [of Normandy] by the name of Englishman alone – fear so sudden that nobody, or almost nobody, thought that there was any safety other than in flight. If in most of the towns and fortresses those captains who had garrisons had not shut the gates, and if the inhabitants had not been restrained by force as well as by fear, it is beyond question that many would have been left totally deserted as certainly happened in some places. Indeed the people, unnerved by a long period of peace and order, simple as they were, generally thought that the English were not men like everyone else but wild beasts, gigantic and ferocious, who were going to throw themselves on them and then devour them.[3]

The experience of Basin and his own family in that year must have been one shared by very many Norman families, rich and poor. Basin's father was a prosperous bourgeois of Caudebec. On the approach of the English in 1417 he fled to Vernon with his wife and children but was driven out of there by the plague and famine which was brought by the influx of refugees. They then sought shelter in Rouen, then at Falaise, before returning to Rouen. They escaped from here before it was cut off by the English, fleeing to Nantes in Brittany. In 1419 the Basin family returned to Caudebec. However, the neighbourhood had became so dangerous by 1431 that the elder Basin again took refuge in Rouen where he died a pauper. These constant flights before the enemy with what possessions could be carried (if one was lucky) on pack-horses or in carts paralleled those of the French in 1940 during the German invasion. The difference was that there was far more danger for the population from English troops in the fifteenth century than from German in the twentieth. Off the battlefield medieval troops had very little discipline. In any case, despite issuing orders that women and clergy were not to be molested, Henry wanted to cow the Normans during the opening stages of his campaign.

The Normans had already been given a taste of the invaders' savagery on several occasions in the recent past. English raiders had devastated part of the Pays de Caux in 1403, burnt Fécamp in 1410, and again laid waste the Pays de Caux in 1413. Since the occupation of Harfleur in 1415 the garrison there had launched a series of minor but vicious raids into Normandy. Norman fishermen and merchants went in terror of English privateers, especially since the 'King's Ships' had wrested control of the Channel from the French. The Monk of St Denis confirms Basin: 'Everyone thought of nothing else but finding refuge in a place with strong fortifications, as if trying to escape from a storm of lightning.'[4]

The new dauphin, Charles, was known to be at Rouen so the English kept a wary eye on him – presumably through spies as well as scouts – while they marched towards Caen. However, the dauphin was distracted by the knowledge that the Duke of Burgundy had seized Troyes at the end of June and was now advancing in the direction of Paris. Since the dauphin's advisers and all the experts considered Caen impregnable he decided to return to the capital to face what appeared to be the more immediate danger. No doubt his military council were somewhat surprised that Henry had not gone to besiege Rouen straight away – the obvious if potentially disastrous course for an invader.

The king planned instead to cut Normandy in two by marching from north to south across it, to force neutrality on Anjou and then, having cut the Seine above Rouen – depriving the city of its communications with Paris – to besiege the Norman capital. Caen, the principal city of western Normandy, was the keystone of the first stage of the operation. Once captured it would provide a perfectly sited base for the conquest of western Normandy from which to launch the second stage. In addition it had a large port, easily reached from England. The plan was undoubtedly Henry's brainchild.

By 18 August the king had joined forces with Clarence's advance guard and invested Caen. It was a rich city, its wealth based on cloth manufacture and its very active river port. The population may have been as large as 40,000. It was famous for its splendid churches – there were over forty – and known throughout Normandy as 'the city of churches'. (The battle of 1944 sent much of old Caen up in flames, the destruction being compounded by modern development and nightmarish industrial estates, yet a surprising amount of the medieval city survives.) It was completely cut off. However, the dauphin's advisers had not been entirely unjustified in supposing it to be a difficult city to attack. The lower half, or new town, was protected by the many-branched River Orne, which made it virtually an island; while the upper half, or old town, was perched on a steep hill below a great citadel. There were strong new walls and many stout bastions, all in good repair, reinforced by ditches filled with stakes and wolf-traps.

Fortunately, the Duke of Clarence had galloped into the suburbs a fortnight earlier and captured two key strongpoints just outside the fortifications before the defenders were able to demolish them, the Abbaye-aux-Hommes and the Abbaye-aux-Dames. At first he had left them in peace. However, when he was asleep in a little garden – lying on the grass in his armour, his head on a stone – a monk, desperate to save his monastery, was brought in and explained that the Abbaye-aux-Hommes was being pulled down. Clarence immediately had ladders brought and in the darkness scaled the monastery's walls. He also seized the other abbey.

In consequence the people of Caen, who had trusted in their new ramparts, were soon to learn that they were already out of date. The Abbaye-aux-Hommes (founded by William the Conqueror who, ironically, was buried here) still stands, only 600 yards to the west of the site of the city walls. Henry installed both his headquarters and his heaviest guns behind the monastery's own thick walls; from here the latter hurled their huge gunstones at the ramparts, concentrating on a single spot low down in the masonry. The towers and roofs of the abbey became gun platforms for light culverins which were able to fire over the walls down into the city, ably supported by archers. On the east side of the city the Abbaye-aux-Dames (founded by the Conqueror's queen) provided another massive gun emplacement even closer to the walls. From both positions cannon were pushed still nearer, behind earthworks and timber screens. A ferocious bombardment ceaselessly battered the city, both night and day. The English guns were so big that the windows of the Abbaye-aux-Hommes shattered at the first discharge. The Monk of St Denis heard that 'they threw enormous stones with a noise like thunder amid fearsome clouds of black smoke, so that one might have thought they were being vomited forth by hell.' He adds that smaller cannon were sending over a 'hail of leaden balls'.[5] These fired with surprising rapidity – a primitive cartridge consisting of a box, filled with powder and topped by a bullet, being inserted into the breech.

The bombardment was then concentrated on the new town, which could only fire back ineffectually using small guns mounted on the ramparts. Besides stone shot, the English bombards fired hollow iron balls filled with flaming tow; the former demolished entire stone houses, scattering lethal splinters – several churches were destroyed – while the latter set many wooden buildings on fire. In addition the English mined, tunnelling beneath the walls, though this was not so effective; the defenders placed large bowls of water on the ramparts, detecting the mines by the ripples, and counter-mined, tunnelling down to attack the English underground.

Soon there were several breaches. During the night, when safe from arrow fire, the citizens blocked them with stones, baulks of timber and sandbags, digging trenches behind them filled with stakes. The king called on the defenders to surrender or expect no quarter but was answered defiantly.

The Earl of March arrived at the beginning of September with reinforcements. He had landed at St Vaast and then marched down through the rich Cotentin, burning, slaying and looting. His arrival made the king decide to storm the city.

On the morning of 4 September, after hearing three Masses, the king ordered a general assault on the lower part of the town. He was rumoured to have had an encouraging vision of a fiery cross. The first onslaught was beaten back with the help of showers of burning oil, powdered quicklime and scalding water, as well as volleys of cross-bow bolts and stones. One young Englishman, Sir Edmund Spring-house, fell into a ditch behind one of the breaches and was burnt alive by the French, who hurled bales of burning straw down on to him, infuriating his comrades. Henry sent in a second and a third wave of men-at-arms, who climbed down into the breaches and then up to engage the enemy hand to hand. The defenders heard an uproar behind them, panicked and gave ground. Clarence had attacked simultaneously from the opposite side of the new town. A man named Harry Ingles clambered over the rubble and led the duke's men-at-arms as they hacked their way in towards the town centre. The royal brothers met in the middle of it, joining forces to mop up what was left of the defence. If the chronicles are to believed, the victors then herded all the population they could find, civilian as well as military, regardless of sex, into the market place where, on Henry's orders, they massacred at least 2,000 of them. Blood ran in streams along the streets. The king ordered the killing to stop after coming across the body of a headless woman with a baby in her lap still sucking at her breast. Instead he sent his men through the streets, crying 'Havoc!' to loot and rape. (Anything of value, however, had to be surrendered to his officials.) Crowds knelt in the street as Henry passed, begging for mercy. On 5 September under his signet he wrote the usual amiable letter to the mayor and aldermen of London: 'God of his high grace sent unto our hands our

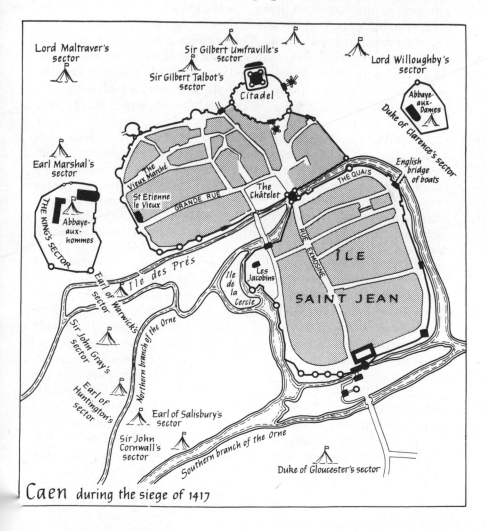

Caen during the siege of 1417

town of Caen, by assault and with right little death of our people . . . we and our host been in good prosperity and health.' One of the greatest historians of the king, Waugh, has written: 'It is humiliating to our pride in a national hero to read the language of those who suffered under his heavy hand, for when the broken spirit of the French began to revive, the foul massacre of Caen was ever foremost in their minds.' (This may be an honest enough admission on Waugh's part but is also a good example of the bias in Henry's favour which still afflicts English historians.)[6]

The old town and the citadel surrendered sixteen days later. The citadel could probably have held out for many months, but its garrison's spirit had been broken by the almost contemptuous ease with which Henry had smashed his way through the new town's supposedly impregnable walls. They can have had little faith in the ability of a relieving force to overcome so terrible an opponent. Moreover, with shrewdly calculated moderation, he offered surprisingly generous terms. The men were allowed to march off with their arms and keep up to 2,000 gold crowns, the women to retain their jewellery.

The fall of Caen, together with the butchery of its citizens, was widely reported. In Venice, Antonio Morosini received letters 'from divers parts' informing him that the king had 'ordered his subjects – barons and knights, and all his men-at-arms – to kill and cut to pieces everyone they found, from the age of twelve upwards, without sparing anybody . . . no one had ever heard of such infamy [nequicia] being committed'.[7] More importantly, as he must have intended, Henry had struck fear into all Normandy. The Monk of St Denis reports that 'by taking the town of Caen, the King of England had inspired such terror in the Normans that they had lost all courage'.[8] Furthermore, he now had a base from which to conquer Lower Normandy where he could be swiftly reinforced from England, since his ships were able to sail straight up the Orne to Caen. Its marble quarries provided him with good gunstones. As at Harfleur, his behaviour was that of a conqueror who intended to stay for good. The citadel – a large square white donjon with four towers at the angles, very like the Tower of London – became one of his favourite personal residences. In his usual pious way he at once installed a lavishly furnished chapel royal in it. He also confiscated many of the best houses in the city, earmarking them for English settlers. Not less than 500 burgesses – perhaps as many as 2,000 – left rather than stay under English rule.

The French, still split disastrously into Armagnacs and Burgundians, and crippled by their interminable civil war, were incapable of uniting against the English exploitation of the situation. However, the Burgundians appeared to be winning. Henry watched Duke John's progress with considerable unease. Although technically an ally of the English, the duke was a Valois and a Frenchman and, should he succeed in capturing Paris and the central government, it was only too likely he would turn on the invaders.

The king therefore concentrated on conquering as much of western Normandy as possible, ignoring the approach of winter. No doubt the Normans expected him to wait for the spring, as was the custom, and give them a breathing space. They were due for an unpleasant surprise. Henry struck southwards in the direction of Rouen, his object being to cut off first Lower Normandy and then Upper from any hope of rescue by either Burgundians or Armagnacs.

Meanwhile Huntingdon and Gloucester were charged with overrunning the western half of the duchy – a task which they performed with efficiency and zest. Other English troops – there cannot have been very many of them – struck south into Maine and the duchy of Alençon. The Monk of St Denis records that they brought 'fire and blood and made everything fall to them, by force of arms, by menace and by terror', storming all the châteaux.[9] 'There was no resistance, save for a few poor companions who held out in the woods',[10] we learn from Jean Juvénal des Ursins. (The phrase *povres compaignons*, which appears so often in Juvénal's writings, seems to mean those fighting for the Armagnac – later dauphinist – cause.) He tells us that 'whenever the English caught them, some they haled off to fortresses, others they threw into the river'. Those thrown in the river would have been bound, since drowning was one of the English methods of disposing of unwanted prisoners who could not pay ransoms, no doubt developed during the Welsh wars. On occasion, as will be seen, Henry himself used it.

In December the king laid siege to Falaise, the birthplace and favourite stronghold of his ancestor, William the Conqueror. Situated on a great crag above the town, its citadel was all but impregnable. It had a most distinguished and gallant soldier as its garrison commander, the Sieur Olivier de Mauny, Charles VI's standard bearer and Keeper of the Oriflamme – the battle banner of France. Very soon, bitter, freezing weather set in – 'winter with great cold grieved both man and beast' *The First Life* tells us – but the king had turf and timber huts built, tents being insufficient. These he surrounded by trenches and a stockade, and 'which, when it was made, seemed not a worse town than that within the walls'. As at Caen his artillery fired ceaselessly, night and day, demolishing houses, churches, and the tower which contained the town clock. He kept Christmas in his shanty town, all but blown down by hail storms, 'And notwithstanding that the sharp winter afflicted both the parties marvellously sore, for all the waters in the valleys were frozen and congealed in such manner that it seemed rather to be crystal or any hard stone than water.'[11] Using gunstones two feet in diameter he finally smashed a breach in the walls on 2 January – the eighth day of Christmas – whereupon the town surrendered.

Even so the citadel of Falaise, on its tall cliff, still remained well out of reach of his cannon, while it proved impossible to tunnel into the rock on which it rested. So, instead, he pushed his leather 'sows', or shelters, up to the foot of the ramparts on the townward side, setting his engineers to work beneath their shelter. The quality of the siege equipment he had brought from England proved its worth and the engineers were able to demolish the masonry in safety with picks and crowbars. On 16 February 1418 the citadel too surrendered. Among the prisoners was a Welshman, Edward ap Gruffydd, who had plainly not forgiven the English for what they had done in Wales. Henry had him hanged, drawn and quartered, the quarters being stuck up at the gates of Caen, Lisieux, Verneuil and Alençon. He had succeeded in taking one of the strongest fortresses in all France, the Verdun of its day. It was truly a shattering blow to Norman morale. Everywhere towns and castles began to surrender to the English king's troops. It was not simply for fear of his terrifying capability as a soldier: Pierre de Fenin, sometime squire and pantler to Charles VI, explains that Normandy 'saw no hope of rescue because of the dissension which then existed among the lords of France'.

The Monk of St Denis says that his pen cannot convey what extreme irritation Henry's 'bragging' caused the French. When briefly restored to lucidity, Charles VI was 'sore afflicted in contemplating the cause for the enemy's arrogance, it being above all the implacable hatred which divided the [French] host'. He tells us that many strong castles in Normandy surrendered to the English king 'by dint of promises rather than naked force. For on his word as a prince he guaranteed, to everybody who yielded, exemption from taxes, freedom to concentrate on farming or commerce, and the re-establishment of privileges as they had been in the time of St Louis, late king of France, on the one condition that they wore a red cross of St George on their shoulder. At the same time he abused the right of kings to punish disobedience. Anyone who rejected his summons [to surrender] and who fell into his hands bearing arms was put to death as guilty of *lèse-majesté*, having first seen him loot and plunder their possessions. If they were young people, not yet old enough to carry arms, or aged men, they had to suffer cruel tortures before being chased into exile. Even mothers were reduced to leaving the country with their children, with the exception of those who resigned themselves to marrying Englishmen.'[12]

However, the monk also gives us a glimpse of what it was like to meet King Henry, and implies that he must have had considerable charm. 'French prisoners who came home to arrange their ransoms, and who had got to know the king's character when in captivity, said that this prince whose exterior and conversation gave every indication of pride and who was generally supposed to be very vindictive, nonetheless behaved in a way worthy of a king and while showing himself pitiless towards rebels treated with the utmost tact those who obeyed him and was anxious they should be shown respect and kindness. He knew how many princes have extended their domains by that sort of behaviour.'[13]

The impression of graciousness is supported by the monk's account of the reports of Henry which French ambassadors brought back the following year. They praised his affability, his courtesy, and his generosity, and told how he had loaded them with expensive presents. They told the monk that, 'He was a prince of distinguished appearance and commanding stature; and although his expression seemed to hint at pride he nevertheless made it a point of honour to treat everybody of no matter what rank or degree with the utmost affability. Always avoiding the long-winded speeches and lectures to which people are ordinarily so prone, he would go straight to the point and confine himself to saying "it's impossible" or "it must be done". When he had spoken these simple words he considered himself obliged to do whatever it was as though he had sworn before Christ and His saints. A scrupulous dispenser of justice, he knew how to exalt the lowly and abase the mighty.'[14]

By the spring of 1418 the king had achieved his first strategic objective, having overrun all Lower Normandy, from Evreux to Cherbourg. The conquered territory was administered by four reliable bailiffs – Sir John Radcliffe at Evreux, Sir John Popham at

Caen, Sir Rowland Lenthall at Alençon and Sir John Assheton at Cherbourg. The administrative centre was Caen, where an English chancellor for the duchy of Normandy was installed, and where the *chambre des comptes* was given an English president; soon a mint would be established at what was to become the second capital of the new Guyenne. He used the stick-and-carrot method – which he had found so effective with the Welsh – to tame his new subjects, alternately terrorizing and wooing the Normans. Anyone with an income of less the £60 a year who would take an oath of loyalty to the king-duke was (on payment of 10*d*) given a 'certificate of allegiance'.

According to Tito Livio of Forli, Henry V's near-contemporary biographer, the king spent the whole of Lent and Easter in prayer, fasting, vigils and almsgiving.

X

The Fall of Rouen

'. . . for iron smiteth not
So sore as hunger doth, if food fail.'

A fifteenth-century translation
of Vegetius's *De Re Militari*

'Unto the French the dreadful judgement day
So dreadful will not be as was his sight'

Shakespeare, *King Henry V*

enry marched out from Caen on 1 June 1418 to conquer Upper
Normandy, his principal objective being the duchy's capital,
Rouen. A week later he arrived at Louviers, a small but strongly
fortified town defended by triple walls, large bastions and many
turrets, all equipped with guns of every type and size. He used an
ingenious siege engine to undermine the triple walls, while using his
own artillery to demolish them with his customary skill. He did not
appreciate being shot at himself. He was conferring with the Earl of
Salisbury in the latter's pavilion when a gunstone fired from the town
walls hit the tent and very nearly killed them. Despite its defences'
reputation for strength, Louviers surrendered after a fortnight.
The king promptly seized the gunners responsible for shooting at
Salisbury's tent and hanged them on tall gibbets.

Even before Henry reached Louviers, disturbing news must have
reached him from Paris of a development which upset the entire
political scene in France. On 29 May the Burgundian captain, Jehan
Villiers de l'Isle Adam, had captured Paris. He and his men had
been secretly admitted at night by a Burgundian ironmonger
through the Saint-Germain gate. The tyrannical Bernard of

Armagnac and his supporters were thrown into prison. A fortnight later a Burgundian mob broke into the prisons and dragged them out, butchering several thousand men, women and children: Count Bernard's body, naked and obscenely mutilated, lay in the gutter for three days, suffering revolting indignities. The Armagnac provost of Paris, Tanneguy de Chastel, managed to escape with the young dauphin, to rally the Armagnacs outside the capital, but the Duke of Burgundy now controlled Paris and was determined to save it from the English.

Duke John at once abandoned his English alliance and reinforced Pont-de-l'Arche. This was the town guarding the River Seine at just the point where the king had intended to cross in order to advance on Rouen. It was a grave setback since the Seine was everywhere wide and deep. The heavily fortified bridge was further protected by the walled and moated town on the south side (from which Henry was approaching) and by a formidable fort with guns at the far end, on the north bank. The defenders had destroyed every boat for miles around.

The river was 400 yards wide and impossible to ford. Its north bank was now guarded by Burgundian troops sent by Duke John. The king selected good swimmers and made them try raising the sunken boats but they were prevented by enemy cannon fire and archery. Then he had small square boats constructed from leather and wickerwork. (These may have been inspired by coracles which he had seen in Wales.) There were some islets between the south bank and the middle of the river and it was possible to push pontoon bridges constructed from hides and poles over, halving the distance. Just before dawn on 14 July, covered by bowmen, Sir John Cornwall and sixty men-at-arms crossed the remaining stretch in the leather boats, a horse carrying two or three light cannon swimming behind. Cornwall was so elated that on the spot he knighted his thirteen-year-old son whom he had brought with him. The bridgehead was speedily consolidated. A full-scale bridge resting on the invaluable leather boats was built and 5,000 Englishmen went over, whereupon the Duke of Clarence blasted the fort into surrender. The 'most devout king . . . fell on his knees and gave thanks in great devotion to the immortal God'. In despair Pont-de-l'Arche capitulated on 20 July.

Monstrelet records that Henry installed a strong garrison at Pont-de-l'Arche 'for dread of which the greater part of the peasantry fled the country with all their possessions'.[1] Not only did he now have

112

a bridge across the Seine but, since it straddled the river and was fortified to control the river traffic, he had effectively cut off Rouen, seven miles downstream, from Paris. The Norman capital suddenly found itself isolated, with no hope of receiving troops or supplies. The king could lay siege without too much interruption to what he described in a news letter to his subjects in London as 'the most notable place in France save Paris'.

Rouen was undoubtably notable, one of the wealthiest and most beautiful of French cities with a population estimated at 70,000. Its cloth and its goldsmiths' work were the staple of Parisian luxury shops, easily transported up river in normal times. Besides a magnificent cathedral and many rich abbeys and priories it boasted nearly seventy churches within its walls. The houses of its opulent merchants were famous for being built and furnished regardless of cost, its guildhalls more splendid than any in England.

Besides being one of the richest and most beautiful of French cities it was also one of the best defended. It contained over 5,000 men-at-arms under the captain of Rouen, Guy le Bouteiller, a Norman nobleman who was an experienced and able commander. There were also 15,000 militia who included a famous force of picked crossbowmen under Alain Blanchard, another veteran. The abundant artillery was directed by a noted gunner, Jean Jourdain, who had a further 2,000 men to operate it. All the Rouennais had complete and justified confidence in their city's tall and massive walls, which covered some five miles. These had recently been strengthened against bombardment by an embankment of earth behind them, while there were sixty towers and five great bastions protecting five great gates – cannon bristled from each one as well as from the ramparts. In every tower there were three guns aimed at three different angles. On the wall between each tower was a great cannon mounted low in the earth and ready to fire. There were small guns at regular intervals on the walls set to shoot at close or long range, and between each tower on the parapet were eight small guns for rapid fire. There was also a trebuchet at each gate. (These details are given by an English eye-witness, John Page.)[2] The city ditch on those three sides unprotected by the Seine had been deepened and filled with wolf traps, and the suburbs had been ruthlessly demolished – even churches had been razed to the ground. Moreover the city had a good water supply and there had been time to bring in large stocks of food. So confident was the garrison of its ability to beat off any attack that it had given asylum to every refugee from miles

113

around. Above all, the Duke of Burgundy had pledged his word that, come what might, he would relieve the city.

Henry and his army reached Rouen at midnight on 31 July. Next morning the Rouennais awoke to find themselves completely surrounded by English troops – the king knew all about psychological warfare. He set up five fortified camps, linked to each other by trenches. His headquarters were in a Carthusian monastery 1,200 yards to the east of the walls. Clarence was in a partially demolished priory to the west, Exeter at the north end, Huntingdon at the south, on the far bank of the river in the rubble of what had been the suburb of St Sever, and Gloucester was a little to the north of Henry. Three huge chain booms across the Seine, supported by several warships – which had been hauled on wheels overland for nearly four miles, sails unfurled to catch the wind – isolated the doomed city still further. In addition a wooden bridge was built over the Seine five miles above Rouen, a remarkable feat of military engineering which the English named 'St George's Bridge': piles were driven into the river bed, then joined by chains on which planking was laid. The besiegers' stranglehold was broken only by the fortified abbey and fort of St Catherine on a steep hill of that name to the east, a few hundred yards south of the king's headquarters. It was partly protected by a belt of marshland and its cannon commanded the road from Paris down which the Duke of Burgundy and his army might march at any moment. Another thorn in the side of the English was Caudebec, a town some miles down stream whose garrison and guns threatened ships bringing supplies and reinforcements up the river to Rouen. However, on 2 September Salisbury stormed the hill of St Catherine and a week later Warwick fought his way into Caudebec.

Henry seems to have anticipated the fall of Caudebec with some confidence to judge from a letter he had written on 16 August to the mayor and aldermen asking them to launch a sort of Evacuation of Dunkirk in reverse: 'And pray you effectually that, in all the haste ye may, ye will do arm as many small vessels as ye may goodly, with victual and namely with drink, for to come Harfleur and fro thence as they may up the river of Seine to Rouen-ward with the said victual for the refreshing of us and our said host.' London responded nobly. According to the accompanying letter it sent: 'thirty butts of sweet wine – ten of Tyre, ten of Rumney, ten of Malmsey – and a thousand pipes of ale and beer, with two thousand and 500 cups for your host to drink.'[3]

His strategy was simple. Since his cannon could make little

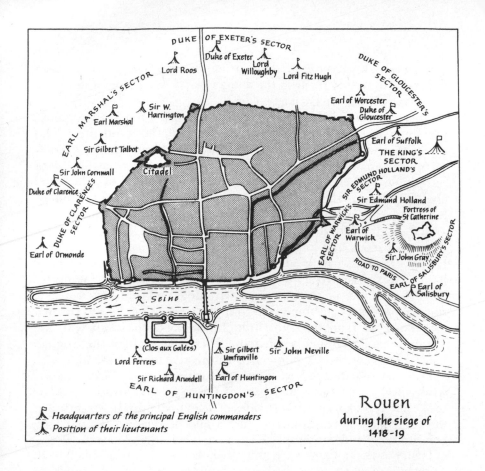

Rouen
during the siege of
1418-19

Headquarters of the principal English commanders
Position of their lieutenants

Map labels:
DUKE OF EXETER'S SECTOR
Duke of Exeter
Lord Roos
Lord Willoughby
Lord Fitz Hugh
DUKE OF GLOUCESTER'S SECTOR
EARL MARSHAL'S SECTOR
Sir W. Harrington
Earl Marshal
Earl of Worcester
Duke of Gloucester
Earl of Suffolk
Sir Gilbert Talbot
THE KING'S SECTOR
SIR EDMUND HOLLAND'S SECTOR
Sir John Cornwall
Citadel
Sir Edmund Holland
Fortress of St Catherine
Duke of Clarence
DUKE OF CLARENCE'S SECTOR
EARL OF WARWICK'S SECTOR
Earl of Warwick
Earl of Ormonde
Sir John Gray
EARL OF SALISBURY'S SECTOR
ROAD TO PARIS
Earl of Salisbury
R. Seine
(Clos aux Galées)
Lord Ferrers
Sir Gilbert Umfraville
Sir John Neville
Sir Richard Arundell
Earl of Huntingon
EARL OF HUNTINGDON'S SECTOR

impression he intended to starve Rouen into surrendering. Now that
Caudebec had fallen food for his men could be brought from England
with ease.

While Henry V was waiting for his blockade to take effect he took
the opportunity to terrorize the country round about – whatever
English historians may say about his desire for conciliation. The Earl
of Ormonde's bastard son, Fra Thomas Butler, Prior of Kilmainham
and of the Irish Knights Hospitaller, arrived with 1,500 saffron-
cloaked Irish kern – knife and javelin men riding ponies, of the type
the king had seen in Ireland as a boy. Knowing perfectly well how
they would behave he let them loose on the local population,
whereupon they raided far and wide to their hearts' content, riding
back with severed heads and even babies dangling from their horse's
necks. Understandably, the Norman peasantry were terrified of
these savages with their war-whoops and bagpipes. Henry himself

115

was shaken by reports of their atrocities and had some of them flogged. He posted them to the danger spots where any attempt at relief was expected to strike first.

The garrison made sortie after sortie from their walls against the English, sometimes in detachments of a thousand men. The besiegers always beat them back though not without loss; the French set man-traps into which they lured their pursuers as they were retreating. When John Blount, the Lieutenant of Harfleur, challenged one of the gate captains to single combat, the Frenchman rode out, knocked Blount off his mount, ran a sword through him and then dragged the body back into Rouen at his horse's tail. Blount's friends had to pay 400 gold nobles to recover the corpse. Henry erected a row of gibbets in view of the walls on which he hanged any prisoners. Alain Blanchard retaliated by stringing up English prisoners on the ramparts, with dogs tied round their necks; some captured Englishmen were put in sacks with dogs and thrown into the Seine. If anything the French won the propaganda war; the Vicar-General of Rouen's spirited excommunication of the English king from the walls was sufficiently impressive to infuriate him.

Food began to be in short supply as early as the middle of August, while the besiegers diverted part of the city water supply. Plague broke out and soon there were piles of dead bodies in the streets. But the Rouennais were confident they would be relieved. It was long before they would contemplate even the possibility of surrender.

Henry was far from sure that their confidence was misplaced. Time and again there were alarming rumours that the Burgundians were marching on Rouen. He kept his men on the alert for their arrival, on one occasion ordering troops to sleep in their armour. Rouen sent daring messengers through the English lines – past the gibbets – begging Duke John to come and save the city. One aged Rouennais priest raised the old Norman cry for assistance against robbers, the '*Haro!*', in front of the duke in King Charles's presence. The duke promised that he would come. In November news reached the by now starving city that a mighty army was on its way to relieve them and would arrive four days after Christmas, whereupon the defenders went to the churches to give thanks to God and ring the bells. In the event the duke reached Pontoise, only twenty miles away, but came no closer. His men began to squabble with the dauphin's troops, who were all Armagnacs, and then the army's food ran out. The relieving force withdrew to Beauvais, still quarrelling, and then disintegrated. Frantic, piteous pleas continued to come

116

from the garrison, beseeching Duke John not to abandon them, to no avail.

John Page, an otherwise completely unknown English soldier who was there, has left a moving account of the siege in doggerel verse, 'all in raff and not in rime'. While convinced of the justice of his king's cause, and that Henry was 'the royallest prince in Christendom', he was a compassionate man who sincerely pitied the unfortunate Rouennais. He says that the time came when they had no meat other than horsemeat and how when that was gone they were reduced to eating dogs, cats, mice and rats, and finally to any vegetable peelings they could find – they even ate dock roots.[4] Pretty girls sold themselves for a piece of bread. The king was unmoved by tales of distress, building massive earthworks and blockhouses, all mounted with cannon, to guard against any attempts at relief or revictualling.

At the beginning of the Christmas season the garrison turned 12,000 'useless mouths' out of the city, in the hope that they would be allowed to depart. But although there were old men and nursing mothers among the groups driven forth from every gate, the king ordered his troops to herd the pathetic exodus back into the ditch, to die slowly from hunger beneath the winter sky and unending downpour. It rained continuously during their weeks of slow death. In the ditch, John Page tells us, 'one might see wandering here and there children of two or three years old begging for bread since their parents were dead. Those wretched people had only sodden soil under them and lay there crying for food – some expiring, some unable to open their eyes and not even breathing, others as thin as twigs.'

> And woman holding in her arm
> A dead child and nothing warm.
> And children sucking on the pap
> Within a dead woman's lap.

One might easily count in the ditch ten or twelve dead to every one alive, who had died so quietly, without call or cry, as if they had died in their sleep. Henry allowed all babies born in the ditch to be hauled up in baskets and christened – after which they were returned to their mothers by basket.

Pious as always, the king marked the feast of Christmas with a truce – to last the twenty-four hours of Christmas day. He sent two priests and three servants into the ditch with food. He also sent his heralds to the captain of Rouen, Guy le Bouteiller, offering a meal to anyone who lacked food, and freedom to come into the English lines to eat it. The captain did not trust him and refused to let the Rouennais take advantage of the offer. Those in the ditch prayed that Henry might 'win his right', if we may believe John Page, 'since Englishmen have tender hearts'.

As John Page also explains (and Vegetius teaches), hunger breaches even stone walls. On the night of New Year's Eve 1419 a French knight at the Bridge Gate was heard shouting that he wanted to talk to a baron or knight with the right ancestry. Gilbert Umfraville shouted back that he was a knight and told him his name. (He was descended from a Norman knight who had ridden with William the Conqueror.) The French knight thanked God 'for you are of the ancient blood of Normandy'. Umfraville arranged for envoys from Rouen to come and discuss with the king the possibility of a parley.

When they arrived the following day Henry, very much in character, made them wait until he had finished hearing Mass. When at last he saw them he had a scowling face. One of them remarked that Rouen was no mean city, whereupon the king replied fiercely, 'It is *mine* and I will have it!' When they pleaded for the folk in the ditch he answered, 'Fellows, who put them there?' Full scale negotiations for surrender began the following day, in two tents in Gloucester's camp. When the ditch was again brought up the king listened coldly and refused to let the 'useless mouths' out, asking who had placed them in it. 'I put hem not there and that wot ye!' He insisted that Rouen was his by right, rebuking the envoys for having 'kept my city, the which is mine inheritance'. He harped at length on this favourite theme; 'Rouen is my heritage'. According to the *First English Life* he demanded, 'Or else, peradventure, you take upon you the judgement of my title? Know you not how many castles, cities and defensible places have been by us obtained and gotten, and how often from the field with victories have we chased our adversaries? Were not these signs of justice?'[5] It was yet another repetition of his claim that God was on his side, that he was justified by signs of divine approval.

The negotiations broke down and the envoys returned to Rouen. However, the city's poor had had enough and accused the rich of being murderers – 'false traitors, assassins and ruffians' – threatening to kill them rather than die of hunger. The envoys went back to argue with the English king. They 'treated day, they treated night, with candle and torches bright'. Finally, largely through the mediation of Archbishop Chichele of Canterbury and the city's clergy,

118

Rouen agreed to surrender within eight days, on 19 January, if it had not been relieved by noon on that date, and to pay an indemnity of 300,000 gold crowns. Eighty hostages were taken – twenty knights or squires and sixty bourgeois – to serve as guarantees until the ransom was paid. On Henry's insistence they also agreed to hand over the Vicar-General of Rouen, Robert de Livet, whose excommunication of him the king had found so insulting, and Alain Blanchard, captain of the crossbowmen. Livet was handed over 'fast bound in irons, from which he never departed until he miserably finished his life', Henry committing him 'unto obscure prison'. Blanchard was immediately hanged from a gibbet.

On the afternoon of 19 January the king, in gold robes of state and seated on a throne, received the keys of Rouen at his headquarters in the Carthusian monastery. He then named the Duke of Exeter as captain of the city, ordering him to occupy it the same night. Next day, escorted by four vested prelates and seven vested abbots, Henry rode up to the main gate. He was met outside it by the clergy of Rouen bearing no less than forty-two processional crosses – each of which he kissed in turn. Then he rode into his city of Rouen, wearing his by now customary gloomy expression, without pomp or trumpets, in black but with a gold train reaching down as far as the ground, on a black charger with black trappings. He was accompanied by a single squire, bearing a lance with a fox's brush at the tip – a favourite Lancastrian badge. He went straight to the cathedral to hear a thanksgiving Mass before installing himself in the castle.

The citizens who watched King Henry ride by were mere skin and bone, with hollow eyes and pinched noses. They could scarcely breathe or talk. (Though the *Brut*, a contemporary English chronicle, claims, 'They cried all "Noel" as high as they might yell.')[6] Their skin was as dull as lead and they looked like those effigies of dead kings one sees on tombs. There were corpses lying in every street and crowds by the hundred begging for bread. The king had food sent into the city, since the Rouennais were now his loyal subjects, but the deaths continued for days afterwards, quicker than the carts could carry them away for burial.

According to the terms of the surrender, save for those specifically excepted, the defenders were to be allowed to leave if they wished to do so. Henry had his own thrifty views on how they should depart. 'The garrison were ordered to march out by the gate leading towards the Seine,' Monstrelet tells us, 'and were escorted by the English as far as the bridge of St George where they were searched by commissaries from the king who took all their money and valuables from them, giving two sous in return. Some noblemen were even stripped of their handsome coats, made of marten skin or embroidered with gold, and made to exchange them for worthless old garments.[7] The proceeds went to swell the royal coffers.

XI

The Norman Conquest – In Reverse

'The King had subdued all Normandy.'

The First English Life of King Henry the Fifth

'If the expression "bled white" was at any time accurate, it best describes the state of the conquered provinces of France under English rule.'

K. B. McFarlane, *The Nobility of Later Medieval England*

When the fall of Rouen became known, the rest of Normandy quickly submitted. Often it was sufficient for Henry's captains to appear in front of a town or a castle for it to surrender. By the spring of 1419 nearly the entire duchy was in his hands. To the east his line of strongholds reached as far as Mantes on the Seine, only thirty-five miles from Paris. He established his headquarters at Mantes as it could be reinforced swiftly by river. To the south there was a similar line from which to launch the conquest of southern Maine and Anjou. Treaties with the Dukes of Burgundy, Brittany and Alençon ensured that no trouble would come from their direction.

The king at once began to make Normandy an independent state, separate from the rest of France. New government departments were set up – a Norman chancery, a Norman seneschalcy (overseeing all civil and military administration), a Norman exchequer and a Norman admiralty (with responsibility for coastal defences). Bishop Kemp of Rochester became the chancellor, the chief administrative official; William Alyngton, the treasurer; and the Earl of Suffolk, the admiral. There were eight *baillis* or regional governors, all Englishmen.

A little too much has been made by English historians of Henry's programme of conciliation; his guarantees of property and privilege, his respect for local institutions, and his strict observance of legality. Admittedly his approach was impressively imaginative, unmatched during the late Middle Ages – though there were no conquests which can really be compared with that of Normandy. However, the reason why the Normans submitted to what the Monk of St Denis calls 'the odious yoke of the English' was that they had seen just how incapable was the French monarchy, torn between Armagnacs and Burgundians, of saving them from sharing the fate of so mighty a stronghold as the ducal capital.

No doubt the king's Norman Conquest in reverse retained Norman institutions, invited Norman noblemen to swear fealty, and employed many Norman clerics in its administration, yet although a few magnates submitted and took an oath of allegiance, the vast majority of the upper nobility refused to do so and were dispossessed. Henry gave their estates to Englishmen, just as William the Conqueror had once bestowed Saxon lands, confiscated from the thanes, on his followers.

The redistribution of land and titles began almost at once. Six great Norman counties were re-allotted during 1418–19; the Duke of Exeter was given that of Harcourt, together with its enormous family stronghold of Lillebonne; the Earl of Salisbury was made Count of Perche; the Earl of Warwick, Count of Aumale; Lord Edward Holland, Count of Mortain; Sir John Grey of Heton, Count of Tancarville; and Sir William Bourchier, Count of Eu. The Duke of Clarence received three viscounties, comprising a vast block of land. (The Duke of Bedford was given nothing for the moment, but by the time he died as 'Regent of France' in 1435, he was Duke of Alençon, Duke of Anjou, Count of Maine and Count of Dreux, to mention merely his most senior Norman dignities.) Lord Willoughby secured the lordship of Beaumesnil with other *seigneuries* and Sir Walter Hungerford became Baron of Le Hommet. Sir Gilbert Umfraville obtained all the estates of his distant kinsman, Pierre d'Amfreville, at Amfreville-sur-Iton (whence his ancestors had come), together with those of the Seigneur d'Estouteville – once commander of the garrison at Harfleur. Lesser men benefited too, such as Sir John Popham of South Hardeford in Hampshire who became Lord of Thorigny, or Sir Christopher Curwen of Workington in Cumberland who became Lord of Cany in the Caux. In all, some 500 fiefs were confiscated from the French in Normandy.

The disadvantage of such grants was that Henry expected military service in return, just as William I had from the thanes' dispossessors 350 years before. His grantees had to carry out specified duties, whether providing troops, garrisoning towns or maintaining their castles and manors as fortresses or depots. Umfraville had to furnish twelve men-at-arms and twenty-four archers for the royal army. Hungerford, the royal steward, was obliged to give the king-duke a lance tipped with a fox's brush every year on the feast of the exaltation of the holy cross – and to produce ten men-at-arms and twenty archers whenever required. Willoughby, besides giving Henry a golden spur at Caen every midsummer's day, was obliged to ride with the king and bring with him three men-at-arms and seven archers for so long as the war against the French should last. On a humbler level a William Rothelane was committed to finding a guard for part of the town of Coutances, and a Hugh Spencer had to find men for the guard at Harfleur. Such small fry were threatened with death by Henry should they ever dare to try to leave Normandy.[1]

Most of the new English lords of this Norman Conquest in reverse were small fry, the smallest sort of gentlemen, if that. They did not belong to distinguished or influential families in England; were not men of landed property. Such inducements as a manor house and an estate, often accompanied by a title, and lucrative employment provided attractive reasons for staying and settling. And they could expect more than the mere income from their estates or increment from office. Every garrison captain received one third of his men's plunder, the 'spoils of war' (while remitting another third of it to the king together with a third of his own). There was also the *pâtis* or protection racket levied on villagers for the maintenance of the local English garrison.

Henry's attempts at full-scale colonization varied from place to place. His settlement of 10,000 Englishmen at Harfleur was almost certainly intended to create a second Calais. At Cherbourg and Caen – and to a much lesser extent at Rouen, Bayeux and Coutances – it is more likely that he was inspired by memories of Wales, where towns originally intended to be entirely English, but with a strong Welsh element, had remained loyal to the Crown because of the large number of settlers. A fair number of the English who settled in Normandy took French girls as wives.

The king also had a policy of conciliation – he did not want his new subjects in permanent rebellion against him. Apart from military posts, the majority of officials save for the most senior continued to be Frenchmen. Nobles who swore allegiance to him were regranted their lands for the feudal dues by which they had formerly held them from the King of France, with no increase. As always in occupied countries, a few inhabitants profited from the new regime, especially lawyers. The structure of Lancastrian Normandy gave them all sorts of new opportunities, since the judicature was separated from Paris and countless fresh prerogatives and offices made for lucrative disputes in the ducal courts. There were also plenty of posts for bureaucrats in the administration. Some Normans may even have welcomed English rule. Most rejected it.

Many Norman nobles, including all the magnates and great landowners, fled to other parts of France. A number of squires held out in the woods, leading a *maquis* against the invaders, with the help of the peasants; but as the occupation dragged on they became discouraged. In the end most resistance of this sort was confined to bands whose members were often as much bandits as partisans. The kingdom was so torn between Burgundians and Armagnacs that even the most stubborn can have seen little hope of success.

Jean Juvénal and the Monk of St Denis tell the story of the young Dame de La Roche Guyon, Perette de la Rivière, whose husband had been killed at Agincourt. One of the greatest ladies in Normandy, she held out for three months in her huge castle, on a bluff overlooking the Seine, against a siege conducted by Warwick and Guy le Bouteiller – the former captain of Rouen who had taken the oath of allegiance to Henry, one of the few Normans of rank to do so. Eventually the English, tunnelling up from caves below the castle, mined its walls. When forced to surrender Perette was told by the king that she might keep her lands if either she took the oath or married Guy le Bouteiller. She refused to swear allegiance or marry someone whom she considered a traitor, particularly when the marriage contract stipulated that any son by Guy would inherit La Roche Guyon, depriving her two sons by her first husband of their patrimony. The Dame de La Roche Guyon preferred to leave Normandy, penniless, with her children.[2]

During the nineteenth century romantic French historians insisted on seeing every Norman highwayman or outlaw as a hero of the 'resistance'. And no doubt, although many of the 'brigands' in the forest were criminals, perhaps the majority,[3] yet a fair proportion

Henry V as a youth. From an early sixteenth-century copy of a lost original.
(The Mansell Collection)

John, Duke of Bedford kneels before St George, from the *Bedford Book of Hours* c. 1423. The small forked beard makes it highly probable that St George is a portrait of Henry V. (The British Library)

Thomas Montacute, Earl of Salisbury – Henry's most formidable commander – with fashionable military haircut. Note his poleaxe. (The British Library)

Henry V's aunt Princess Elizabeth Plantagenet and her third husband, Sir John Cornwall KG, one of his most daring commanders. From a window formerly at Ampthill in Bedfordshire.

Henry V's father-in-law, King Charles VI of France, with his counsellors.
(The Mansell Collection)

Henry V's brother-in-law the Dauphin, with King Charles VII, as one of
the Three Magi. From a miniature by Jean Fouquet. (Giraudon)

A room well known to Henry V – the ruins of the dining hall of Kenilworth Castle in Warwickshire. (John Cooke Photography)

The château of Lassaye in Maine. Destroyed in 1417 to stop it being used as a base by the English, it was rebuilt in 1458 with cambered walls designed to resist siege artillery of the type used by Henry V.
(S. Mountgarret)

A hunting scene of a sort very well known to Henry V. In the background is his favourite French residence, the castle of Bois-de-Vincennes. From the *Très Riches Heures du duc de Berry*. (Giraudon)

Henry V's official residence in Paris, the Louvre, as it was in his time. From the *Très Riches Heures du duc de Berry*. (Giraudon)

were definitely partisans. When the English captured someone in Normandy they would only allow him to ransom himself if he could prove he came from territory which had not yet submitted to the English king – by, for example, showing that he belonged to a dauphinist garrison. Otherwise, from as early as February 1418, by Henry's express orders, he was treated as 'a brigand and our enemy' and hanged. The English deliberately refused to discriminate between partisans and common criminals, both swinging side by side from the same gibbet.

It is obvious from an edict issued by Henry the year before he died, sent to every *bailli* in Normandy, that he himself was convinced that all too many brigands were noblemen. He says 'many nobles together with men of the common people' (*plures nobiles et alii populares*) had either joined 'Our enemies' (the dauphinists) or were else living in woods and caverns as robbers – tacitly admitting that they were prepared to lead a miserable hunted life rather than take an oath of allegiance to him. Whether the brigands were *maquis* or bandits, Basin makes it plain that everyone thought they only existed in such numbers because of the English occupation – 'as soon as the English were chased out of Normandy and made to go home, the country was delivered from this pest.' Furthermore the bishop has no doubt that many 'brigands' were motivated primarily by dislike of the occupation:

There were a very large number of ruined and desperate men who, from idleness, hatred of the English, coveting other people's goods or knowledge that the long arm of the law was seeking them for some crime, had left their fields and houses and, instead of living in towns or castles held by the French, inhabited the most inaccessible depths of the woods in the manner of wild beasts or wolves. Maddened and half-crazed by hunger they would go forth, usually by night when it was dark, to break into the houses of peasants, seizing their goods and dragging them off as prisoners into impenetrable forest fastnesses and there, by all kinds of ill treatment and torture, they would force them to bring great sums of money at an arranged time and place as ransom to purchase their liberty (together with goods indispensable for such a way of life). Failure to deliver meant that those whom the peasants had left as hostages would suffer the most inhuman tortures or the peasants themselves, if the robbers could catch them, would be murdered or else their houses be mysteriously set alight at night and burn down . . . above all they attacked the English, killing them without pity whenever they had the chance.[4]

125

This picture is a little suspect since the author had once been the 'collaborationist' Bishop of Lisieux, a willing tool of the English, with good reason to detest such men. Undoubtedly a fair proportion of those hanged by the occupation as 'brigands' were dauphinist partisans who received food and shelter from the peasants. Writing about 1470, Basin was sure of one thing about the rebels, reiterating again and again that they had only been there because of the English presence – 'the country could not be saved from or cleansed of this pest until the English domination was over and it was returned to the French, its natural masters.'

Emigration was ultimately a far more damaging form of resistance to the English than guerilla warfare in the woods. Some noblemen emigrated simply to protect their families but most did so to avoid taking the oath of allegiance. A substantial number of clergy refused to swear allegiance to Henry, including two archbishops of Rouen – only three Norman bishops would so so – and many emigrated, friends collecting their stipends for them since otherwise they might have starved. (Some clerics who stayed pretended they had taken the oath.)

However the vast majority of emigrants, those whom Normandy could least afford to lose, were peasants between the ages of twenty and thirty. They were driven away by war taxation and the brutalities of the army of occupation. Most went to Brittany though some went as far away as Flanders. Henry and his officials were so alarmed by the loss of labour that they made serious efforts to lure the men home.[5] This constant bleeding-away of the population was disastrous for Norman agriculture.

It was not just Frenchmen who left. As early as 1416 men were deserting from the Harfleur garrison, sneaking home across the Channel. By the autumn of the following year this trickle of deserters had grown to a flood from all over Normandy. In September 1418 the king wrote to the sheriffs of England complaining of soldiers who 'without our licence have in great numbers falsely and traitorously withdrawn and returned to our kingdom of England'. By 1418 he was ordering the garrisons at Calais and Harfleur to hang any deserters they could catch. A system of passports was introduced, while Sir Richard Walkstede was given the task of searching every vessel which sailed from Rouen harbour. If such measures prevented men from crossing the Channel they did not stop them deserting. Those forced to stay in France went in fear of being hanged and like the 'brigands', many took to the woods and lived by robbery.

126

Deserters were not the only English to add to the misery of the French country people; the troops who remained with their garrisons were often almost as much of a pest. There was no authority, such as military police, to stand in their way. In February 1418 Henry ordered all garrison captains to punish soldiers who 'oppressed and pillaged the people'. In theory discipline was enforced by the Constable of England, Clarence, and by the Earl Marshal, Lord Mowbray. Although they appointed commissioners, their control over garrisons was minimal. Every captain received a copy of the king's regulations to read to his men. They were surprisingly specific, especially with regard to prostitutes – whose money must be confiscated and arms broken – and sanitation: troops had to 'bury their carrion and bowels about their lodgings and within earth, that no stench be in their lodgings'. There must be no robbing, no seizing of food or livestock.[6]

Inevitably the garrisons lived off the country. Their pay was usually in arrears; when a rudimentary commissariat was set up to feed them it proved inadequate. A fair proportion of troops were pardoned criminals and in any case there must have been that instinct for vandalism which often emerges among groups of ignorant and aggressive young men who find themselves in a foreign country. The best soldiers are prone to looting, even the British and Americans during World War II, not to mention the *Wehrmacht*. The occasional murder of a comrade did not incline the English to treat the population any more gently. Since the labour force had already been depleted by the plagues which followed the Black Death, the occupation made it still harder to till the soil – good farmland began to revert to forest. Landowners suffered a dramatic drop in their incomes. Moreover, trade was badly hit by the disruption of communications with the rest of France.

English historians express surprise that so few troops held down Normandy, arguing that it shows acceptance of English rule. The answer lies in the mobility of widely spaced but carefully sited garrisons, often consisting of no more than a dozen archers. Since these were mounted they could cover long distances swiftly along the excellent Norman roads – which compared very favourably to roads in England – to relieve each other or enforce obedience by nicely calculated atrocities.

In the meantime Henry never missed an opportunity of claiming he enjoyed divine favour and his merciless orthodoxy and puritanism impressed many churchmen. One such was the Spanish

127

Dominican, Vincent Ferrer. A hell-fire preacher, Vincent travelled everywhere with an entourage of penitents which included flagellants with bleeding backs. His mission was the denunciation of vice and corruption. When he consecrated the Host at Mass he wept so infectiously that the whole church resounded with the congregation's wailing. In May 1419 he came to Caen and preached before the king and his court, publicly rebuking him for killing so many Christian men and women who had never done him any harm. Henry listened impassively. Afterwards he had Vincent brought to him. His first words were, 'I am the scourge of God sent to punish the people of God for their sins.' When Vincent emerged after being closeted alone with him for three hours the simple friar told the waiting courtiers, 'This morning, before I came hither, I believed that the king your master had been the greatest tyrant among other princes Christian; but now I perceive the contrary, for I assure you he is the most perfect and the most acceptable unto God of all them that be here present this day, and his quarrel is so just and so true that undoubtedly God is and shall be his aid in these wars.' (One can only guess that Henry had been arguing his view that he had a mission to give good government to France.) This incident, dutifully and perhaps too imaginatively recorded by the Earl of Ormonde, illustrates both the sheer force of the king's personality and his conviction that God was on his side.[7]

He advertised the fact that he had come to stay through the medium which circulated most widely – the currency. Some time between January and September 1419 he issued gold *moutons*, and silver and base-metal *gros*, all modelled on French coins and probably struck at Rouen. The gold piece bore the letters *HFRX*, which stood for *Henricus Francorum Rex*; revealingly, the legend on the reverse was *Christus vincit, Christus regnat, Christus imperat* ('Christ conquers, Christ reigns, Christ is emperor'), the words of a popular and triumphantly aggressive plain chant motet. The *gros* were inscribed *Sit nomine Domini benedictum* ('May the name of the Lord be blessed.') Clearly, as in Wales and at Agincourt, the king ascribed his victories to divine favour.

Not everyone shared Henry's belief that the English cause was just. A dialogue between France and Truth, written by an anonymous French moralist in about 1419, records another view. 'The war they have waged and still wage is false, treacherous and damnable, but then they are an accursed race, opposed to all good and to all reason, ravening wolves, proud, arrogant hypocrites, tricksters without any conscience, tyrants and persecutors of Christians, men who drink and gorge on human blood, with natures like birds of prey, people who live only by plunder.'

From Monstrelet we learn that, 'At this time the frontiers of Normandy as far as Pontoise, Clermont, Beauvais, Montdidier, Breteuil, Amiens, Abbeville and St Valéry were overrun by the English and laid waste with fire and sword; on their raids they carried off much booty . . . the poor people were left defenceless, with no other resource than to offer up their prayers and lamentations to God.'

At the Tower of London the captive Duke of Orleans wrote how in France kings, princes, dukes, counts, barons and knights, merchants and common folk must all pray for peace 'because evil men overwhelm noble blood' which can no longer protect its fellow countrymen:

> 'Priez, peuples qui souffrez tyrannie,
> Car vox seigneus sont en telle faiblesse
> Qu'ils ne peuvent vous garder pour maistrie,
> Ni vous aider en votre grand destresse.'

XII

The Murder of John the Fearless

'. . . soldiers waged into France for to make much murder of blood'

Bishop Reginald Pecock

'Enemies have struck deep into the heart of France and enriched themselves.'

Jean Juvénal des Ursins

Henry was not going to be content with Normandy. He wanted all France. He knew that he did not have the resources to conquer the entire country by force of arms so he decided to see what diplomacy could do. During the first weeks of the siege of Rouen he had negotiated with the late Constable–Count of Armagnac, and had tried to play him off against the Duke of Burgundy. When the count was murdered the king foresaw that his party would survive its leader's death, just as it had that of Orleans. However, after an attempt to meet the dauphin, the Armagnacs' new leader, had failed in March 1419 Henry reverted to wooing the Burgundians.

There were several meetings between Henry and Duke John in the spring and early summer. At the first encounter 'the duke saluted the king, bending his knee a little and inclining his head', Monstrelet reports. 'But the king took him by his hand, embraced him and showed him great respect.'[1] There seemed to be a real chance of an alliance, even if Duke John was also negotiating secretly with the dauphin. Early in June there was a meeting at Meulan attended not only by Henry, Clarence, Gloucester and Burgundy, but also by Queen Isabeau and Princess Catherine. The king – presumably frustrated by his self-imposed celibacy – was enchanted by the girl.

He regarded her as the only possible bride for him, if contemporaries are to be believed. He stated his terms: Catherine, with Normandy and Aquitaine in full sovereignty.

He had asked too much. If genuinely anxious for a settlement with Henry and clearly prepared to concede a great deal, Duke John and Queen Isabeau dared not yield on sovereignty; to break up the kingdom of France in this way would destroy their prestige and their credit. Henry would accept nothing less. Before leaving Meulan he told the duke, 'Fair cousin, we wish you to know that we will have the daughter of your king or we will drive him and you out of his realm.' 'Sire,' answered John, 'you may be pleased to say so, but before you can drive my lord and myself out of this realm I make no doubt that you will be heartily tired.'[2] Henry had failed. He could not fight successfully an alliance of Burgundians and Armagnacs. And it quickly became obvious that Duke John had made up his mind to seek a reconciliation with the Armagnacs.

The name '*Jean sans Peur*' bestowed on Duke John had a certain irony. In reality 'Fearless John' was a paranoiac who at Paris slept in a specially built tower which contained a single, easily defendable bedroom and a bathroom. (The Tour d'Artois, it still stands in the rue Etienne Marcel, a last fragment of the otherwise long-vanished palace of the dukes of Burgundy.) He would only go out with heavily armed bodyguards. He had reason to fear. Not only had he murdered the Duke of Orleans and others, but the Armagnacs blamed him for the massacres in Paris when some of their comrades had been made to jump from the Châtelet's battlements on to the spears of the mob waiting below. He publicly admitted to having been persuaded by the Devil to kill Orleans and was suspected of being a warlock. A letter urging further evil deeds was widely circulated, addressed as follows:

Lucifer, emperor of the deep Acheron, king of Hell, duke of Erebus and Chaos, prince of the Shadows, marquis of Barathrum and Pluto, count of Gehenna, master, regent, guardian and governor of all devils in Hell and of those mortal men alive in the world who prefer to oppose the will and commandment of our adversary Jesus Christ, to our dearest and well-loved lieutenant and proctor-general in the West, John of Burgundy.[3]

Yet the duke was even more frightened of Henry than he was of the Armagnacs.

The king resumed the offensive. Very early on the morning of 31 July the Earl of Huntingdon and the Captal de Buch rode to Pontoise through the darkness. It had a garrison of 1,200 men under Marshal de l'Isle Adam and was considered sufficiently safe to be visited frequently by Charles VI's court. In the gloom the captal's troops stole up to the town ditch through vineyards just outside and hid there, waiting for a signal that Huntingdon's men were in position. At 4.00 a.m. they scaled the walls with ladders and, despite a fierce response by the garrison, so damaged a gate that Huntingdon was able to gallop straight in. The town was then sacked horribly, its citizens losing everything they possessed – not to mention the atrocities to which their women were subjected. The English 'gained great riches for it was full of wealth' says Monstrelet. On hearing the news Henry had a *Te Deum* sung at Mantes. He rode in a week later, writing exultantly to the mayor and aldermen of London that its capture surpassed any previous gain. Not only had he taken a vast military depot stocked with arms and provisions valued at two million crowns but he now possessed an advance base on the River Oise from which to threaten Paris, a mere twelve miles away. Even if his communications might be dangerously extended and he was alarmingly far from his main bases, he had shown the Burgundians that he was in earnest when he threatened their duke at Meulan.

Today Pontoise is part of the Paris conurbation but when one visits it one can still see why it was of such vital importance in 1419. On a mighty bluff (near the modern railway station) the citadel's ramparts were only 150 yards from the bank of the River Oise, so that gunners and archers could shoot down on to this crucial waterway up which even now barges bring food to Parisians. Moreover the Oise is sufficiently narrow to be easily blocked by a bridge of boats or a boom. An English garrison could not only stop supplies going up the river but could also raid Paris without warning.

The fear inspired by the English is vividly attested by the Bourgeois of Paris, an anonymous chronicler who lived at the French capital throughout these grim years. He was probably a canon of Nôtre Dame. He tells us that about ten o'clock in the morning on the feast of St Germain

twenty or thirty people entered Paris through the Saint-Denis Gate, in a state of terror like persons who had just escaped death, which indeed was true enough: some of them being wounded while others were faint

132

with fear, cold and hunger, and all looked more dead than alive. Stopped at the gate and asked why they were in such a sad condition, they began to weep, saying, 'We are from Pontoise, which for sure was captured by the English this morning; they killed everyone who crossed their path; and we count ourselves very lucky to have escaped from them, for no Saracens ever harmed Christians so sorely.' As they were speaking the gatekeepers saw a huge crowd approaching, men, women and children, some wounded, others stripped of their clothes; one of the men there had come to seek shelter with two babies in a basket under his arm; many of the women were bareheaded, while others were only in their bodices or their shifts. . . three or four hundred people lay about, bemoaning their sufferings, the loss of goods and friends, since very few among them had not lost a relation or a comrade at Pontoise. And when they thought of those who were in the hands of those cruel tyrants the English their anguish was such they could scarcely bear it, being weak from lack of food and drink. Some pregnant women gave birth during their flight, dying shortly after. Nobody had a heart hard enough to contemplate their misery without shedding tears. They continued to arrive throughout the following week from Pontoise and the district around, reaching Paris in a daze like a great flock of sheep.[4]

The Bourgeois goes on to tell us that after capturing Pontoise the English terrorized all the area around Paris but did not assault the city. They contented themselves with 'pillaging, killing, robbing, taking prisoners whom they would free only when a ransom had been paid'. He continues, 'In those days the only news one heard was about the ravages of the English in France every day; they took towns and castles, spread ruin throughout the entire realm, sending everything, loot and prisoners, back to England.'[5]

'Booty was one of the chief military objectives, and no one, peasant or townsman, clerk or knight, was immune from loss at the hands of enemy raiders,' says McFarlane. 'Civilians were as fair game as combatants . . . Clearly the plunder of France was no small matter; and equally clearly the English got far more than they gave. Fighting most of the time on alien soil, they could and did strip it of everything in the line of march.'[6] A particularly vile practice was the kidnapping of boys and girls, to be sent across the Channel and sold as indentured servants.

The English of all classes, and no doubt the Welsh too, must have been staggered by the wealth of French cities and towns and by the fertility of French farmland. London was only half the size of Paris (which had a population of perhaps as many as 200,000) while no

English city could rival Rouen. Much of England was still sheep country and had no grain lands like the *plat pays*. Vines were unknown (save for a few rare monastic vineyards producing thin and eccentric beverages). The sheer amount of wine in France – in those days produced even in the region around Paris – astonished the English troops, who frequently drank themselves into a stupor, to the fury of Henry and his commanders. This was truly a promised land for looters. At first there can have been little trouble in persuading men to stay and settle.

It should not be forgotten that Henry's conquests in north-western France included part of Maine. Using Alençon as a base, his troops occupied a block of territory which stretched as far south as Beaumont-le-Vicomte and even a little further – there were constant raids down towards Angers. These southern conquests were extremely insecure, the strongholds constantly changed hands. As early as 1417 the English had attacked the great château of Lassay (between Mayenne and Alençon), severely damaging it; in 1422, presumably in response to raids, the dauphinists demolished it, to stop the English from using it as a base. The dauphinists walled the small town of Ste Suzanne a little further south, huddled beneath an already grim twelfth-century castle on a high cliff, creating something very like a Gascon *bastide* (or fortified frontier town). The menace of Henry's invasion was transforming the landscape of north-western France. Villages, monasteries and even churches were fortified against the English.

The king also encouraged his captains to raid deep into enemy territory over the understandably ill-defined frontier. Just what this involved may be glimpsed from an often quoted minute to the Royal Council by one of his minor commanders, a veteran of the Agincourt campaign, who later became one of the most famous soldiers of the Hundred Years War – Sir John Fastolf. Although written thirteen years after Henry's death it accurately describes a type of operation launched all too often by his men. In Fastolf's opinion the most effective way of dealing with the French was to send small raiding parties of 750 lances into their territory from June to November 'burning and destroying all they pass, both houses, corn, vines and all trees that bearen fruit for man's sustenance' while all livestock 'that may not be driven off . . . be destroyed'. The object, Sir John explains bluntly, was to drive the enemies thereby to an extreme famine. No doubt he was doing no more than echo Vegetius, but this can scarcely have been of much comfort to the farmers

134

in the path of such raids – if they managed to escape with their lives.[7]

It is known from the accounts of the Treasurer-General of Normandy, William Alyngton, that money was spent on spying. The captain of Calais had agents – the ancestors of MI6 – to warn him of any threats to the isolated city, and Henry employed these to discover French objectives and troop dispositions in Picardy. It is likely that every garrison captain made similar use of spies, whether on the frontier to report on enemy troop movements or inland to ferret out conspiracies. We even know of an English couple called Mr and Mrs Piket, who in 1420 had to leave Angers hurriedly for La Rochelle when the dauphin sent men to arrest them – they had been gathering information for Sir John Assheton, the *bailli* of the Cotentin.

Duke John was deeply alarmed by the failure of the negotiations at Meulan in June and the realization that the English king was not to be bought off. He was probably even more frightened by the man himself. Although scarcely an idealist, the duke saw that the only chance of saving France was a military alliance between Burgundians and Armagnacs, or at least between Burgundians and dauphinists; if he could dominate the weak and colourless young heir to the throne, he might be able to wean him away from his hardline Armagnac friends. Accordingly, a treaty between the duke and the dauphin was signed at Pouilly-le-Fort on 11 July 1419. In it both stated that they would resist 'the damnable aggressions of the English, our ancient enemies' which were exposing the entire kingdom of France 'to the most cruel tyranny, perhaps even to total ruin'. The Parisians went wild with joy, dancing in their city's streets where they set up tables to feast in celebration. They were justified in rejoicing – the new alliance was France's last hope.

During the first half of July Duke John had had three meetings with the Dauphin Charles which had been without incident. Fear of the English king made the duke forget about the enmity of the irreconcilable Armagnacs who constituted the bulk of the future Charles VII's entourage – men thirsting to avenge their foully murdered leader and comrades. John was still more shaken when Henry captured Pontoise. The situation was growing desperate, and the treaty of Pouilly-le-Fort had not brought military co-operation against the English any closer. He seems to have decided that at all costs he must see the sixteen-year-old dauphin again and impress upon him the urgency of the crisis.

135

On 10 September the two Valois kinsmen met by appointment for a further discussion. The rendezvous was some forty miles from Paris, on the fortified bridge of Montereau over the Seine where the Yonne flows into it. Barricades had been erected at both ends of the bridge with a wooden pen in the middle in which, each escorted by ten chosen advisers, they could meet safely without any fear of an army of the other's supporters rushing forward to seize them. The duke's worst nightmare was to come true; it was a cunningly planned Armagnac plot to trap and 'execute' him. No one will ever discover what exactly took place. What is known is that after Duke John had knelt on one knee before the dauphin, who raised him to his feet, there was a short conversation between them, then a sudden mêlée and John lay dead. A plausible reconstruction is that someone, probably Tanneguy du Chastel – a redoubtable Breton thug and former henchman of Louis of Orleans – had suddenly struck the duke in the face with a small battleaxe, cutting off part of his chin and knocking him down; and as he lay on the ground someone else pulled up his armour to thrust a sword into his belly, finishing him off. He was not killed in self-defence, as the Armagnacs afterwards claimed. Almost certainly the dauphin was implicated; he never punished anyone for the crime and in later years heaped honours on Tanneguy who undoubtedly had a hand in the killing. A Carthusian monk, showing the duke's skull to François I in the sixteenth century, commented succinctly that the English entered France through the hole in Duke John's head.[8]

The Armagnacs, the one faction committed unequivocally to Charles VI's son, had not merely done themselves terrible damage in French public esteem but had very nearly ruined their patron's cause. There was no chance now of any *rapprochement* with the Burgundians. The real losers were France and the French people, left at the invaders' mercy. The Bourgeois, however much a committed Burgundian supporter he seems to have been, was justified in claiming that the Armagnacs had already brought much misery upon France as it was. 'Normandy would still be French, the noble blood of France would never have been spilt nor the realm's greatest lords carried off into exile, nor the battle lost nor so many good men killed on that dreadful day at Agincourt, where the king [of France] lost so many of truest and most loyal friends had it not been for the pride of that wretched name of Armagnac.' The dauphin shared in the Armagnacs' disgrace, since everyone knew that he was their puppet. Moreover, while the French continued to be divided the

136

English were united in waging what for them was undoubtedly a national war.

On hearing the news of his father's murder the new Duke of Burgundy, Philip 'the Good', took to his bed where he threw himself about, gnashing his teeth and rolling his eyes. This was probably more the effect of rage than of grief. (During all too many well attested paroxysms of anger he was said to turn blue in the face.) He had seen how Duke John had been repaid for his desire to save France and his sense of family loyalty, and could think of nothing but revenge. At a meeting held in Arras a month after the 'bridge of Montereau' the entire Burgundian faction – including its supporters in Paris – urged him to ally with Henry. A man of Flanders by upbringing, he knew very well how anxious his Flemish townsmen were to maintain good relations with their business friends in England. An English alliance would mean the acquisition of large chunks of northern France. In any case he had little alternative.

Henry reacted predictably, loudly and cynically lamenting the death of 'a good and loyal knight and honourable prince' (a blackly humorous description), while – to judge from the accounts in more or less contemporary chronicles – it was abundantly clear that he realized that he could now obtain almost anything he wanted. Waurin records how he swore that by the help of God and St George he would have the Lady Catherine though every Frenchmen should say him nay. Ten days after the murder Queen Isabeau wrote exhorting him to avenge Duke John and it seems that at the same time she asked Duke Philip to protect her from her son. She knew what Henry wanted and was prepared to co-operate. Negotiations between the English and the Burgundians began at Mantes at the end of October. Henry told the envoys that if their duke tried to take the French crown he would make war on him to the death. He expected to marry Catherine and inherit the crown from King Charles, who however might keep it during his life, while queen Isabeau was to retain her estates. These were the terms which would eventually be agreed by the Treaty of Troyes in April 1420 and make him 'heir and regent of France'.

Meanwhile at Mantes, according to Tito Livio, the king 'gave not himself to rest and sloth but with marvellous solicitude and diligence he laboured continually. For almost no day passed but he visited some of the holds, towns and [strong] places. And everything that they needed he enstored. He ordained in all parts sufficient garrisons for their defence. He victualled them. He repaired their castles,

137

towers and walls. He cleansed and scoured their ditches.'[9] He did not neglect to let London know what was happening, writing under his signet on 5 August 1419 to the mayor and aldermen that the enemy would not make peace and that therefore he must continue the war.

A further meeting of Burgundian notables at Arras warned Duke Philip that if he allied with the English there was a danger that not only would Henry drive the king and queen out of France but many of the French people as well, replacing them by English lords, knights and priests; this warning surely reflects the impression made by news of what was happening in Normandy. On the other hand most of Philip's subjects believed in the dauphin's guilt and wished that the duke would avenge his father's murder. Philip was a Valois too, the great grandson of King John II who had been defeated at Poitiers, and it might be asked why he did not put in a bid for the throne himself instead of letting the Englishman take it. But Philip could not fight both the Armagnacs and the English; in any case the latter now had a name for near invincibility. By allying with Henry he doubled his territory and blocked the return to power of the hated faction which had killed his father so foully.

The king's hold over large areas of France was to be made infinitely more secure by the alliance with Burgundy and by the feud between Burgundians and Armagnacs. Any Frenchman who had little love for the Englishman but feared the Armagnacs was forced to support him. This was particularly true in the capital where, in the light of the bloody massacres of recent years, every Parisian had good reason to dread the return of the dauphin whose Armagnac followers would surely take the opportunity of settling old scores as bloodily as possible. The Bourgeois of Paris shudders as he recounts how the city was full of rumours of fiendish Armagnac atrocities – each report of the dauphin's forces raiding anywhere in the vicinity of Paris being greeted with horror.

Henry was perversely anachronistic in his insistence on seeing the throne of France as something which was neither more nor less than a personal inheritance. Yet at the same time he was fully aware of the power of nationalism – from his Welsh campaigns and from his English subjects' frenzied rejoicing at his victories. Sometimes when talking to Frenchmen he even referred to 'our way' and 'your way'. Where, on the other hand, he was centuries before his time was in presenting the dispute over the French throne as a struggle between personalities. No modern politician contesting the leadership of a party or the presidency could have sold his case more shrewdly. He

138

offered himself as an experienced and proven leader, a superb soldier and brilliantly efficient administrator who could give outstandingly good government, impeccably fair justice and, above all, peace. At the same time he contrasted his rival with himself – as an immature degenerate, a murderer rejected by his parents, condemned by the law of the land, the willing tool of vicious and revengeful party bosses.

The King of England realized that he was now the most powerful man in France, against whom no one could hope to stand successfully, and that he was on the verge of a diplomatic triumph. He continued to batter his way mercilessly towards Paris while at the same time mopping up any Norman strongholds which still held out for the King of France. He moved his headquarters from Mantes to Pontoise on 6 August, Clarence raiding savagely up to the very gates of Paris. Gisors, the easternmost strongpoint in Normandy, fell to him on 23 September 1419, and St Germain very soon after; Gisors threatened the Burgundian border, St Germain Paris. The Burgundians might still control the capital but they had to accept that Henry was certain to capture it and that with Paris they would lose their hold over that tattered symbol of phantom authority which was poor, mad King Charles VI. They were forced to accept that their only course was to follow their instinct to avenge Duke John's killing and ally with the English, however much good reason they had to dislike them. The English king knew that he could demand what he wanted from the Burgundians – their acquiescence in his conquering not merely vast tracts of France but the French crown itself. In early December his troops finally obtained the surrender of Château Gaillard on its great cliff overlooking the Seine. It had been popularly regarded by the French as the strongest fortress in the realm.

Constructive negotiations commenced as soon as the Burgundian envoys arrived at Mantes on 26 October. Despite their being received 'very benignly and feasted', Henry repeated what he had told Duke Philip's father; that unless their master agreed to his terms he would conquer France by himself. This time he set a deadline for agreement – Martinmas, 11 November. He again made clear just what he wanted – there never was a more expert practitioner of *realpolitik*. He demanded the hand of Catherine of France and his recognition as heir to the French throne; while Charles VI might retain the crown till his death, Henry must be Regent of France during his mad fits; and the Duke of Burgundy would have to

139

acknowledge Henry as his sovereign after his crowning. As the English king saw clearly, Philip had much to gain from an agreement; not only would he have the chance of increasing his territory but he would be protected from the dauphin and the Armagnacs. If some Burgundian supporters feared that Englishmen might monopolize all positions of power and influence in France, it was obvious that Henry V would never allow so dangerous a situation to develop. A treaty was signed with Duke Philip on Christmas Day, 1419. All that remained was to persuade the French king and queen to disinherit their son.

The dauphin was accused of killing Duke John on the bridge at Montereau and the accusation was used as a pretext for depriving him of his inheritance. Even had he been tried and found guilty there was no law or precedent for excluding him from the succession, while the notorious insanity of the French king made it impossible for him to set his son aside with any convincing show of legality. Nevertheless, the infuriated Burgundians' desire for revenge enabled Henry to use the accusation as grounds for usurping the youth's birthright.

The English king had convinced himself that in creating a dual monarchy, in which each realm would be governed according to its own laws, he was securing what was rightfully his. He believed that he alone could impose the same good government on France which he had given England. His entire political programme was based on these two firm convictions.

Henry tried indefatigably to surround dauphinist France with a string of diplomatic alliances, some of them dynastic. Excellent, although not particularly profitable, relations were maintained with the Emperor Sigismund, while the three important Elector-Archbishops of Cologne, Triers and Mainz all received English subsidies. A trade agreement was negotiated with Genoa.

The king also tried, unsuccessfully, to marry his brother Humphrey of Gloucester to the daughter of Charles III of Navarre, whose realm adjoined Guyenne. His most ambitious attempt at a dynastic alliance was in 1419 when he sent John Fitton and Agostino de Lante to Naples to explore the possibility of his brother John of Bedford being adopted by the Neapolitan queen. Bedford was thirty while Joanna II was forty-four, a widow with a discarded second husband. She was childless and clearly infertile, a byword for promiscuity and had a thoroughly sinister reputation. She had made the first move in the negotiations, offering to create Bedford Duke of Calabria – the title traditionally borne by heirs to the Neapolitan throne – and to acknowledge him as her official successor, besides handing over to him all citadels and castles in her possession. Probably just as well for Bedford, nothing came of this exotic project.

English links with Scandinavia were closer than at any time since the eleventh century. Henry's sister Philippa was the queen of Eric XIII, King of Sweden, Denmark and Norway. Her husband's great-aunt, St Bridget, had presided over the creation of the triple monarchy, now in a state of chronic unrest. The links had been responsible for the foundation of the Bridgettine monastery at Twickenham, its first nuns and monks being Swedes from Vadstena. Probably they were also why Henry employed the Dane, Sir Hartung von Clux (whom he made a Knight of the Garter) in so many capacities. Hartung led embassies to the Emperor Sigismund and also fought in France. In 1417 he brought four men-at-arms, nine archers and, most unusually, two crossbowmen to the invasion force. Later that year he was appointed captain of Creully and he was among the first to be given a Norman estate.

Henry's diplomacy reached as far as the land of the Teutonic Order on the Baltic. That extraordinary country, stretching from the Neumark of Brandenburg to the Gulf of Finland, was ruled by celibate German knights who waged war on Europe's last pagans, the snake-worshipping Lithuanians, and less admirably on the Catholic Poles. In 1410 the latter had inflicted a crushing defeat on them, killing their '*hochmeister*'. However, the Order remained rich and powerful, with its capital at the Marienburg and commercial centre at Danzig, it was of vital importance in Baltic trade and still wielded considerable international influence; in 1407 the Duke of Burgundy had tried to involve the *hochmeister* in a war with England. Every year a fleet sailed from Danzig to England, joining the fleet of the Hanse towns en route, laden with Prussian goods – corn, silver, furs, falcons and amber. It took home English cloth which was sold all over Poland and western Russia. It was important for the English to keep on good terms with the knights. In 1419 Friar Netter led an embassy to them, and also to King Ladislas of Poland with whom the Order was still at war.

The man whom Henry used most for diplomatic missions was Sir John Tiptoft, the former speaker and treasurer. He played an invaluable part in the negotiations to isolate France before the campaign of 1417, visiting the emperor and many German princes, the Kings of Aragon and Castile, and the republic of Genoa. He was among the commissioners who tried to manoeuvre the French into

141

accepting Henry's terms in 1419. During all this time he was also Seneschal of Guyenne, having been appointed in 1415, shortly before Henry sailed on his Harfleur expedition, to the most important office in the duchy.

The king never had time to visit Guyenne, although he demanded more and more money from it. He paid the duchy careful attention nonetheless, as is shown by his appointment of Tiptoft, and by that of Sir John Radcliffe as Seneschal of Bordeaux. He was tactful when dealing with the citizens of Bordeaux, writing frequently to the mayor and burgesses to tell them of his progress and asking them to send him news of themselves. The Gascons were firmly tied to England, partly because it bought so much of their wine, and they rejoiced at their king-duke's victories in the north. He employed Gascon troops, one of his most redoubtable captains being the Captal de Buch, whom he made a Knight of the Garter. Yet Guyenne had its problems, suffering from dauphinist raids and brigandage. It was essential to make sure of two great southern magnates whose territories bordered the duchy, the Counts of Foix and Albret. This involved Henry in much tortuous diplomacy and a considerable outlay in cash.

Tito Livio tells us that the most devout king of England returned to Rouen to keep the feast of Christmas, 1419. However, although Henry himself may have been given up to devotion during this sacred season of the year, at the same time he sent his captains out to conquer further tracts of France. The English troops, who 'feared not the death for the recovery of the king's right . . . remained conquerors in the field and put their adversaries to flight, of whom they first slew many and many they maimed'. Meanwhile, Henry 'persevered in the city of Rouen lauding and honouring the sole creator and redeemer of the world'.[10]

XIII

'Heir and Regent of France'

'No king of England, if not king of France'

Shakespeare, *King Henry V*

'Shall I tell of the ruin of Chartres, of Le Mans, of Pontoise – once a most distinguished and flourishing place – of Sens, of Evreux, and of so many other places which, taken by trickery, perfidy or treachery, not just once but again and again, were completely delivered up to pillage?'

Thomas Basin, *Vie de Charles VII et Louis XI*

In February 1420 Duke Philip of Burgundy made public knowledge the treaty which he had agreed with the King of England at Christmas. Joint Anglo-Burgundian military operations had already begun. While the Burgundians had no objection as Burgundians to capturing and besieging Armagnac strongholds in northern France, as Frenchmen they disliked intensely the English practice of massacring or taking prisoner Armagnacs who had surrendered only after Burgundians had offered them life and a safe-conduct. Yet somehow the uneasy alliance survived, and even prospered. The two armies captured many towns and cities – among them Rheims, where the kings of France were traditionally crowned.

It was essential for Henry and Philip to obtain the support and co-operation of Charles's queen, Isabeau of Bavaria, who claimed to be Regent of France. Fat and fortyish – she had been born in 1379 – at her court in Troyes she surrounded herself, as she had always done, with gigolos and a menagerie including leopards, cats, dogs, monkeys, swans, owls and turtle doves. Despite having given her husband twelve children she was notoriously promiscuous. Preachers rebuked her publicly to her face for making her court an 'abode of Venus'. After Agincourt the English king had told Charles of Orleans that he need not be surprised at being defeated, on account of the sensuality and vices prevalent in France – he was referring to the court of Queen Isabeau. One of her affairs had left her with a bitter and ineradicable hatred of the Armagnacs. In 1417 King Charles had briefly recovered his wits, whereupon the late Count Bernard of Armagnac had informed him that his consort was sleeping with the young Sieur Louis de Boisbourdon; the king immediately had Boisbourdon arrested, horribly tortured, tied in a sack and thrown into the Seine to drown, while imprisoning his erring wife at Tours under a penitential regime. Previously she had been inclined to prefer Armagnacs to Burgundians but this episode made her change her mind. In response to her anguished pleas, Duke John sent 800 men-at-arms to rescue the Queen from a miserable captivity and helped her establish her court at Troyes. The incident had also set her against the Dauphin Charles, who had taken the opportunity to plunder his mother's treasury. Isabeau was unreliable, vicious-tempered from gout and a prey to agrophobia. Yet, while largely disinterested in politics, she possessed a powerful sense of self-preservation.

The alarming English warrior king was an ally who could ensure her survival and her luxuries. Understandably, any comparison with the Dauphin Charles made the latter seem a doomed weakling in her eyes. When the dauphin's chosen friends killed Duke John on the bridge of Montereau, they had branded him indelibly as a murderer, however much he might protest his innocence. Besides appropriating his mother's money and jewellery, he had excluded her from any share of power. Even so, she had tried to reach some sort of understanding with him, but the Burgundians skilfully blocked her attempts. They also ensured indirectly that she was kept short of money – the dauphin being as yet too naïve to offer her financial assistance – and promised her through Duke Philip's mother (her Bavarian aunt) that if she did as they wished they would see she continued to live as she pleased. In addition King Henry sent a personal envoy, Sir Lewis Robsart, a naturalized Englishman whose first language was French, to convince his prospective mother-in-law that he would give her anything she wanted. As early as January 1420 Isabeau issued an edict publicly condemning her son Charles and his actions, recognizing Henry and Duke Philip as her husband's official allies. Soon it was widely if erroneously believed that she had confessed that Charles VI was not the father of the Dauphin Charles; while undoubtedly she had taken many lovers and it is not entirely impossible that he really was a bastard, it is extremely unlikely that she would ever have admitted it. (During the mid-1420s her son is known to have been extremely worried about his parentage.) The bastardy story was certainly circulated for all that it was worth by Henry's agents.

In March 1420 King Henry marched through enemy territory to Troyes in Champagne where King Charles, Queen Isabeau and their daughter Catherine were waiting for him with their cousin, Duke Philip. Henry was accompanied by Clarence and Gloucester, since the Armagnacs were within striking distance with a string of fortresses stretching from south of Paris along the Seine and the Yonne. Henry went by way of St Denis, where he paused to pray, and under the walls of Paris, whose citizens cheered him from the walls – presumably in the belief that he would bring peace rather than from affection. When his army entered Champagne the king issued the remarkable order that no man should drink the local wine 'so famous and strong' (*The First English Life*'s wistful description) without watering it. Just before he reached Troyes he was met by the Duke of Burgundy and a host of Burgundians on horseback, who escorted him into the city. Philip and his court were in black armour with black horsetrappings – the duke's swept the ground – and squires bore black banners seven yards long.

At Troyes Henry knelt before the mad French king who was seated on his throne. For some time Charles VI could not be made to understand who Henry was, but finally muttered, 'Oh, it's you! You are very welcome since it is you. Greet the Ladies.' The English king then greeted Queen Isabeau and at last Catherine of France, spectators observing that the kiss 'gave him great joy'.

On the following day the treaty was solemnly ratified in the cathedral of Troyes in the presence of King Henry and Queen Isabeau – though not of Charles VI – its articles being read out before the assembly. Charles was to remain King of France for as long as he lived, but at his death his crown would pass in perpetuity to Henry and his heirs. Henry, henceforward to be styled 'heir of France' was also to be regent of the realm advised by the French estates; he promised to bring to obedience those areas of France still ruled by the 'self-styled dauphin of Vienne'. Furthermore 'considering the horrible and enormous crimes' perpetrated by the latter,

Charles VI, Henry and Duke Philip agreed never to negotiate separately with the dauphin. The English king was to marry the Princess Catherine who, instead of having to bring a French dowry with her, would receive that of an English queen to the amount of 40,000 French crowns per annum, the cost to be borne by the English exchequer. Queen Isabeau was to be maintained as a queen for as long as she lived. Any Burgundian whose lands had been appropriated by the English was to be compensated out of territories to be conquered from the dauphin.

Henry also pledged himself to guarantee France's traditional laws and institutions and to appoint Frenchmen to French offices. There was to be perpetual peace between England and France, and after Charles VI's death their sovereign was to be one and the same man. The peace would extend to a defensive alliance and to a measure of free trade. 'All hatreds that may have existed between England and France shall be put an end to, and mutual love and friendship take their place.' Moreover, Henry promised that with regard to King Charles and Queen Isabeau, 'We shall regard them as Our father and mother, and honour them as such, and as it fitteth such and so worthy a prince and princess, to be honoured especially before all other temporal princes of this world.' (His blatant failure to observe this clause caused genuine resentment even among Burgundians.)

In January the following year the dauphin (and his advisers) were to issue a manifesto against 'the damnable treaty for which Henry of England has asked'. It stated that 'the honour of the fleur-de-lys and the right to the crown of France cannot and must not be given away to foreigners, especially those who are our ancient enemies.' More subtly, it claimed that the treaty would subject the clergy, nobles and commons of France to 'shameful servitude'. This claim was designed to offset Henry's carefully calculated campaign to assure the French that nothing in their laws, customs or privileges would change – which was why he had abandoned the old Plantagenet claim in return for adoption by Charles VI.

In Troyes Cathedral, on the same day that he signed the treaty, the new 'heir and regent of France' was betrothed to Catherine, after which there were twelve days of feasting until the marriage on 2 June. His bride had been born in 1401, the youngest daughter of Charles VI and Isabeau of Bavaria – and sister to Richard II's little Queen Isabel. She was therefore half German. One does not receive the impression of a strong personality. She seems to have been attractive, to judge from her husband's well-attested raptures at the portrait of her which her mother had sent him (which has not survived) and Monstrelet assures us that she was 'very handsome'. She may have inherited Isabeau's legendary sensuality, while she undoubtedly transmitted her father's schizophrenia to her only child by Henry. After the king's death she fell besottedly in love with a humble gentleman-in-waiting from Anglesey, Owain Tudur, her Clerk of the Wardrobe, whose father was the Bishop of Bangor's butler. (She had four children by him, apparently after a secret marriage, one of whom was to be Henry VII's father.) As will be seen, it is likely that the king's true feelings for her were essentially dynastic, and that he felt little affection for her.

A folk song, the *Mariage anglais*, commemorates the wedding. It tells how Catherine begged her brothers to stop Henry taking her away – 'I would rather have a French soldier than an English king' – and how there was not a lady in all Paris who did not weep to see their king's daughter leave with an Englishman. When serenaded by his musicians she cried out scornfully that the *'maudit anglois'* could not sound like 'the hautbois of the King of France'. At supper she told the king when he tried to help her to the dishes, 'I can neither eat nor drink when I look upon you.' When English ladies tried to undress her, she ordered 'the accursed English' to leave her – 'I have plenty of folk from my own country to serve me.' Yet when it came to midnight she was still awake and yielded to her husband.

The seal of Queen Catherine

Retourne-toi, embrasse-moi,
Mon cher Anglois!
Puisque Dieu nous a assemblés,
Faut nous aimer.[1]

Perhaps the *Mariage anglois* really does convey what Catherine of Valois felt about Henry. It certainly provides a clue to how some Frenchmen thought of him. The Monk of St Denis's comment on the king was, 'If he is the strongest, all right then! Let him be our master, just so long as we can live in the lap of peace, safety and plenty.'[2] Both song and chronicle preserve a sense of hopelessness induced by unending civil war. However, the Lancastrian monarchy brought none of these things to its 'kingdom of France'. Henry had promised 'good governance' and an end to corruption and extortion. In the event he was able to do nothing against the entrenched interests of the Burgundian officials who ran the kingdom. Nor was he able to rid it of dauphinist raiders, who often threatened Paris itself.

Having spent a honeymoon of only two days, Henry left Troyes with Duke Philip to march on the dauphinist city of Sens, which quickly surrendered. The Anglo-Burgundian army then laid siege to Montereau, where the duke's father had been murdered nearly a year before. English and Burgundians, the latter roaring for revenge, stormed Montereau on 24 June. The governor, the Sieur de Guitry, and most of the garrison took refuge in the heavily fortified castle which adjoined the town but eleven of them were caught. Monstrelet recounts what then took place:

> The King of England sent the prisoners from the town under strong guard to parley from the ditches with the men in the castle and persuade the governor to surrender the place. When they were within hearing they fell on their knees and begged him piteously to yield, for by doing so he would save their lives and in any case he could not hold out much longer against such a large force. The governor replied that they would have to look after themselves as he was not going to surrender. Abandoning all hope of life, the prisoners then asked to speak with their wives, friends and relatives in the castle and everyone said goodbye with tears and lamentations. When they were brought back to the army the English king had a gallows erected and hanged them in full view of the castle. The king also hanged a running footman who always followed him when he rode out, holding the bridle of his horse. He was a great favourite of the king but, having killed a knight in a quarrel, was punished.[3]

148

The fact that the knight had been killed accidentally made no difference whatever to Henry. Meanwhile in the town Duke Philip had his father's corpse disinterred, 'a melancholy sight, for he was still in his pourpoint and drawers'. After it had been suitably clothed and placed in a leaden casket packed with salt and spices, it was sent to the Burgundian family mausoleum at Dijon for reburial. The Sieur de Guitry surrendered on terms on 1 July, marching off with his garrison.

The Anglo-Burgundian army, 20,000 strong, marched to Melun nearby, investing it on 9 July. Here both defences and defenders were unusually strong. The city centre and citadel were on a small island in the Seine, linked to the rest of the city on either bank by fortified bridges, each section forming a separate stronghold. The captain of Melun, the Sieur Arnaud Guillaume de Barbazan, was more than just a fire-breathing Gascon: he was a leader of magnetic personality who inspired his 700 troops (who were clearly 'picked men'), enthusiastically supported by armed citizens. Henry pitched his camp on the west side of the river, Duke Philip on the east. The king built a pontoon bridge over the Seine, screened his gun emplacements with earth ramps and timber stockades, and protected his lines from enemy sorties by trenches. As usual his artillery fired night and day. It included a particularly large cannon, a gift from the City, and named in consequence the 'London', which had arrived unexpectedly. However, the English gunnery had little effect on the walls of Melun. The Burgundians became so exasperated that they launched an assault by themselves, despite a warning from Henry, and were bloodily repulsed; they began to squabble with their allies, the Prince of Orange taking his contingent home in disgust. The Duke of Burgundy stayed; indeed many of his leading supporters were most anxious to wage war at the side of the English king, since it was their sole hope of recovering estates appropriated by the Armagnacs.

Henry and his Burgundian allies tried mining. The miniature paintings of medieval sieges in the illuminated manuscripts show cannoneers in gleaming armour and smartly clad archers shooting gracefully at some fairy-tale castle, their commanders watching from gorgeous silk pavilions. The reality was not quite so elegant. Usually, as at Melun, mining was needed to help the guns smash a breach in the defences; this entailed tunnelling beneath the foundations, frequently from a long distance away, then propping the tunnels up with pit props, and finally firing the props to bring the

149

walls above crashing down. At Melun the soil was unsuitable because the river was so near and the miners had to dig knee deep in mud and water. The defenders countermined to break into the tunnels and attack the besiegers. These desperate hand-to-hand combats in fetid darkness lit by guttering torchlight between half-naked men slipping in the mire must have been indescribably brutish, far removed from the chivalrous combats recorded in the chronicles. The king himself went down into the mines to take part. On one occasion he crossed swords over a wooden barrier in a dimly-lit tunnel with an unusually tough adversary, who turned out to be Barbazan, the enemy commander – when Barbazan realized whom he was fighting he insisted on withdrawing.

Henry had his wife installed at Corbeil nearby, then in a house which he had specially built near his headquarters. Each day his minstrels serenaded her with an hour's concert at sunrise and another at sunset. He also kept in his camp Charles VI and James I, the captive King of Scots. He made the former summon the garrison to surrender but it shouted back that while it honoured a French sovereign it would never kneel to an English king. A similar appeal by James to Scotsmen in the garrison met with a similar response.

After four months' resistance there was good reason for the English to grow alarmed, even if the walls were by now no more than mounds of rubble barely higher than the ditches. More and more Burgundians were deserting (although the duke was able to obtain reinforcements), dysentery had broken out among the English, and it was known that the dauphinists were assembling a relief force. Even if they could not save Melun they might well cut off the Anglo-Burgundian army, which was now seriously depleted. An epidemic broke out among the English. There was gloomy news from across the Channel. In Venice the diarist Antonio Morosini received a letter from London dated 8 September 1420 reporting that the plague was raging there, with 400 people dying every day.

The defenders had to live on horseflesh for three months, but at last, when they had gone without any meat and drink for nearly a week, Barbazan gave up hope and surrendered, on 18 November. The garrison's lives were spared but both soldiers and civilians were to remain prisoners until ransomed and anyone remotely associated with the murder at Montereau was to be handed over bound. Everything in Melun became the spoils of the victors. Umfraville was made its captain.

There was a marked lack of magnanimity in Henry's implementation of the terms. He had been irritated rather than impressed by the heroism of the defence. Boat-loads of the more valuable prisoners, some 600, were sent down the Seine to Paris: many who could not organize payment in time died in confinement.[4] He wanted to execute Barbazan, who only escaped by invoking the laws of chivalry and claiming that since he had crossed swords with the king in the tunnel he was his brother-in-arms. Henry contented himself with condemning Barbazan to perpetual imprisonment and incarcerated the man in an iron cage, first at the Bastille and then at Château Gaillard (where he remained for many years). Large numbers of Armagnacs were executed on the non-proven grounds that they had been involved at Montereau. The king also hanged twenty Scots on the even more specious pretext that they had disobeyed their captive monarch's summons to surrender. He had two monks in the garrison put to death for having brought messages to it.

Henry was 'much feared and dreaded by his princes, knights and captains, and by people of every degree', Waurin informs us, 'because all those who disobeyed his orders or infringed his edicts he would put to death without mercy'.[5] The pitiless ferocity of his letter-of-the-law justice was in evidence at Melun. Shortly after it fell Bertrand de Chaumont, a northern Frenchman who had fought by the king's side at Agincourt and had since loyally served in his household, was accused and found guilty of helping Armagnac friends from the garrison to escape; the Armagnacs had been at Montereau during Duke John's murder and, even if blameless, had faced certain death if they fell into Henry's hands. The Duke of Clarence interceded for Bertrand, pleading for his life. 'By St George, fair brother, had it been you yourself We should have done likewise,' answered the king, who had Bertrand beheaded immediately. Jean Juvénal, recording how the man was executed without a trial, comments 'but then Henry was an Englishman' ('*mais il estoit Anglois*').[6]

As for the prisoners, Jean Juvénal tells us that, 'the hostages and anyone else whom they had captured were brought back to Paris by boat. Some were confined in the Bastille of St Antoine, others in the Palais, the Châtelet, the Temple and in various other prisons.' Here 'several of them were put in deep ditches, especially at the Châtelet, and left there to die of hunger. And when they asked for food and screamed from hunger, people threw straw down to them and called them dogs. Which was a great disgrace to the king of England.'[7]

XIV
The Fall of Paris 1420

'Come on! With us ye shall go see the King!'

A fifteenth-century translation
of Vegetius's *De Re Militari*

'Hélas, doulce France, doulce ville de Paris.'

Jean Juvénal des Ursins

The Anglo-Burgundian army, pausing to collect King Charles at Corbeil, returned to Paris. Henry rode in beside his dazed father-in-law while behind them rode the Dukes of Burgundy, Clarence and Bedford at the head of a glittering cavalcade which nonetheless had some sombre notes – the English king's squire bearing his strange ensign of a fox's brush on the tip of a lance, Duke Philip and his knights all in black. The heir and regent went at once to Nôtre Dame to pray at the high altar, before installing himself in the Louvre. Within hours of their arrival English troops had seized all strongpoints in the French capital, which they were to occupy for seventeen years; they captured the Bastille with a simple subterfuge; a knight engaged the Burgundian castellan in conversation until the soldiers were able to creep up and rush the drawbridge. Led by clergy, dons from the university and lawyers from the *Parlement*, the Parisians greeted the visitation with seeming joy, singing *Te Deum*, encouraged by the wine flowing from the public fountains which the city fathers had prudently provided to sweeten their mood. However alien, this terrifying foreign king might at least bring peace, rescue them from an unending nightmare of civil war and bloodshed. Next day Isabeau and Catherine arrived in their litters, the fountains flowing this time with rose water as well as wine.

The Parisians quickly had good cause to curse the heir and regent. Medieval currency was based on bimetallism and on a bewilderingly complex structure of monies of account – the pound sterling, the pound Scots, the pound *tournois*, the pound *bordelais* and the pound *parisis*, the exchange rate between them fluctuating from place to place. Throughout the century the amount of gold and silver available for coinage diminished steadily, with an accompanying rise in the value of both metals. There was a constant temptation for governments to lower the weight of coins, altering exchange rates to their own advantage. Almost as soon as Henry secured control of Paris the rate was altered to the detriment of the pound *parisis*, producing soaring inflation; within a week of his arrival there food prices more than doubled. The effect of endemic warfare on an agricultural economy always on a knife-edge – so finely balanced that Paris's entire food supply could be endangered by a heat wave or a cold snap, let alone an influx of refugees – had already been disastrous. Soon corn, flour and bread were beyond the purchasing power of the poor.[1]

It is from the Bourgeois of Paris that we know that Parisians blamed the rise in food prices on the new exchange rates at Rouen. His journal has been described as a chronicle of nourishment – or, rather, of under-nourishment. By Christmas, Paris was in the grip of full-scale famine. Everywhere one heard little children crying, 'I'm dying of hunger.' Boys and girls, in bands of twenty or thirty, rooted for scraps on the city's rubbish tips as they died from starvation and cold. Those who pitied them had nothing to give. There was no corn, no wood and no coal, and it was the coldest winter for forty years. People ate pigswill and cabbage roots, even the tripes from dead dogs. Thousands died, and wolves swam the Seine to eat the unburied corpses lying in the street.[2]

Meanwhile Henry and Charles presided over a meeting of the States General, which obligingly endorsed the Treaty of Troyes, and also agreed to a calling-in of the present currency and a re-coinage. This resulted in the coining of the beautiful Anglo-Gallic gold *salut*, which bore the arms of England and France held by an angel and the Virgin. On one side was the inscription *Henricus Dei Gratia Rex Angliae, Heres Franciae* and on the other the presumptuous *Christus Vincit*. (This fresh devaluation made the famine still worse.) Later the Duke of Burgundy's filial desire for revenge was partly assuaged

153

by Charles VI obediently holding a *lit-de-justice* at the Hôtel de Saint-Pol. The 'heir of France' sat with him on the great cushions, to hear the *Parlement* of Paris pronounce the dauphin and his principal henchmen guilty of Duke John's murder. They were summoned to Paris where they were to make the *amende honorable* and be drawn in a tumbril through the public places of Paris bearing lighted torches. When, not unexpectedly, the dauphin and his friends failed to appear within three days, he was banished from the realm of France and debarred from inheriting the French crown by reason of his 'horrible and dreadful crimes'.

Although cowed by years of massacre and famine, and also leaderless, the Parisians could not entirely repress their dislike of the English and their icy arrogance, nor of the foreign king who was to be imposed on them when Charles VI should die. The latter began to be held in considerable affection, according to the Bourgeois of Paris, by the ordinary people of Paris – '*le menu peuple*' – who were to throng the streets in tears when he died. They did not enjoy the occupation of their city by foreigners. Although certain modern English historians claim that it is anachronistic to speak of 'national' feelings at this date, there is at least one contemporary witness who tells us just what the French thought about the English presence in their city.

If Georges Chastellain was a Flemish noble by birth, born at Ghent in 1405, he regarded himself as 'a loyal Frenchman' and always wrote his verses and his history in French. No doubt he suffered from the fashionable pessimism of the age – 'I, man of sadness, born in an eclipse of darkness, and amid thick fogs of lamentation' he says in the foreword to his chronicle – yet his testimony has unusual insights, even if it is occasionally inaccurate. A squire to Duke Philip the Good and Herald of the Order of the Golden Fleece he met all the famous people of his day and was very well-informed. He writes of 1420:

> The city of Paris, ancient seat of France's royal majesty, then seemed to have changed in both name and location, because this king and his great English people [*son grant peuple anglais*] made a new London of it no less by their rude and proud manner of talking as by their language, going everywhere through the city all of which they held as masters. And they went with their heads high like stags, staring all around them, glorying at the shame and ill-fortune of the French, whose blood they had shed in such quantities at Agincourt and elsewhere, and so much of whose heritage they had taken from them by tyranny . . .

For he [Henry V], and also the English lords who were there in much pomp, and more arrogant than can be imagined, had no respect whatever for any lords of France who were present so that it seemed indeed to the English lords and knights that the heritage of the French belonged to them, that the latter's rule and lordship should be taken away by those of English name, whether they liked it or not. Thus did it appear, in truth, since from that time on all the realm and its business was governed and guided by the hand of the English king, and all its places and charges were bestowed and changed at his pleasure, turning out even those men put in place by the two dukes of Burgundy, father and son, and in their stead putting in Englishmen and people of that nation, foreigners unsuited to the nature of the country . . .

Such changes in places and charges did the King of England make on his coming to Paris that in secret many French hearts were sore stricken with sadness, had they dared show it, alas! Watching he who came upon them [Henry] as he was entering Paris they cried 'Noel! Noel!' and rejoiced since they hoped for peace, yet they knew only too well their misfortune and their servitude. And I call to mind often how men came to Jerusalem and stole the ark of the covenant, *arcam foederis*, and violated the temple and the holy places, and how the people there were treated and served scurvily, all their glory and past happiness abased and turned to shame and wretchedness. So it was with the English king and the French. For them every road led to sadness, and it gave him great joy to have done this.[3]

There is other testimony besides that of Chastellain.

The Burgundian nobles, most of whom were Frenchmen, found Henry's coldness and stiff pride repellent. He rebuked Jehan de l'Isle Adam, a valiant marshal of France, for appearing in his presence in a rough grey coat and for then daring to look him in the face when explaining why. (l'Isle Adam had been the garrison commander at Pontoise when it was surprised and captured by the English in 1419.) The king was ill-pleased by the marshal's proud answer that Frenchmen thought it unmanly to lower their eyes when speaking to anyone however high his rank might be. 'That is not our way!' he retorted angrily.[4] Even in those days Frenchmen considered English manners cold and unnatural, and must have thought them peculiarly detestable in invaders. Yet they could do little to express their burning resentment while the Burgundians and Armagnacs hated each other more than they did Englishmen.

Peeresses crossed the Channel to wait on Queen Catherine – and to share in their menfolk's spoils. An anonymous Norman chronicler records: 'The king of England kept his Christmas at Paris in the Hôtel des Tournelles; and there were there the ladies of England who had come to the queen, namely the Duchesses of Clarence and York, the Countess of March, the countess marshal and other noble ladies from the realm of England.'[5]

Parisians were ashamed by the contrast between the splendour of the English king and his court at the Tournelles and Charles VI's miserable condition at the Hôtel de Saint-Pol. They were strangely devoted to their crazed monarch, perhaps partly because he was a focus for anti-English feelings and partly out of pity for his madness. The Hôtel de Saint-Pol was a fine enough palace but the French king, madder and dirtier than ever, was 'poorly and meanly' served by a scant and shabby staff according to Monstrelet, who comments how this must have been 'disgusting for all true and loyal Frenchmen'.[6] Queen Isabeau, no doubt to her fury, had to stay by his side, while every French noble of importance was either with the Duke of Burgundy or the dauphin or else dancing attendance on the 'heir and regent' at the Hôtel des Tournelles. No doubt many cynical French courtiers fully expected that, in view of Charles's age, anyone so much younger, as the Englishman, must soon enter upon his 'inheritance'.

Yet, for all Henry's ability it was undoubtedly usurpation. In 1435 the legal faculty of Bologna gave their verdict that the Dauphin Charles's succession to the throne had been guaranteed by his investiture with the Dauphine in 1417, that Charles VI was not entitled to disinherit him simply on account of Duke John's murder, that the king had been of unsound mind when he did so, that a father could not be both judge and accuser. However, the House of Lancaster had already shown in England that it knew both how to usurp and how to keep a throne.

Admirers of Joan of Arc – whether hagiographers or Bernard Shaw – have given an impression that Henry's brother-in-law was a poor creature, at best a late maturer. Even Edouard Perroy subscribed to this view of him. 'Physically and morally, Charles was a weakling, an unpleasant degenerate,' he writes. 'Puny in size, spindly, [he had] a face devoid of expression in which little frightened eyes, cunning if somnolent, lurked behind a great long nose . . . Roaming gloomily from palace to palace, silent, underhand, superstitious, this retarded adolescent would need to be buffeted much more by misfortune before he could show that he was a man and become a king.'[7] Such a portrait verges on caricature. Admittedly,

156

by comparison with, for example, the flamboyant figure of Philip of Burgundy, it is not easy to obtain a strong impression of the dauphin's personality across the centuries. Undoubtedly he had an unimpressive physique and was fearful to the point of paranoia. A patron of astrologers and the occult, he was a solitary, bookish person who disliked fighting, hunting, tournaments and the normal amusements of fifteenth-century noblemen. The runt of Isabeau's litter, whose two elder brothers had died young, he had never been intended for a throne. Nevertheless there are indications that he matured sooner rather than later. Chastellain, who had considerable respect for him, remarks that 'what he lacked in courage, which was not in his nature, he made up for in shrewdness'.

Like Henry V, the future Charles VII grew up early. Born in 1403 he began presiding over royal councils in 1417 when still only fourteen. A year later he took the title of Lieutenant-General of France (the old French term for regent) and at once became a rallying point for opposition to the looming Anglo-Burgundian domination. He attracted an extremely able and distinguished following. If he was inscrutable he knew very well how to charm – he was said to have a very pleasant voice. Chastellain describes him as being extraordinarily subtle. If he did not care for war he could be both ruthless and violent, as he showed by his complicity in the murder of Duke John on the bridge at Montereau.

In his own way, despite his diffidence and lethargy, this cynical and highly intelligent young man was extremely formidable. However, during his early years he allowed incompetent favourites too much control of policy while his supporters were dangerously unruly; consequently he had difficulty surviving the sinister intrigues of the court of Bourges. He possessed no standing army and no money to pay one, although it has been estimated that the potential revenues from his territories, comparatively undevastated, amounted to at least three times those of Lancastrian France; monies were not properly collected or else embezzled. One day new officials would collect his taxes more efficiently and he would build an army. In the meantime he faced two opponents of genius: Henry and later Bedford. But one should not make the mistake of underestimating the Dauphin Charles.[8]

The dauphinists made much of Henry not being the rightful heir of Richard II, which must have infuriated the king. (As late as 1435 Jean Juvénal was still referring to the usurpation.) In the spring of 1421 Henry had an unpleasing reminder that opposition to the

157

House of Lancaster was not yet dead in England. A close kinsman of the Earl of March, Sir John Mortimer, was arrested on suspicion of treason and sent to the Tower; it can only have been that he was plotting to place his cousin on the throne. The alarm was taken so seriously that he was incarcerated in a dungeon underground. Sir John escaped early in 1422 but was recaptured and again imprisoned in the Tower. He was to escape for a second time in 1424, to be recaptured once more, whereupon he was legally murdered – hanged, drawn and quartered – on the specious charge that his escape had been 'treason'. Throughout Henry's reign, the House of Lancaster remained nervous about public attention being drawn to March's claim to the throne.

News from home that his presence was required there, after three years away, persuaded the heir of France that he must return to England even though it was the sacred season of Christmas. En route he could inspect his duchy of Normandy. On 27 December he left Paris for Rouen, leaving the Duke of Clarence in charge of France, and Exeter in charge of his new city of Paris, both ably supported by his best commanders. On the road to his Norman capital he caught up with Queen Catherine and her ladies who had left some days previously – when her farewell to her mumbling father had deeply moved spectators. With them rode the Duke of Bedford, the Earls of March and Warwick, and the captive King of Scots.

XV
Lancastrian Normandy

'une longue calamité'

Robert Blondel,
Complanctus bonorum Gallorum

'les povres compaignons des frontieres'

Jean Juvénal des Ursins

The Duke of Normandy and his duchess kept the feast of the Epiphany, always a day of celebration and banqueting, at their beautiful new palace castle of Rouen. The building was not only the symbol of English occupation. It was also a symbol of the impoverishment of the citizens since its gleaming magnificence was in striking contrast to the rest of the city.

For the Norman capital remained largely in ruins throughout the English occupation. Its suburbs, together with any buildings outside the main walls, such as abbeys and churches, which might be used for offensive purposes, had been demolished by the Rouennais themselves in 1418 before the beginning of the siege. Others inside the walls had been destroyed by cannon fire during the siege. Some buildings were requisitioned by the English and not restored to their proper use; among these was the badly damaged abbey of Saint-Ouen, much of which served as a barracks. The citizens were crippled financially by the enormous collective ransom which Henry was still extorting from them. Even he realized they could not find 300,000 gold crowns at once and, after painful wrangling over the value of a crown, it was agreed that it should be paid in annual instalments of 80,000 crowns. After eleven years only 260,000 had

159

been extracted, despite the seizure of hostages. The Earl of Warwick, who negotiated the compromise, was merciless in hunting down those who ran away to neighbouring towns to avoid paying their share, seeing that they suffered 'imprisonment of their bodies and sale and exploitation of their goods on account of the debts they properly owe to the king'. The impoverishment and depopulation of the local countryside, and of many Norman towns and villages, did not make for prosperity. Above all, the miserable state of occupied Paris (so graphically recorded by the Bourgeois) deprived Rouen of much of the former market for its luxury goods.[1]

Henry presided over a meeting of the three estates of Normandy – nobles, clergy and bourgeois – which he convened at Rouen. It was also attended by representatives from the estates of the other 'lands of the conquest', territory conquered before the Treaty of Troyes. We do not know how many attended. The king-duke exhorted them to be faithful to the provisions of the Treaty of Troyes, explained he was well aware of the lamentable state of the coinage, and asked for advice on the general state of Normandy. Supposedly as a result of their advice, he announced the imposition of a silver levy in order to strike better coins. He also announced the welcome introduction of a uniform standard of weights and measures throughout the duchy, adopting Rouen's standard for grain. The Earl of Salisbury paid ceremonial homage for his county of Perche, to remind everyone that there was now a new social hierarchy.

The military establishment was exclusively English, from the lieutenant-general down. All captains and lieutenants (commanders and deputy commanders) of garrisons were Englishmen. Besides the towns, there were no less than sixty castles with garrisons. It seems that there were probably about 5,000 English troops in northern France at the time of Henry's visit to the duchy (a handful of rank and file being renegade Frenchmen). Some 1,600 of them were on the new state's southern frontier from Avranches to Verneuil, another 1,600 on the eastern frontier from Pontoise up to Eu, and a further 950 in the Seine valley; of the rest 1,400 were distributed among the castles of the English *seigneurs*, while there were perhaps 150 more along the road leading from Cherbourg through Caen to Evreux. For the moment they had an extremely energetic leader in the king's lieutenant, Clarence.

A substantial number of garrisons were in towns or castles on the rivers. Not only were these of vital importance for defence, but their barges provided the chief means of travel and trade; the Seine and

160

the Oise played a part in the life of northern France comparable to that of the Missouri and the Mississippi in the old American South, if on a smaller scale. It was essential to control them. Castles along their banks, particularly those which guarded crossings, were occupied by the English who rigorously checked the credentials and cargoes of every boat passing and extracted tolls. At the same time those versatile craft, ballingers, patrolled the river, looking out for enemies on the banks as well as afloat. Reinforcements could be brought very quickly to any fortress under attack. This was of the utmost help to such a small occupying army, whose men had to be dispersed in penny packets. The average strength of the lesser garrisons was a mere three men-at-arms and nine archers – though at the little castle of Pont d'Oue which guarded the bridge over the River Vire there were only eight men under a captain in 1421. The garrisons of privately owned strongpoints were even smaller.

On the civil side, pre-conquest institutions had been taken over as far as was feasible, and traditional privileges were respected. Henry tried to woo the poorer classes, the lesser bourgeoisie and the country people. In 1419 he had issued an ordinance allowing all whose houses were of small value to return to them. He also reduced substantially the gabelle, the hated tax on salt. On the other hand noblemen, whether knights or squires, who had left the duchy were still being shown scant mercy. The king ordered his *baillis* to discover the names of those nobles who had gone off to join the Armagnacs or the 'brigands'; it appears that some had entrusted their châteaux or manors to their wives while they themselves were away fighting the English – their estates were now confiscated. The duchy remained so troubled that between May 1421 and September 1422, 386 brigands were captured and hanged. Probably in consequence of this situation Henry had to change his attitude towards the recalcitrant Norman nobility; at the end of 1421 he offered men of all classes a full pardon so long as they returned and took the oath of allegiance before Candlemas (2 February) 1422 in the presence of the nearest *bailli* or garrison commander on the frontier. However, during his visit at the beginning of 1421, Norman nobles if discovered to be absent were still being expropriated as rebels, and 'voluntary absence' was deemed an act of rebellion against the king-duke. He continued to use this as a pretext to obtain lands for his grants to English settlers.

The fate of the exiled nobles was grim, as we know from Robert Blondel. As a young man (he was born about 1390) Blondel had fled in 1418, at the latest, from the Cotentin where his grandfather, the squire Guillaume Blondel, was Seigneur of Ravenoville near Valognes. He took refuge in Paris, where he studied at the university and entered the Church. He wrote three works denouncing the English conquest of Normandy. All are especially interesting in that they describe what happened to the refugees. In the *Complaint of All Good Frenchmen* of 1420, Blondel laments how, 'Captive Normandy lies under the yoke of the leopard [of England]. Some are laden with chains while others are dying under torture. There are those who have been killed by the sword, those who have fled the soil of their fathers, those who have despaired and died, ground down by the sheer weight of tyranny. The unhappy exiles lack everything, even somewhere to find a refuge.'[2] Looking back from 1449 – 'soon thirty-five years will have gone by' – he complains how:

> Before the war we were renowned, rich and powerful. Today, broken and crushed by want, we lead the life of beggars. Many among us who are noblemen are forced to take up the most menial employment; some work at the tailor's trade, others serve in inns, while English cowherds and yokels from the scum strut through our country, grown rich on our inheritances and sporting stolen titles of duke, count, baron or knight.[3]

He also refers to 'my country's incredible devastation'.

Devastation certainly existed in Henry's time. In December 1421 he issued instructions to the wolf-hunters of the Pays de Caux:

> It has come to Our knowledge that, since these our present wars began and because of them, wolves, she-wolves and other ravening beasts have greatly increased in Our said duchy and especially in the bailliwick of Caux, that they have piteously devoured several human creatures at which Our suppliant subjects are so sore affrighted in their simplicity that they dare not stay in their houses in unfenced towns or villages or leave their children, and neglect their labour; so that the said cruel beasts have very much diminished the livestock and produce of the said land, which is nearly devoid of people.

Similar missives of the same date were addressed to wolf-hunters at Carentan, Cherbourg, Bayeux, Gisors and other Norman towns.

Most of the devastation was caused by the English garrisons rather than by wolves. For the troops, whether *baillis*, captains,

162

men-at-arms or humble archers, were paid erratically. We know that the Earl of Suffolk and Sir Thomas Rokeby received six months' pay for their men in 1417 but nothing more until mid-1418 and then only enough money for a single quarter. In January 1418 Sir John Pelham wrote from Caen 'I am here without wages'. In the summer of the same year a soldier at the siege of Cherbourg complains in a letter of 'the long time we have been here, and of the expenses that we have had at every siege that we have come to, and have had no wages since that we came out of England, so that we have spent all that ever we had, wherefore I beseech you heartily to send me £20'. At the end of 1419 Sir Gilbert Halsale, captain of Evreux, complained he had received neither pay nor provisions since Michaelmas and warned that his men were going to desert, a warning he repeated in 1420 – they were at last paid sometime during the summer.[4] Inevitably the troops supported themselves by robbing the peasants.

Henry made superhuman efforts to remedy the situation, personally sending the orders for the payment of each garrison to the treasurer of war. At first the money came from the English exchequer, but later it was supposed to be provided mainly by the Norman treasury. The system did not function properly for the simple reason that the king was often too short of ready cash; the pay of the vitally important garrison at Calais was years in arrears, despite his wish that soldiers should be paid on a monthly basis. He also tried to stop his men living off the country by establishing a commissariat to feed them, something which even Napoleon would find difficult in occupied territory. The Norman *vicomtes* began supplying the troops with cattle and sheep on the hoof, as well as with wine and cider. In 1420 two royal victuallers were appointed under the treasurer-general of Normandy to deliver food to garrisons, while provisions were shipped over from England. Whether because the operation was too ambitious, or whether as a result of corruption or inefficiency, it failed to solve the problem. Henry was fully aware of the dangers which must ensue. His council said that the king's soldiers 'should be compelled to pay for their victuals in the country, the which must needs be done or else, without recovery, Normandy should be lost from him'.

In December 1418 all those who had been injured or plundered by English garrisons were told they might apply to the *vicomtes'* courts for redress. In April 1419 Henry gave strict orders that nothing must be taken by troops or officials without down payment in good money. In August that year he commanded the drawing up of a strict code of behaviour for garrisons. In January 1421, during his visit to Rouen with Catherine, the king issued a revealing 'ordinance':

> The king, learning how some of his English subjects have carried out unjust requisitions and inflicted violence on the poor people, because of which it is feared that merchants may abandon their trade and peasants their labour, forbids the people of the open countryside [*'plat pays'*] being made to pay tolls at the gates and bridges of towns and fortresses; the requisitioning of horses and beasts of burden without their owners' consent; the taking of livestock, victuals, wine or merchandise except for the proper price.

Fines and imprisonment were stipulated. Yet in April 1421 Henry again had to forbid stealing and unofficial levying of the *pâtis*. Next month Sir John Radcliffe was sent on a tour of inspection to make sure that captains and their garrisons were obeying the king's orders. But in December the same year we find Henry issuing a further edict in which he complains angrily that his soldiers are still ravaging the countryside; he threatens them with imprisonment if they are caught infringing his ordinances – and with hanging if caught doing it a second time.[5]

For, while a ferociously effective disciplinarian on campaign, the king had no really effective means of controlling his men from a distance. Basin, who spent many years in Normandy and in Paris when both were under the English occupation, speaks of 'the insolent and undisciplined English army [*insolens illa et indisciplinata . . . Anglorum milicia*]'. Medieval armies were usually without much discipline and tended to rob and bully. Henry, desperate to win popularity with the French, was one of the few commanders who tried to do something about it. He appointed special commissioners to inspect garrisons; the office of Seneschal of Normandy was revived, its holder being charged with investigating the troops' conduct. It was in vain. There was trouble from all ranks. In 1420 the inhabitants of Mantes complained to the king about the extortionate behaviour of the Earl of March. Then there were the deserters; in August 1422 Henry commissioned the captain of Pont-de-l'Arche to arrest 'certain vagabond English who wander from place to place robbing and inciting the soldiers to desert'.[6] But he was not in a position to apply the one cure for the problem – to see that the troops received regular pay. Even his administrative genius could not discover an alternative to wages.

His prohibition of tolls was not without irony. It seems they were forbidden only if unofficial. Monstrelet records that no one was allowed to enter or leave any of the towns occupied by the English without an expensive permit costing four sous – 'a useful source of income for the king' observes the chronicler. For Henry's thunderbolts at troops who extorted money were directed only against those who did so without authorization. He derived considerable revenue from the *pâtis, courses, sauvegardes, billets* and *congés* levied in his name.[7] It is unlikely that the French relished paying dues of this sort officially any more than they did unofficially. Nor is it likely that English troops were any gentler in extracting them.

The attempt to transform Harfleur into an another Calais by replacing its inhabitants with Englishmen was soon recognized as a failure, even if some merchants accepted the royal offer of houses there. (And apparently were still doing so in 1419 when the lieutenant, Sir Hugh Lutterell, was empowered to grant dwellings to any Englishman who applied for them.) The English presence in Harfleur was essentially a military one since, as a seaport, the town commanded the mouth of the Seine. By 1417 at latest Henry had changed his mind, abandoning mass colonization in favour of small settlements which could be integrated into the surrounding community. The settlement at Caen was started immediately after the city's capture and, clearly by deliberate design, was very much smaller than that at Harfleur, its members living side by side with the French population. Caen was the capital of western Normandy and the centre of the new regime's financial administration; by the beginning of 1418 a Norman treasury and *chambre des comptes* had been installed in the city. It was in urgent need of English merchants, soldiers, and of bureaucrats. The merchants' task was to revive prosperity after the sack and the departure of 500 bourgeois to Anjou. The garrison numbered fifteen men-at-arms and forty-five archers. One of the latter, John Milcent, who became a man-at-arms and was to style himself '*bourgeois de Caen*', received no less than five houses in the city in early 1421 (with the obligation of manning the watch for four nights a year). There was a particular demand for bureaucrats. In 1419 the *chambre des comptes* recruited as auditors Roger Waltham, John Brinkley and William Wymington (who married a French girl); in the following year they were joined by John Chepstowe, a priest accountant. A few merchants became tax officials, such as Nicholas Bradkyrk, a draper from London.[8]

English control of the duchy was constantly threatened. Two exiled Norman grand seigneurs, members of the great family of Harcourt, led their private armies against the English from time to time. They were the Count of Harcourt himself and the Count of Aumale, both of whose counties had been taken away from them by King Henry. The former, Jacques d'Harcourt, who switched his allegiance from the Burgundians to the dauphinists in 1422, led a small force of Norman exiles based in Picardy which occasionally raided across the ducal frontier. His cousin Jean d'Harcourt, based in Anjou, led a similar band on raids of the same sort deep into Normandy; in May 1422 Aumale and the Vicomte de Narbonne with 2,000 men seized Bernay, killing 700 English. Henry gave instructions for all castles which could not be garrisoned adequately to be demolished lest they become rallying points for brigands – 'concursus brigandorum'.

Even the ducal capital was sometimes at risk. In July 1419 the Earl of Warwick was sent in haste to Rouen by the king to investigate a plot which had recently been detected, presumably a plot to hand the city over to the dauphinists. A similar plot was uncovered in 1422, led by one of the richest goldsmiths in Rouen, Robert Alorge, who was executed. In December 1421 captains of riverside castles were warned to be on the alert to safeguard the capital. Traffic along the Seine was checked constantly, boats moored in unassigned places being sunk.

What unsettled Normandy still more was that, although Henry hoped to reconcile the Normans to his rule, he was forced to impose a new and crushing tax burden on them. The king-duke had to maintain his towns, castles and garrisons, and to subsidize the further enormous war effort needed to subdue the rest of France. He realized that England could not, would not pay any more, as Parliament was beginning to make very clear indeed. He therefore had no alternative than to tax viciously the lands of the conquest. Since Normandy was the land most firmly under English control it was to be the greatest milch cow of all. The Norman estates received some idea of what was in store for them at their meeting with Henry early in 1421.

All classes, even the normally exempt nobility, would have to pay heavier taxes than ever before. Yet the invasion had wrought havoc with the Norman economy. Agriculture, markets and exchanges had collapsed, and seemed unlikely to revive because of the general insecurity. The merchant fleet of every port had been requisitioned to ferry supplies for the English troops from across the Channel. Emigration by the thousand had ruined such industries as Caen's already declining cloth trade; many exiled weavers set up their looms in Brittany, competing with those who had stayed at home. There were exiled Norman craftsmen all over France, while some of the duchy's ironworkers had fled as far as Germany.[9] The bourgeoisie were additionally demoralized by being rounded up as hostages and shipped over to England; they were always under pressure after any plot or raid in which complicity was suspected. Crushing taxes discouraged everybody. The situation was to improve to some extent under Bedford, a more flexible and humane ruler than his brother, while the new security of the Channel could offer fresh opportunities to Norman ports. Indeed Bedford's regency was a period of genuine prosperity for the Normans, at least when compared with conditions during his brother's reign.[10]

The Normans regarded Henry with awe and fear, in contrast to Bedford of whom they were later to be genuinely fond. English historians tend to dismiss Robert Blondel's references (in his account of the expulsion of the English from Normandy) to Henry because he wrote long after the king's death. Yet Blondel was only three years younger than Henry and appears to have a reasonably reliable memory. He describes him as 'the ferocious and savage king' (*'ferox et immanis rex'*), as 'a tyrant', as 'cruel'.

Attitudes towards the English occupation varied according to class. The nobility's position was complicated by the fact that marriage and kinship linked them to other noble families all over France and thus to the interrelated and tightly interwoven groups of cousins who made up the nuclei of the dauphinist and Burgundian factions. Norman nobles who were Burgundians were in two minds whether to support or defy the regime; all had kinsmen who had killed, or who had been killed by, dauphinists – one Burgundian source says that the dauphinists committed worse crimes than any ever commited even by demons. The bourgeoisie's instincts as business men made them prefer 'collaboration' with the occupation to resistance – a reaction not unknown during World War II – since they were primarily concerned with the safety of trade and commerce and there were opportunities for profit as tax farmers. (They would be reasonably contented with the relative prosperity which later resulted from Bedford's shrewd and tactful administration, finding the man and his measures far more sympathetic than his brother.) The class which above all disliked the English was the ordinary people, who suffered most from the attentions of the soldiery and had to pay the bulk of the new taxes.

English settlers were quickly made aware that they were unwelcome in Normandy. The words 'son of an Englishman!' were often heard in taverns when drink inflamed tempers, recognized as a deadly insult, the equivalent of 'son of a Whore!'. [11] Some clergy refused publicly to pray for King Henry. Norman farmers and merchants sold grain to dauphinist garrisons across the frontier. The entire countryside was hostile. When travelling, especially through woodland, English troops always had to be on the alert. Whether in citadels or castles, garrisons never dared to relax their guard for an instant. The *bocage*, or hilly, wooded country, was especially perilous; much of the Duke of Exeter's county of Harcourt was *bocage* and his officials were too frightened to collect his rents. There was danger everywhere – danger from dauphinist partisans, danger from brigands. Mass executions and hostage-taking did not solve the problem. The regime held but was always insecure.

It is scarcely surprising that many settlers soon grew homesick for England. The confiscated lands given to them were often no better than wasteland because there were not enough peasants left to work them. They were treated as interlopers and enemies by the local population. Despite the ferocious penalties, they tried to return across the Channel in large numbers. In April 1421 Henry sent orders to the captains of Honfleur and Dieppe, to the lieutenants of Harfleur, Caen and Cherbourg, to stop anybody of any nation (including *'personas anglicas'*), regardless of rank or sex, from departing 'without our special licence'. All who attempted to leave Lancastrian Normandy without a passport were to suffer death and the confiscation of their property. Even these draconian measures were of no avail. The colony at Harfleur, once 10,000 Englishmen strong, had melted away to a mere handful by the time the French recaptured the port in 1435. After the king's death the regent, Bedford, showed, by letting settlers go home if they wished, that he regarded his brother's attempts at colonization as a serious error of judgement.

Henry and Catherine rode out from their Norman capital on 19 January. They were accompanied by the Duke of Bedford, the Earl Marshal, the Earls of March and Warwick, many knights and gentlemen and the great ladies, and King James, their escort consisting of a force of picked men-at-arms and archers. There were loyal greetings and ceremonial gifts as they progressed through Amiens and other towns on their way to Calais. The king was particularly pleased at the compliments paid to his queen by his French subjects – though these may secretly have been inspired more by Catherine being the daughter of their lawful Valois sovereign than by her beauty. At Calais they received a wildly enthusiastic, and no doubt genuinely sincere, welcome from its inhabitants before setting sail.

XVI

'Rending of Every Man Throughout the Realm'

'The sieges hath . . . consumed innumerable goods of his finance, both in England and in France, and in Normandy.'

Sir John Fastolf

'What king that doth more excessive despenses
Than his land may to suffice or attain,
Shall be destroyed.'

Thomas Hoccleve, *The Regement of Princes*

The royal party landed at Dover on 1 February 1421. A huge crowd had assembled on the beach to greet it, barons of the Cinque ports carrying the king and queen ashore on their shoulders through the shallows. Henry was received by his English subjects, in Monstrelet's phrase, 'as one of God's angels'. He at once went to Canterbury with his wife, cheered every step of the road, to offer thanks at St Thomas's shrine and be welcomed by Archbishop Chichele. He then rode up to London to organize Catherine's reception, leaving her to follow by litter. They were reunited at Eltham on 21 February, entering London the same day.

The mayor, Will Cambryge, aldermen, sheriffs and officials of the City guilds, together with a whole host of Londoners dressed in their best, met them at Blackheath to escort them in. They were welcomed by pageants and tableaux no less splendid than those which had greeted the king after his return from Agincourt. As in 1415, everyone was edified by Henry wearing purple, the colour of Christ's Passion, when he went to give thanks at St Paul's.

170

Two days later Catherine, in white, was crowned and anointed Queen of England by the Archbishop of Canterbury in Westminster Abbey. Afterwards she presided in her crown over her coronation banquet in Westminster Hall – Henry being absent, according to custom. Since it was Lent the menu consisted of countless dishes of fish and sweet puddings, the former ranging from sturgeon, salmon and sole to whelks, conger and porpoise. The royal cooks had surpassed themselves in creating 'subtleties' – pastry tableaux which appeared between courses – though a tigress led on a chain by St George might have been liable to misinterpretation. Throughout, the queen was served on bended knee by her brothers-in-law, Bedford and Gloucester.[1]

After three-and-a-half years' campaigning Henry was no longer the smooth-faced youth of the National Portrait Gallery. His crowned effigy on a stone screen at York Minster, begun about 1425, has recently been identified as a portrait. Unexpectedly, he wears a small forked beard like Richard II. Beneath a thick crop of elaborately curled hair his face is handsome and commanding, but undeniably tense and careworn.[2] The beard (also shown on the obverse of his Great Seal) provides the clue to another unsuspected likeness. A miniature of St George in the *Bedford Book of Hours* not only depicts the saint in the gilded armour, Garter cloak and pudding-basin crop affected by the king but with a small forked beard. In the present writer's view this too is a portrait of him.

During Henry's absence overseas his régime had held up very well, partly because of Bedford's effectiveness as regent, partly because of pride in his triumphs over the French. There was no trouble from Lollards, now a hunted remnant; Sir John Oldcastle had been caught in 1417 and roasted alive as he swung in chains from a gibbet. Supporters of King Richard and the Earl of March had all but given up the struggle (even if March's kinsman Sir John Mortimer was still plotting). The Welsh had stayed cowed while the 'Foul Raid' by the Scots under the Duke of Albany and the Earl of Douglas had met with the usual fate of Scottish invasions, having been routed with contemptuous ease by the Duke of Exeter. The restoration of law and order had also survived apart from certain outbreaks of violence in the north of England and on the Welsh border, but that was only to be expected in those chronically unruly areas. Coastal and merchant shipping remained free from the threat of privateers which had been such a menace in the decades before Henry's accession. Not only had the French privateers been put out

171

of action completely but the Castilians had been deprived of their bases in French ports by his occupation of Normandy and alliances with Burgundian Flanders and Brittany, while the 'King's Ships' patrolled coastal waters with reassuring efficiency.

Nonetheless, there were noticeable tensions. Not everyone had profited from 'spoils won in France' and all too many people associated the war with high taxation. In 1416–18 Archbishop Chichele had referred more than once to clerics who were growing tepid in their prayers for the king's success; the clergy disliked paying taxes as much as anybody else and were seemingly less than enthusiastic about unending campaigns which drained their pockets. The Parliament of 1419 had voted smaller sums than ever before for the war, while that of December 1420, just before Henry's return, had complained of its petitions always being sent abroad for the king's consideration (although he was meticulous in answering them, even during the most demanding campaigns) and showed itself so unwilling to vote any further war taxation that he had waived his demands.

As McFarlane pointed out, 'Henry does not seem to have bothered his head over much about the financial soundness of his enterprise; he needed money but was quite indifferent to the means by which it was procured . . . Modern estimates, based on an imperfect understanding of the principles of medieval book-keeping, have unfortunately disguised the real gravity of the position.'[3]

Every government department was deep in debt and, with hindsight, it can be seen that unless the war ended soon the monarchy faced inevitable bankruptcy. The king's scheme to pay for his campaigns with money from his conquered French territories was simply not working; it is known that during the last year of his reign the Norman revenues brought in only £10,000 despite his steep increase in taxation. His English subjects would have to foot most of the bill, as they were beginning to realize with growing irritation.

By 1421 Henry's financial situation was already desperate. Almost £40,000 of his father's debts and his own personal debts were unpaid, he had not yet reimbursed several senior commanders for their very considerable outlay during the 1415 campaign and he owed wages to most if not all of the garrison captains in France. The Calais garrison's pay was in arrears to the tune of £28,710 (it would mutiny in 1423). At home he owed nearly £7,000 (10,000 marks) to the Earl of Northumberland for policing and defending the eastern stretch of the Scots border. A general loan approved by Parliament in 1419 had produced derisory sums since he had not been in

England to extract it. The City of London, which had advanced over £6,000 in 1415 and again in 1417, would now lend only £2,000 for a fresh campaign. It was unlikely that Parliament would grant more taxes and even he dared not override it.

He decided to make a fund-raising tour of the kingdom. The ostensible reason for the ensuing royal 'progress' was to show Queen Catherine her new country and to visit holy shrines. Commissioners were to follow in his wake to extort loans by whatever means they could from noblemen, gentry, clergy and burgesses, even from yeomen and artisans, although the sums extracted from the latter might amount to no more than a few pence.

However, France was never out of his mind for one moment. On 27 February 1421 he wrote to his officials across the Channel:

> We have understood by your letter to us, sent desiring to wit if ye should ordain masons and carpenters for repairment of our castle of Pontorson. Wherefore we will and charge you that you ordain that it be repaired and amended as well as the two towers at the bridge . . . and we have certified our cousin of Suffolk how that we have charged you therewith. And also we have charged our foresaid cousin that the governance of Avranches and of the country thereabout be amended.[4]

Before embarking on the tour Henry went to Bristol and then to Shrewsbury to investigate reports of disturbances on the Welsh border. Then he joined Catherine at Leicester where they celebrated Easter. We know the way that they travelled on their tour from the chronicle of John Strecche, the canon of Kenilworth, who immortalized the story of the dauphin's tennis balls. First they visited Nottingham, then Pontefract and then York. The king did not forget to visit the shrines of his two favourite Yorkshire saints, John of Bridlington and John of Beverley. The bones of the second, who died in 721, had been translated (ceremonially reinterred) at Beverley Minster on 25 October 1037. Since Agincourt was fought on a 25 October, Henry attributed his victory to John's intercession, making the Church in England alter the day in the Sarum and York rites from the feast of the Gallo-Roman Crispin and Crispinian to that of an Anglo-Saxon bishop's translation. After this he and his queen went to Lincoln for the consecration of a new bishop.

At Lincoln news came from France. His brother Clarence, after a most successful raid into Maine and Anjou during which he stormed many castles, had been defeated and killed at Baugé near Angers by

173

a force of French and Scots. The 'Marshal of France' (Gilbert Umfraville), the 'Count of Tancarville' (John Grey) and Lord Roos had died with him while the Earls of Huntingdon and Somerset, Lord Fitzwalter and Sir Edmund Beaufort had been taken prisoner. At midnight two Scots earls, Buchan and Douglas, wrote from the battlefield to tell the dauphin of his victory, sending Clarence's banner with their letter. For a moment it seemed that the entire English conquest was threatened. The king did not reveal the dispatch's contents to his courtiers until the following day. They marvelled at his self-control.

Baugé had been lost by Clarence's foolhardiness in charging 5,000 enemy troops with 150 men-at-arms. Umfraville and Huntingdon had tried to dissuade him but he wanted a victory to rival Agincourt. The English had been beaten, a contemporary wrote, 'by cause they wolde nott take with hem archers, but thought to have doo with the ffrenshmen them selff wythoute hem. And yet whan he was slayne the archers come and rescued the body of the duke . . . god have mercy a pon his soule, he was a valyant man.'

Salisbury, who brought up the archers, extricated what remained of the English force with considerable difficulty. To cross the Loire he had to construct a bridge out of carts and fencing. He found an even more ingenious way of bridging the River Sarthe. He made his men wear white crosses like dauphinists and, having convinced some local peasants that he was a Frenchman, ordered them to build a bridge for him. Once over he had the peasants put to death.[5]

The French had killed the head of the English government in France – heir to the throne of England – besides eliminating half the king's best commanders. Had the French caught Salisbury, the English might have been driven out of France thirty years earlier than they were. Although he had escaped, the dauphinists were understandably elated. Wild rumours spread throughout France; it was even believed that Henry himself had been killed. A tactful astrologer consulted by John Stewart of Darnley prophesied that both the English king and Charles VI would die in the very near future.

It is clear that Henry had given the strictest instructions never to offer battle without archers, and understood perfectly why his brother had been routed. Basin says the king commented that if Clarence had escaped with his life he would have suffered the death penalty for disobeying orders. Nevertheless it was a fearful blow to Henry and not just because he had lost a brother. (Clarence and he had never been very close, even if his succession to the throne put an end to their rivalry. Significantly, he had omitted the duke from his will in 1415.) So disastrous a defeat gave the lie to his loudly proclaimed conviction that his cause had the Divine approval, that God invariably fought on his side.

He travelled back to London by himself, by way of King's Lynn, Walsingham – where he prayed at the shrine of the Virgin – Norwich, and other East Anglian towns. Catherine took a different route, through Leicester, Stamford, Huntingdon, Cambridge, and Colchester before rejoining her husband at the capital. It seems that commissioners accompanied both of them. Strecche informs us that, 'From the cities thus visited the king and queen received precious gifts of gold and silver from citizens and prelates . . . Moreover the king demanded and received from the more powerful men of the realm, such as merchants and bishops, abbots and priors, a great deal of money.'[6] Together with his efforts in London, the tour produced loans amounting to some £9,000, an enormous sum for such an operation at that period.

This 'rending of every man throughout the realm, be he rich or poor' – Adam of Usk's description of fund raising – did not enhance the war's popularity. Adam adds that the king's unceasing demands for money for his campaigns were beginning to infuriate his subjects – 'the grievous taxation of the people to this end being unbearable, accompanied by smothered curses'. While the English admired, even revered, the man, they were growing alarmed by his ambitions overseas.[7]

When Parliament met in May the Commons complained, politely but resentfully, of poverty and distress among the king's subjects and probably – though there is no definite evidence – refused the permanent taxation which was the sole hope of reducing the steadily growing deficit in the royal budget, a deficit which increased alarmingly each year. They would only grant a subsidy of a fifteenth, less than ever before. With even more reluctance the clergy granted a tenth.

The conclusion is inescapable that the English had seen the Treaty of Troyes as a danger signal; with reason they expected countless new campaigns for which Henry would demand ever increasing sums of money. They based their resistance to any further demands of this sort on the treaty's constitutional implications; in their view the war was now one between the French monarchy, in the person of the 'Heir of France', and his father-in-law's rebellious

175

subjects, and Englishmen could not be expected to pay for it. However much he may have disliked it privately, the king was too shrewd a politician to oppose such an argument head-on, and he had clearly anticipated it, to judge from his response. He had asked for no fresh taxation in the Parliament of December 1420, nor did he now – 1421 was the first year of his reign when no new taxes were collected. He would have to make good the shortfall by private borrowing on a nationwide scale, as he had already begun to do. Henry refused another Commons request (inspired by the Treaty of Troyes, and the fear that the monarch would be abroad for long periods) that parliamentary petitions might be answered by the king's lieutenant at home in England; he would continue to consider them personally, even on campaign, as hitherto – when he had time to do so. For all the enthusiasm of their welcome, and their pride at humiliating the hereditary enemy, the English were definitely beginning to tire of their hero king always being overseas – creating a dual monarchy, with France as an equal, had considerably less appeal than a war of straightforward plunder. However, no one dared to criticize publicly Henry's foreign ambitions.

The seriousness of the king's financial problems can best be understood by appreciating that when he died the government would have to face a deficit of £30,000, together with debts of £20,000. This was against a total annual revenue of just over £56,000, inadequate for the crown's expenses in peacetime, let alone in wartime. He had only been able to pay for his campaigns by living hopelessly above his means without any thought of a reckoning.

Henry seized every possible opportunity of raising money. He even exploited the popular belief in magic, at the expense of his own family. Everyone believed in wizards and witches. We know from John Lydgate's *Troy Book* (written between 1412 and 1420) that a witch could tell the future by astrology, though usually employing necromancy or calling up demons to do so, and change the weather, raising up storms of lightning, hail and snow, of cold and ice. (Just as Owain was reputed to have done.) She could even turn old men into young ones, besides being able to do more unpleasant things.

On 25 September 1419 the Archbishop of Canterbury wrote to his bishops to inform them that the king desired their prayers for protection against the supernatural machinations of necromancers who were trying to destroy him. (Necromancers were magicians who brought dead bodies to life, to work evil spells for them.) There was nothing much out of the ordinary about this request. What was truly startling, however, was the arrest of Joan, the queen dowager, four days later on such a charge. According to the parliament rolls her confessor, Friar Randolf, a Franciscan of Shrewsbury, had accused her 'of compassing the death and destruction of our lord the king in the most treasonable and horrible manner that could be devised'. The *Chronicles of London* are more explicit; she had attempted 'by sorcery and necromancy for to have destroyed the king'. Friar Randolf was arrested in Guernsey and brought to Henry's field headquarters at Mantes, where the king interrogated him personally before ordering that he be taken to London and imprisoned in the Tower. Two other members of the queen dowager's household were also arrested, a groom called Roger Colles and a maid named Peronell Brocart – nothing is known of their subsequent fate.

Admittedly Joan of Navarre's father, King Charles the Bad of Navarre, had had an unfortunate (and possibly justified) reputation for sorcery, as many people must have remembered. It was also true that her son by her first marriage was Duke John of Brittany, who disliked the English; that another of her sons, Artus de Richemont, had been captured at Agincourt after being so hideously wounded in the face that he looked like a frog and was still languishing in captivity in England. (Oddly enough, in later years there were to be rumours that Richemont practised sorcery.) Yet Joan had always been on the best of terms with Henry and indeed with all her other stepchildren ever since she had married their father in 1402. Good-looking, elegant and amiable, she seems to have been generally liked. There was no apparent motive for her trying to kill the king. In the event she was never brought to trial, while the friar who had accused her stayed in the Tower until he was killed there in a fight with a mad priest. (Save for a brief episode after Henry's death when he was extricated for a short period by his literary patron the Duke of Gloucester.) Nevertheless Joan, who had been deprived of all her possessions and revenues four days after her actual arrest, remained a prisoner for nearly three years. What was so curious about her captivity, which was mainly at Leeds Castle in Kent, was that it was so very comfortable. She had nineteen grooms and seven pages and was provided with every luxury, entertaining the Duke of Gloucester and the Archbishop of Canterbury who both came and dined with her; Bishop Beaufort stayed with her as her guest for several days, as did Lord Camoys.

The late A. R. Myers' explanation of this extraordinary episode is almost certainly the correct one, and demonstrates just how ruthless

Henry V could be, even towards the most harmless members of his own family. The plot can only have existed in the mind of Friar Randolf, presumably crazy and recognized as such by the king. But the queen dowager was entitled to a dowry of over £6,000 a year, a very heavy expense for a government whose total regular income was little more than £56,000; during her imprisonment she never cost more to keep than £1,000 in any one year. An increase in revenue of £5,000 per annum would have been of crucial importance to a ruler who was only just staying afloat financially. It also explains why Joan was never brought to trial; if she had been, she would have been acquitted, thus depriving the government of her dowry. On his deathbed Henry ordered her release and the restoration of her possessions and income 'lest it should be a charge unto Our conscience', a tacit admission that the whole affair had been trumped up. For the rest of her life until her death in 1437 she was treated with the utmost respect and consideration. Clearly, few people had believed in the story that she was a royal witch.

One aspect which Myers ignores is that Joan's son was the Duke of Brittany. John V had not seen her for many years, and was in any case a man with little family feeling. Nevertheless it would be extremely embarrassing for the duke if his mother was proved publicly to be a witch – he was not to know there was no case – and on at least one occasion he demanded to know what was being done with her. John was flirting with the dauphinists – later he would briefly desert his alliance with the English – and Henry would have had no scruples about using this particular threat against him.

Another relative was even more profitable. Few English prelates, not even Cardinal Wolsey, have been as blatantly avaricious as the king's uncle, Bishop Henry Beaufort. In 1417 he had resigned the chancellorship of England and gone to Constance where a council of the Church was seeking to end the schism. When a new pope, Martin V, was at last elected, he curried favour with him. Martin hoped to extinguish the Statute of Provisors, which did not allow papal nominations to English benefices; he therefore appointed Beaufort papal legate in England and offered him a cardinal's hat. In 1419 Beaufort was warned by his angry nephew, who confiscated the bull naming him legate, that he had infringed the Statute of Provisors and risked losing all his goods and being degraded from his see. Most unwisely, Beaufort tried to obtain a fresh bull. Henry, through the bishop's cousin and confidant, Thomas Chaucer, who was secretly in the king's pay, informed him that he was facing ruin in earnest.

178

The example of Joan of Navarre had not been wasted. Beaufort became so terrified that in 1421 he lent his nephew over £17,000, increasing his loans to him to the enormous sum of £38,000.

An estimate submitted to Henry in May 1421 showed him that he was operating on the brink of financial disaster, as he must have guessed in any case. He was obsessed with money. We know from an undated letter that, despite all his difficulties, he had at one period during his reign reserves kept at Harfleur of £30,000 in gold coin, £2,000 in silver coin and blocks of silver weighing half a ton.[8] He was not above checking figures himself. Early in 1421 he examined the accounts of a former Keeper of the Great Wardrobe, a man who had been dead for four years, accounts which in any case would have automatically been audited by the treasury sooner or later, and indicated items which he wished to be queried. It was not that he was in any way a miser. It was simply that he was determined to find the resources to pay for his conquest of France – resources which only existed in his imagination.[9]

His desperation at this date is understandable. Parliament had refused to grant more money at a moment when still more bad news was coming out of France. Dauphinist morale had soared after Baugé while that of the English sank correspondingly. The latter no longer seemed invincible, as they had ever since 1415, a consideration of vital importance for scanty forces occupying a vast area of territory and defending very long frontiers.

Salisbury, the new King's Lieutenant, assembled fresh troops, sent out scouts to locate the various uncoordinated dauphinist forces about to march into Normandy and attacked each separately in turn, causing the dauphin to abandon the siege of Alençon and any idea of invading Normandy. The earl then raided deep into Anjou, afterwards reporting to Henry that 'we broughten Hom the farest and grettest Prey of Bestes' – meaning that whole herds of horses, cattle, sheep and pigs had been seized from the wretched peasants – and that he and his men were rested and ready to strike again.[10] Even so, Salisbury had been very lucky that the enemy, who vastly outnumbered his little army, had not joined forces to invade Normandy. Instead they turned west and laid siege to Chartres.

Yet the dauphin's change of direction was alarming enough. For he took Montmirail and menaced Paris. The capital was now more or less blockaded by his skirmishers, whom Parisians were threatening to admit in the way they had Burgundians in the past. The Duke of Exeter and his tiny garrison were cut off. Fortunately for the

179

English the dauphin was badly advised and did not concentrate his troops. As it was, Henry was on the verge of losing Paris.

In addition there was trouble in Picardy. Here Jacques d'Harcourt (whose county of Tancarville in Normandy had been confiscated by Henry and given to the late Sir John Grey) was attacking isolated English and Burgundian strongholds with some success. It is likely that his activities seriously alarmed both the burgesses of Calais and Duke Philip. In the king's words, Picardy needed 'better governance'.

Somehow, in the midst of all these urgent preparations for war, King Henry found time to turn his pious attention to the Benedictines, whom he decided were in dire need of reform. He may have had political motives, or at least been influenced to some extent by memories of the monks' former political sympathies. The community of Westminster had included some strong and vociferous supporters of Richard II and those of Shrewsbury and Wenlock had connived at Sir John Oldcastle's escape despite his heresy – almost certainly out of distaste for the Lancastrian usurpation. The 'old English black monks' could be undeniably aggressive; a monk archdeacon of Westminster was reputed to wear full armour on occasion. Men who did not accept that God had inspired the House of Lancaster's seizure of the throne of England must surely have unsound spiritual as well as political values. Yet his interference in their affairs, in almost Tudor style, probably stemmed even more from his determination to assert the royal will in every area of ecclesiastical life. A complaint by 'certain false brethren' that the Benedictines had slackened in the observance of their rule met with a most sympathetic hearing from the king. He consulted the prior of Mount Grace Priory in Yorkshire, Dan Robert Layton, (himself a former black monk) as to what to do; the Carthusians, 'never reformed because never deformed', were the most respected religious brotherhood of the age on account of their austerity and genuine sanctity, though as hermits they were scarcely best suited to advise monks who lived a communal life.[11]

On 5 May 1421 the king addressed a special assembly of nearly 400 Benedictines in the chapterhouse at Westminster, exhorting them to mend their ways. He reminded them how generous his ancestors had been to them, how this generosity was inspired by a desire for their prayers, but how such prayers could continue to be effective only if the brethren returned to a proper observance of their rule. He read out Prior Layton's criticisms and suggestions. A committee was appointed by the monks to report on the problems. In the event Henry soon returned to France and the black monks neatly shelved the matter. Had the king lived another decade they might well have had to implement draconian proposals.

Henry had never intended to leave France for very long and preparations for a new expeditionary force had been in hand from the moment he returned to England. It consisted of a mere 900 men-at-arms and 3,300 archers, which was all the king could afford, though it was supported by a mass of supernumeraries such as gunners, sappers and engineers. The expedition assembled at Dover and was ready to embark at the end of May, a fine feat of logistics. Henry's decision to sail to Calais instead of Harfleur – the nearest bridgehead into endangered Normandy – has been criticized but is understandable. The threat to Picardy was too grave to ignore and it was essential to reassure Duke Philip and the Burgundians. Moreover the voyage from Dover to Calais took only a few hours if tides were properly calculated, as opposed to perhaps several days sailing from Southampton to Harfleur.

XVII
Meaux Falls

'For other weapon is there remedy
But on the dart of hunger is to die.'

A fifteenth-century translation
of Vegetius's *De Re Militari*

'In the year of 1422 I saw a foreign king gain glory from our shame and ignominy, batten on our plunder, cast scorn on our exploits and our courage.'

Alain Chartier, *Le Quadrilogus Invectif*

Henry marched out of Calais almost as soon as he landed, early in June 1421. His first step was to send a relief force to the beleaguered Exeter at Paris. He took his main army, even smaller in consequence, down to Montreuil, twenty-five miles south, to confer with the Duke of Burgundy. Here the king agreed to dispatch the bulk of his troops to Chartres to relieve the besieged Burgundians, while he himself went on to Paris with a handful of men. Duke Philip rode with him as far as Abbeville and en route they had a day's boar-hunting by way of relaxation. One may be sure that it was suggested by the duke – nothing so frivolous would normally have occurred to Henry on campaign.

He entered Paris late in the evening on 4 July. He found the Duke of Exeter in control, more or less, though presumably very glad to see him. For not only had the capital been menaced by foes outside the walls but there had been considerable unrest within.

Much of the unrest had centred around l'Isle Adam. Chastellain (who almost certainly met the marshal) tells us that, after secret instructions from Henry before his departure from Paris the previous

182

December, Exeter had him suddenly arrested and sent under strong guard to the Bastille – now the English headquarters. According to Chastellain, 'when the rumour ran through the city that l'Isle Adam had been seized a large mob of common people took up hatchets and hammers [*à hacques et à macques*], planning to rescue him and remove him by force from English hands, but found themselves facing six score of English archers, all with bows strung, shooting at them . . . And so he was put in the Bastille and held in prison so long as the king his enemy lived who, had it not been for fear and favour of the Duke of Burgundy his master, would have had his head off.'[1]

Henry's appearance had a calming effect on the Parisians, since we hear of no more disturbances of this sort. He found time to visit his parents-in-law, Charles VI and Queen Isabeau, at the Hôtel de Saint-Pol and to hear Mass at Nôtre Dame. However, he left his French capital after spending only four days there.

The king then went to his old headquarters at Mantes. Here he conferred once more with the Duke of Burgundy before setting off to relieve Chartres. However, as he approached the city he was told that the dauphin had already abandoned the siege and was hastily retreating southwards into Touraine, on the unconvincing pretexts that he was running short of food, that the weather was bad, and that his men were deserting. The true reason was of course that he had heard of his supplanter's return and was not going to risk a battle. King Henry thereupon marched on Dreux instead, some fifty miles west of Paris. This was the only substantial stronghold left to the dauphinists on this side of the capital, on the border between Normandy and the Île de France. It was invested on 18 July, the direction of the siege being entrusted to the Duke of Gloucester and the King of Scots. Despite a gallant defence by both its garrison and its townsmen, Dreux surrendered on 20 August, and at the news a whole string of lesser dauphinist strongpoints north and west of Chartres also opened their gates to the English.

The king then struck down towards the Loire, hoping to bring the enemy to battle but, says the *First Life*, 'against him came no man, nor no enemy abode his coming'. He heard that the dauphin was assembling a big army near Beaugency on the north bank of the Loire. Accordingly, on about 8 September he stormed Beaugency (though its citadel held out), and then sent the Earl of Suffolk across the river with a small detachment to see if he could locate the enemy army or provoke it into action by inflicting as much damage as possible. However, the dauphin was not to be drawn. Henry then marched along the north bank of the Loire to Orleans nearby, burning its suburbs in which his men found much-needed provisions. He set up his camp outside but his army, by now probably numbering less than 3,000 men, was too small to besiege so large a city with any prospect of success. After resting his men for three days, he swung north-east towards Joigny.

What Jean Juvénal calls 'a marvellous pestilence of stomach flux' had broken out among the troops. Henry provided as many carts as he could for those who could not walk. Nevertheless, 'Dead soldiers were found along the roads . . . and others [still alive] in the woods around Orleans by country folk who had gone there to hide and keep out of the way, and who killed many of them.'[2]

In addition, so one gathers from the *Croniques de Normandie*, Henry had lost not only many men during his march from sickness but others who collapsed from hunger, besides having to abandon a great number of horses, carts and pack-mules through lack of fodder. He nonetheless kept on undaunted. One has to respect such a leader.

On 18 September he captured Nemours and on 22 September Villneuve-le-Roy on the River Yonne, which had been preventing supplies from Dijon reaching Paris. He also took another dauphinist stronghold, Rougemont, which he stormed with a speed that astounded its dazed defenders. Infuriated by the loss of a single English soldier durings its taking, he had it burnt and its entire garrison drowned in batches in the Yonne, including some who escaped but whom he caught later; sixty men in all. Jean Chartier observes of Henry that he was a very hard and cruel dispenser of justice.[3] According to the king's lights this was 'justice' – as defenders of a fortress taken by storm such men had no right to their lives in the military code of the period.

Describing the siege of Rougemont, Chastellain, who must have met many veterans who had fought against Henry or at his side, gives some idea of what it would have been like to face him. 'The English king had them attacked most fiercely, assaulted lethally from every side, did not give them rest or respite, scarcely let them draw breath, harried them to death. If I do not describe the [castle's] fortifications, which were the best possible, it is because they could not save them.'[4] Colonel Burne thinks the secret of Henry's success as a soldier was 'a double foundation of discipline and fervour' – discipline unusual in field armies of the period, coupled with his ability to communicate a savage self-righteousness. (Something not seen in English troops until Cromwell's New Model Army.) Burne

184

also considers that his meticulous preparations before taking the field contributed a good deal; in advance of his last campaign, one in northern France which he did not live to fight, he arranged for the citizens of Amiens to provide food for his troops, even fixing the prices.[5] Above all, he was undoubtedly a born leader of men, instilling in his men his own ferocious dynamism and dogged determination. It is unlikely that his heath was good, though we do not have precise details; more than one important meeting had to be postponed because he was unwell (such as the crucial encounter with Queen Isabeau in June 1419'. We know from Walsingham that the illness which killed him was of long standing.[6] Yet he let nothing deter him. If a singularly gloomy man, as he showed at moments of triumph, he can at least never be accused of pessimism in battle. According to the Monk of St Denis he maintained extraordinary equanimity during both setbacks and triumphs. He used to tell troops who had been defeated, 'You know, the fortunes of war tend to vary. If you want to make certain of winning, always keep your courage exactly the same regardless of what happens.'[7]

The monk also tells us that Henry imposed the strictest discipline. As during the Agincourt campaign, he prohibited 'the vile prostitutes' under ferocious penalties from plying their trade in the English camp as they did in the French. On this topic the king remarked sententiously that 'the pleasure of Venus all too often weakened and softened victorious Mars'.[8] Admittedly, contrary to a popular misconception, venereal disease certainly existed during the fifteenth century. Yet the prohibition, together with restrictions on drinking when possible, may well have contributed to the high rate of desertion from his armies. (As Bacon observes, 'I know not but martial men are given to love. I think it is but as they are given to wine, for perils commonly asked to be paid in pleasures.') In a letter home one of Henry's men longs to go 'out of this unlusty soldier's life into the life of England'.

Having cleared the Yonne valley the king marched north-west on as broad a front as his tiny army could manage, presumably to mop up any more pockets of resistance, besides inflicting as much devastation as possible. He divided it into three columns, the one to the east crossing the Seine at Pont-sur-Seine, the second to the west crossing at Nogent and the third continuing along the Yonne.

The men suffered considerable hardship. The three columns of weary English troops rejoined each other at Meaux, having successfully concealed that this was Henry's real objective. Jean Juvénal

185

tells us that its inhabitants had been so unwise as to send envoys to the king at Paris, complaining that he was waging total war on them and setting all the country round Meaux on fire. 'To which he replied it was on purpose and that he would lay siege to them and take them, and as for the fires which they said he had started in the countryside, that was merely the custom of war, and war without fire was like sausages [*andouilles*] without mustard.'[9]

The town of Meaux was the biggest dauphinist stronghold near the capital. On a bend of the Marne, it was divided by the river into two sections, the old town, and the market, which was protected on three sides by the river and on the fourth by a canal.

In addition, Meaux possessed unusually formidable defenders. Its captain was Guichard de Chissay, a brave and resourceful commander, who had excellent lieutenants in Louis de Gast and in the Bastard of Vaurus and his cousin Denis de Vaurus. The garrison was composed of a ferocious mixture of brigands and deserters, some of them English and even Irish, who knew they could expect no mercy if they fell into the king's hands. The most desperate of them all was the Bastard of Vaurus, little better than a brigand chief, who had a well-deserved reputation for cruelty. Outside the town there was an elm-tree called the 'Tree of Vaurus' on which he hanged his victims, eighty of whose corpses were dangling from it in 1421; on one occasion he had had a pregnant girl tied there for the night – when she gave birth to a child, wolves came and ate both mother and infant.[10]

By 6 October Henry had invested Meaux. Although he knew that the siege must be a long one, as usual he ignored the medieval convention of going into winter-quarters. Meaux was too valuable a prize. Not only would its capture remove a threat to Paris and please the Burgundians, but the many lesser dauphinist strongpoints which depended on it would be frightened into surrendering. He was undeterred by the small size of his army which by now numbered no more than 2,500 men. At least he had two fine captains with him, in the Duke of Exeter and the Earl of Warwick.

Remorselessly the king set about the reduction of Meaux. He divided his army into four, positioned east, west, north and south of the town. Warwick commanded the division to the south on the far side of the Marne, Henry building a pontoon bridge over the river. The king's headquarters were about a mile from the town walls, at the abbey of St Faro. He had huts and dug-outs constructed to protect his troops against winter weather, and trenches to guard

186

them against sorties by the garrison. Guns, siege engines, munitions and food were shipped upstream from Paris. He concentrated his artillery fire on carefully selected sections of the walls and gates.

For months the siege seemed to make no progress whatever. The abominable weather hampered the English severely. It rained steadily throughout December so that the Marne burst its banks, to sweep away the pontoon bridge and cut off Warwick against whom the garrison made sorties by boat. The river also flooded the besiegers' huts and dug-outs, deprived their horses of forage and rendered the ground unfit for mining. Dysentery and other sicknesses afflicted the miserably cold and damp English. Food supplies broke down. There were many desertions and it has been estimated that by Christmas Henry's army had dwindled by twenty per cent.

The king maintained discipline in his own imaginative way. When dauphinists ambushed and cut to pieces an English foraging party, one man escaped by running away. On being informed, Henry had a deep pit dug and ordered the deserter to be buried alive in it.[11]

The writer known as 'pseudo-Elmham' preserves a rumour, possibly contemporary, that the king's army never suffered so much harm during any of his sieges as in this one. Besides the epidemics and other hardships, the defenders fought unpleasantly well. Henry's redoubtable uncle, Sir John Cornwall, had to be sent home in a state of shock, swearing that he would never again fight Christians, after his promising seventeen-year-old son had been killed by a cannonball taking his head clean off his shoulders. The king himself fell ill and a physician was summoned but he soon recovered. (We have no details of his malady.) Some captains advised him to abandon the siege. He was undoubtedly worried; in December he contemplated hiring German or Portuguese mercenaries. Yet nothing could shake his determination. By sheer strength of personality he prevented a collapse in morale, forcing his troops to hold on till the weather improved and the epidemics subsided. Inside Meaux they began to run short of food.

It was not only those engaged at Meaux, besiegers or besieged, who were suffering. The Bourgeois of Paris records:

> The King of England spent Christmas and the Epiphany at the seige of Meaux; his men pillaged the entire Brie and, however hard they tried, no one was able to sow crops . . . most of those working the land ceased to do so, abandoned their wives and children and fled in despair, saying to each other, 'What can we do? Let everything go to

187

the Devil! It doesn't matter what becomes of us. It serves one better to do evil rather than good, it's better to act like Saracens instead of Christians, so let's do all the harm we can. They can only catch and kill us! Because of misgovernment by traitors we've had to leave our wives and families and flee to the woods like hunted beasts.'[12]

The Bourgeois laments that in Paris 'God knows how much the poor suffered from cold and hunger!' He tells how everywhere in the capital one heard people crying, 'Alas! Alas! Most gentle living God, when are you going to put an end for us to this cruel misery, to this wretched existence, to this damnable war?'[13]

Yet Henry's heart is said to have been filled with great gladness and, according to Waurin, 'throughout the kingdom [of England] there was perfect joy displayed, more than had been seen there for a long time.'[14] News had come of the birth of a son to Queen Catherine at Windsor in December. Now there was an heir in blood to the dual monarchy of England and France. No doubt in his pride as a father, and in his delusion that the hand of God was always benevolently evident in his destiny, it never occurred to him that the future Henry VI, bred from the diseased Valois stock, might be anything other than a great king. It would be another hundred years before a tale became current how he had foretold: 'Henry born at Monmouth shall small time reign and get much, and Henry born at Windsor shall long reign and lose all, but as God wills so be it.'

Nevertheless the defenders of Meaux were holding their own, if only from desperation. One day early in 1422 some of them brought a donkey up onto the walls, beating it savagely until it brayed, and shouted down at the English that here was their king. They would live to regret it. Nothing could ever shake Henry's determination, no display of confidence by the garrison, no amount of casualties or desertions, no bad weather, illness or shortage of food – not even the salt fish of the Lenten fast when it came. Although he lodged a mile from Meaux, either at the abbey of St Faro or at the castle of Ruthile, he was far too dedicated a soldier not to spend much of his time in the front line with his men in their waterlogged trenches and dug-outs, superintending the bombardment.

He was employing more cannon than ever before – bombards, culverins and serpentines – more guns of all shapes and sizes arrived every day. Some may be seen at the Musée Militaire in the Invalides at Paris. He also had ribaudequins which were battle carts mounting several small cannon side by side, fired simultaneously and intended for close-quarters fighting. It was not easy to transport the bigger guns, some of which were enormous; most came by boat from Rouen and were then brought up by ox-carts to the siege-lines to be mounted in specially constructed wooden firing frames. The rough tubes which formed their barrels were rarely, if ever, straight, so that accuracy was impossible. Gunpowder was crudely mixed and unreliable. Considerable skill was needed to load; gunners filled the firing chambers three-fifths full of powder, leaving a fifth as an air pocket and a final fifth for the elm-wood tampon on which the gunstone rested, with a ratio of one part powder to nine parts stone. Barrels had to be swabbed out meticulously after each discharge. It was difficult to calculate trajectories with such weapons. Even so, at short range a barrage of gunstones could do terrible damage, battering down ramparts and smashing through house walls and roofs inside a city, as well as demoralizing a beleaguered garrison. When such bombardments continued ceaselessly by day and by night, regardless of expense, as they did during all Henry V's sieges, the effect was horrific. The king's passion for artillery had never flagged since his first use of it against the Welsh at Aberystwyth.[15]

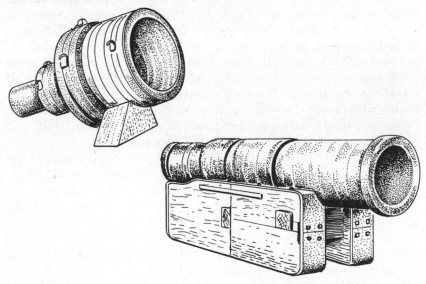

Two types of bombard These were far more effective than is generally appreciated, firing stone cannonballs weighing nearly 1000 lbs which, besides demolishing masonry, shattered into lethal fragments – 'stone shrapnel'.

As the siege dragged on, the garrison began to feel that they would have more hope of surviving if the defence was conducted by an unusually experienced and skilful commander. They sent to a famous dauphinist captain, Guy de Nesle, Sieur d'Offrémont, who agreed to come and take over. Early on 9 March, accompanied by an escort of 100 men-at-arms, he made his way in the darkness with great daring through the sleeping English lines to a pre-arranged spot below the ramparts. Here the garrison let down ladders to a plank over the moat. The man in front of Guy on the ladder dropped a box of salt herrings he was carrying which fell onto Guy, knocking him off the ladder into the moat; he clutched at two lances held down to him but, no doubt in full plate armour, was too heavy to pull out. His frenzied splashing aroused the English sentries and he was taken prisoner.

Guy's failure dismayed the garrison of Meaux so much that they withdrew from the town the same day to the market which they thought would be easier to defend. They broke down the connecting bridge over the canal and took the remaining food with them; it would last longer if there were no non-combatants to feed. Henry rode in immediately and before evening his guns were firing from the town into the market. He then used a portable drawbridge, mounted on a siege tower on wheels, to straddle the gap made by the defenders in the bridge joining the town to the market. Next he bombarded the fortified mill-towers so that the Earl of Worcester's men-at-arms could charge over the drawbridge and storm the towers. The assault was successful, though Warwick's cousin, the Earl of Worcester, lost his life when a stone was dropped on his head from the battlements. Now the English had a foothold on the market island, while the garrison was no longer able to grind its corn into flour.

All this time Henry's attitude to paperwork remained as Napoleonic as ever. A stream of edicts, ordinances and letters, including answers to petitions from England, went out from his headquarters beside Meaux during the siege, possibly the most gruelling experience of his life. Even during the worst months he was constantly sending orders and instructions dealing with a truly immense range of affairs. The supply of munitions naturally ranked high among these. On 18 March 1422 he wrote to his officials: 'We will and charge you that, in all the haste ye may, ye send unto our cofferer to Rouen all the gunstones that been at our towns of Caen and Harfleur, with all the saltpetre, coal and brimstone that is at Harfleur.'[16] An order for iron is in the same letter, an order which occurs frequently in his correspondence. A special official, the King's Clerk of Ordnance, was attached to his headquarters, having responsibility for communications with the artillery depot at Caen and the royal arsenal at Rouen; the Norman administration had been given military duties by Henry, the civilian *vicomtes* being charged with supplying garrisons with cannon. The king insisted on efficiency – his letters always end with a variant of 'faileth not in no wise'.

He was obsessed by the problem of supplies. Buying arrows was just one aspect. He purchased 150,000 arrows in England in 1418, a figure which had risen to nearly half a million by 1421; in addition the arsenal at Rouen seems to have manufactured them and in 1420 his commissioners were instructed to press-gang fletchers (arrow makers) to work there without pay. Then there was the question of finding enough remounts, which he appears to have contemplated solving with a huge royal stud. (In April 1421 a commission was issued to a John Longe to travel through England looking for 'destriers, coursers and other horses suitable for the king's stud' and purchasing their use.[17] Weapons, transport, food, finance, military discipline, law and order, diplomacy, affairs in England, all received his meticulous attention.

Meanwhile at Meaux, English cannon had been mounted on a small island in the Marne, protected by earthworks and shelters of heavy timber, from where they battered the adjoining market relentlessly at close range. Warwick contrived to erect a 'sow' (a mobile leather shelter on wheels) on the tiny strip of land between its walls and the water, using it to capture an outwork where he mounted a forward battery. Hungerford used wooden bridges to bring guns nearer the wall at another side. Landing on the island, sappers started a mine. At Easter, Henry allowed a truce, launching a general assault shortly afterwards. It was beaten back. But the defenders were beginning to despair. What finally broke their spirit was the sight of a floating siege tower, higher than the market's walls, carried on two barges and designed for men to attack the rampart tops from the Marne side over a drawbridge. (It was never used, though the king, nothing if not a professional, had it tested after the place had fallen.) At the end of April the garrison in the market sent envoys to negotiate a surrender.

On 10 May Meaux surrendered after a resistance of seven months. It had only fallen because of Henry's brilliant siegecraft and sheer technical expertise, as a siege it was a genuine masterpiece, as has often been claimed. After the city had finally surrendered he observed the conventions of medieval warfare in leaving its defenders their lives – though nothing else – save for twelve who were specifically excluded from mercy by the articles of surrender. The Bastard of Vaurus and his cousin had their right hands stricken off, were dragged on hurdles through what was left of the streets of Meaux, then beheaded and hanged from their own infamous tree; the bastard's head was displayed on a lance stuck in the ground beside it, his body at the foot, and his banner thrown over it – the ultimate heraldic symbol of derision. A trumpeter called Orace, 'one that blew and sounded an horn during the siege', was taken to Paris for an agonizing public execution in punishment for some unrecorded insult to the king. Louis de Gast was also taken to Paris for execution. Their heads were stuck on lances and put on show at Les Halles.

Almost at once Henry sent 100 particularly valuable prisoners to the Louvre, roped in fours, for shipment to Normandy and thence to England to await ransoming. A few days later he sent another 150. According to the Bourgeois of Paris, probably a spectator, these were chained in twos by the legs, and 'piled up like pigs'; they were given only a little black bread and water.[18] We learn from Jean Juvénal that they were incarcerated in prisons all over Paris, including the Châtelet – a place of ill omen and terrible memory for Armagnacs. There was no organization for feeding such large numbers of prisoners and, according to Jean Juvénal, many died of starvation – some tearing flesh from their comrades' bodies with their teeth before their own death. Presumably they were not worth much money.[19] The Bishop of Meaux received somewhat better treatment before being taken away to await ransom in England, where he was to die. In all, as many as 800 of those who had surrendered were shipped over the Channel; it is likely that the majority never returned to France, ending their days in semi-slavery as indentured servants. In addition, 'All the bourgeois and anyone else in the market was forced to hand over any valuable goods they possessed,' says Jean Juvénal. 'Those who disobeyed were treated very savagely, and everything contributed to King Henry's profit. There was more than this. After the bourgeois had lost all they had, several of them were made to buy back their own houses. Through such confiscation the king extorted and amassed large sums of money.' Bullion, jewels and every conceivable sort of valuable – including an entire legal library – was stored for the time being in special depots at Meaux, together with armour, weapons and other munitions, to await the pleasure of a monarch who had made plunder a fine art.

One prisoner who was very lucky indeed to escape with his life was Dom Philippe de Gamaches, Abbot of St Faro, the nearby monastery which had been Henry's headquarters throughout the siege. Dom Philippe, a former monk of St Denis, together with three other monks from that abbey, had put on armour and taken up swords to fight the English. The chronicler monk of St Denis – who presumably knew them – tells us that the Bishop of Beauvais had given them all permission 'to fight for the country' ['*pugnareque pro patria*']. The bishop was none other than Jean Juvénal des Ursins. Fortunately for Philippe, his brother was dauphinist captain of Compiègne; he purchased the abbot's life by handing the town over to the English – Henry had intended to drown him.[20]

Baugé was avenged. Moreover a whole string of dauphinist fortresses surrendered in consequence, including Crépy-en-Valois and Offremont – the castle of the Guy de Nesle who had fallen into the moat at Meaux. Henry rode through the countryside receiving the surrender of each stronghold in person, mopping up any local resistance.

Then he celebrated by going to Paris to meet his queen. Monstrelet says that he and his brothers greeted Catherine 'as though she had been an angel from heaven'. The son and heir who was the cause of so much congratulation had been left behind in England. The reunion took place at the great castle of Bois-de-Vincennes just outside Paris.

Today Vincennes may seem gloomy, a soulless barrack of a place. It has unhappy memories; the Duc d'Enghien was shot in the moat in 1804 as was Mata Hari in 1917, it was General Gamelin's headquarters in June 1940 after which foreign troops occupied it again for four years. Yet Henry's fondness for Vincennes is understandable. Originally a hunting lodge, being in the woods it was ideally situated for the king's favourite relaxation – if ever he had time. Catherine's grandfather, the great King Charles V, had completed the *donjon* during the 1370s and it was here that Henry lived; his bedroom may still be seen. There were three mighty gatehouses and six tall towers, all linked by curtain walls, and providing enviable accommodation for his high ranking-officers. A hunting scene in the *Très Riches Heures du duc de Berry* shows the fortress-palace in the background, much as it must have looked at this time, and one can see why the Monk of St Denis calls it 'the most delectable of all

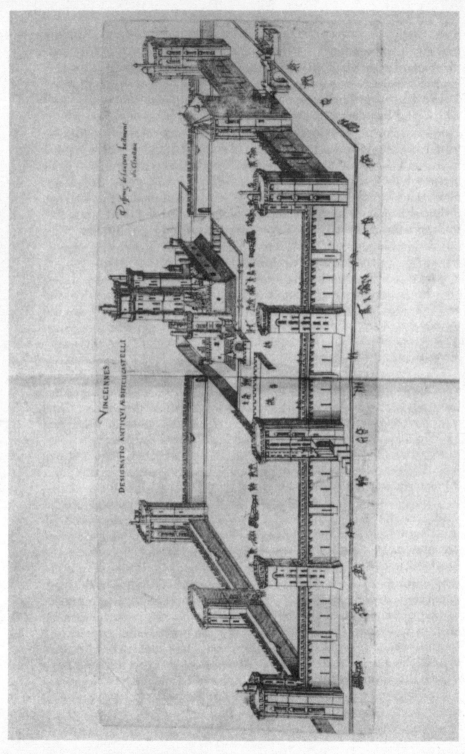

Vincennes in 1576, still just as it had been in Henry V's time. The *donjon* (or keep) within the inner moat is where the king died in 1422.

the castles of the king of France'.[21] Moreover Vincennes was only three miles from Paris – close enough to overawe the capital if need be, and sufficiently far away to avoid any danger from the mob or dauphinist plots.

At the Louvre, says *The First English Life*, echoing Monstrelet's chronicle, 'on the proper day of Pentecost the King of England and his queen sat together at their table in the open hall at dinner, marvellously glorious, and pompously crowned with rich and precious diadems; dukes also, prelates of the church and other great estates of England and of France, were sat every man in his degree in the same hall where the king and queen kept their estate. The feast was marvellously rich and abundant in sumptuous delicate meats and drinks.'[22] Unfortunately the splendid effect was somewhat tarnished by no food or drink being offered to the crowds of spectators, as had always been the custom in former days under the Valois monarchs.

The *Brut of England* records with relish, 'But as for the King of France he held none other estate nor rule but was almost left alone.'[23] Charles VI stayed forlornly at the Hôtel de St-Pol, deserted by his nobles since, so Monstrelet informs us, 'he was managed as the King of England pleased . . . which caused much sorrow in the hearts of all loyal Frenchmen.' Chastellain comments indignantly that Henry, this 'tyrant king', despite promising to honour his father-in-law of France as long as he lived, had made 'a figurehead [*un ydole*] of him, a cipher who could do nothing'. Chastellain too says that the spectacle brought tears into the eyes of the Parisians.[24]

Henry spent two days in early June at the Hôtel de Nesle, where he watched a cycle of mystery plays about the martyrdom of his patron, St George. These were staged by Parisians who hoped to ingratiate themselves with the heir and regent of France, their future sovereign. Shortly afterwards he and Catherine, taking with them King Charles and Queen Isabeau, left the capital for Senlis.

A week later a Parisian armourer, who had once been an armourer to Charles VI, together with his wife and their neighbour, a baker, were caught plotting to let the dauphinists into Paris. A strong force of the enemy were standing by in readiness near Compiègne. The civil authority beheaded the armourer and the baker, and drowned the woman.[25]

XVIII
Lancastrian France

'ung royaulme dyabolique'

Jean Juvénal des Ursins

'"The three Frances". In its simple way that formula marks one of the most sombre moments in the nation's history.'

Jean Favier, *La Guerre de Cent Ans*

There were now three Frances – ruled respectively by the heir and regent, the Duke of Burgundy, and the dauphin. As Chastellain puts it, Henry V 'came into France at a time of divison, and amidst this division estranged still further by his sword those who were divided'.

In 1422 Henry's position in France appeared most impressive. 'All the country across the Loire is black and obscure, for they have put themselves into the hands of the English,' laments Jean Juvénal. Invincible in the field, a commander to whom no fortress was impregnable, the king controlled a third of the country and the capital. It genuinely seemed that one day he might be crowned and anointed at Reims with the oil of clovis as king of France. Some modern English historians give an impression that France was too divided by regional loyalties, so much without a sense of nationalism that the inhabitants of Lancastrian France accepted the regime, that a Franco-English monarchy might have survived. Certainly many Frenchmen 'collaborated' but to claim, like one distinguished twentieth-century English historian, that the Rouennais 'settled down without a murmur under the sway of a descendant of their

196

ancient dukes', is a distortion.[1] Henry's so-called policy of conciliation was accompanied by what Edouard Perroy terms 'a regime of terror'.[2] When Perroy wrote this he himself was on the run from the Gestapo.

Discussing 'Lancastrian France' one has to distinguish between the duchy of Normandy (with the neighbouring territory conquered before the Treaty of Troyes) and the small area including Paris which was technically Henry's 'kingdom of France'. The duchy was very much an occupied country whereas the kingdom was more like a puppet state. In the latter all officials save the military were Frenchmen. Most of them were Burgundians and the appointment of many must have been due to Duke Philip's influence, though not invariably – there were occasional grumbles at the removal of Burgundian nominees. The English population of 'occupied' Paris was seldom more than 300; at one moment (after Henry's death) the garrison in the Bastille consisted of eight men-at-arms and seventeen archers. The official in charge of Parisian police was a Frenchman, and so was the president of the *parlement*. So few English can scarcely have been much in evidence in a city whose population remained at well over 100,000 despite famine and a mass exodus. Jean Favier says that one was most likely to see them in the taverns, and they were good customers of the Glatigny prostitutes or at the Tiron brothel.[3]

However, the Parisians' comparative freedom from English rule must not be seen out of context. The 'lands of the conquest' were a mere dozen miles away, while Paris was ringed by fortresses with English garrisons, the nearest being at Bois-de-Vincennes only three miles off. The one at Pontoise numbered 240 men and reinforcements could be rushed up river into the capital at a moment's notice. On occasion the force at the Bastille could show that it was perfectly adequate for cowing the Parisians, its archers running through the streets and shooting at them and at their windows indiscriminately. Moreover it was backed up by a large *milice* recruited from the citizens; crossbowmen and spearmen who could at least be trusted to fight against the dauphinists of whom they were even more frightened than of the English. The former Armagnacs, who called such militiamen '*faux français*', had some nasty massacres to avenge and their raids on the city's suburbs rivalled those of the English in ferocity. This relative freedom and the dauphinist threat did not mean that the Parisians were any the more inclined to like Henry's troops. That staunch Burgundian, the Bourgeois of Paris, pitied the

197

king's prisoners, and the city's prisons were filled to overflowing by his prisoners more than once.

Even an English chronicler, Walsingham, has to admit that Henry was most unpopular in Paris, that force was sometimes needed to control its people.[4] Some of its clergy were openly dauphinist. In December 1420 the chapter of Nôtre Dame elected Jean Courtecuisse Bishop of Paris – a man of exemplary life who was an avowed dauphinist – despite Henry's attempts to bully the canons into choosing a Burgundian nominee. At one moment Exeter, the military governor, put two of them under house arrest. The chapter also refused to contribute to the cost of a detachment of militia which the city had to send to the siege of Meaux. Visiting Nôtre Dame Henry gave the derisory (for a king) offering of two nobles – a noble was worth a third of a pound. Eventually he persuaded the pope to appoint Courtecuisse to another see.

There is more than enough evidence to show that in both the kingdom and the duchy the French population bitterly resented the English presence; the way in which invaders from across the Channel had taken advantage of their civil war to conquer and dominate them. Agincourt was a truly national catastrophe, shared by Burgundians and Armagnacs alike, its memory remaining firmly in their minds. The latter blamed the English for their sufferings even more than they did the Burgundians. 'This storm of misery unleashed on us by the people of England,' ('*le gent d'Angleterre*') says the chronicler Jean Chartier.[5]

Bishop Basin gives a horrific picture of the sort of lives which English settlers must have lived in Lancastrian France. Although he is writing specifically about a truce in Maine and Anjou during the 1440s, such conditions must have been the norm everywhere, from the very beginning. His is the evidence of an eyewitness who had lived under the English occupation until he was nearly forty:

> Shut up for years without almost any respite behind the walls of towns, castles or fortresses, living in fear and danger as though condemned to life imprisonment, they were marvellously happy at the thought of emerging from their long and frightening incarceration. It was sweet to them to have escaped all the perils and alarms among which they had lived since childhood till the days of white hair or extreme old age.[6]

Moreover we know that in Normandy, for example, the population had fallen by a half after eight years of English occupation, partly because of famine but principally because of emigration by all classes – whether dispossessed seigneurs, ruined bourgeois, starving peasants or despairing beggars. Admittedly the misery from which they fled was partly due to dauphinist raiders and brigands but neither would have come but for Henry's invasion.

Most of the Normans, Picards and Champenois who emigrated did so because of social and economic distress.[7] The presence of more than sixty garrisons in the countryside meant ruin for many farmers in the conquered territories. Since these were irregularly paid and there was no real commissariat despite Henry's efforts, the troops had little choice but to continue living off the country, requisitioning food, drink, fodder and anything else they wanted from the locals; even the irreplaceable oxen which drew the ploughs might be slaughtered, while horses and farm carts must have been taken on a very large scale. No doubt the big Percheron horses made excellent remounts for men-at-arms. The peasants were further demoralized by having to pay protection money and tolls, by the harassment of their womenfolk and by all the evils which accompany armies of occupation. In Normandy, where the English were most numerous (and which had suffered a series of bad harvests before their arrival), agriculture all but collapsed. As has been seen, the king was unable to control his troops.

Worse still, many soldiers regarded the country people – which meant the overwhelming majority of Frenchmen and Frenchwomen – as their natural prey. Again, Basin writes of what he had witnessed himself:

> The troops on both sides, constantly raiding each other's territory, dragged the peasants away to their castles and fortresses where they incarcerated them in noisome prisons or at the bottom of deep pits, torturing them in every conceivable way, trying to force them to pay the heavy ransoms which they demanded of them. In the cellars and vaults beneath every castle or tower one would always find poor peasants snatched from their fields, a hundred or two hundred, sometimes even more, depending on the number of kidnappers. Often many, incapable of paying the sums demanded, found no mercy from the raiders and died from hunger, weakness or vermin.[8]

Some enterprising English soldiers did not even bother to imprison their prey, like an archer from the Alençon garrison who simply went round the local villages by himself seizing the peasants' goods 'for ransom', forcing them to buy back their own property, until in despair they beat him to death.[9]

Jean Juvénal's diocese of Beauvais was in conquered territory and in a letter of 1440 to the estates general he recounts what his people had suffered over the years: 'The poor have been killed, taken prisoner and dragged off, plundered, robbed and tyrannized, have lost their flocks, and the land is all destroyed and desolate, while the churches and houses have been broken into, burnt and wrecked and lie in ruins, and they have killed many of my poor people in prison or by some other means.' While admitting that many of these evils – 'cruel, damnable and detestable tyrannies' – have been inflicted by brigands or French troops, he regards the English as primarily responsible; 'they have committed all the crimes and inhumanity that any enemy could'. He complains that: 'little children have been led away into captivity and God knows what sort of life they lead in England among those who trouble and tyrannize us.' (There was a market for such children in England, where they were sold as 'servants' – a euphemism for slaves.) He continues, 'many little maidens, virgins and well born too, have been taken off by force or some other means and made the chambermaids and bawds of lewd youths, thieves, murderers and vagrants.' The bishop tells how at St Médard near Noyon in Picardy the English 'found a church which had been fortified a little as a refuge for poor labourers; and this they took and set on fire, killing two or three hundred'. Monstrelet confirms him, recording that 'over 300 persons or more' were burnt to death. No wonder that Juvénal regarded the death of Henry V as among 'the marvels wrought by God'.[10]

Many peasants fled to the towns, to starve in deserted houses as 'useless mouths'. It has been calculated that even in good times a quarter to a third of the population of late medieval towns were indigent. In any case, as Juvénal explains, the townsmen too were in despair since 'most of the seaports as well as the ports along the river have been destroyed and there is no more trade'.[11] In addition Henry's devaluations of the currency, together with the new taxes, caused them serious hardship. At the end of 1421 Henry imposed a silver levy throughout the lands of the conquest on all ranks of society on (according to Monstrelet) 'churchmen, knights, squires, ladies, damsels, burgesses and anyone thought able to pay it, in accordance with the pleasure and discretion of the tax collectors'. Needless to say, there were 'great murmurings and discontent'. The realm's gold crowns had already been devalued in October from nineteen to eighteen sols. When a new silver coinage was issued by Henry it contained so little silver as to be almost valueless, if Chastellain is to be believed. The merchants, no less than the peasants, suffered from robbery and kidnapping. (A pardon dated November 1424 was granted to one Enguerrand de Monstrelet, 'captain of the castle of Freneuch', exempting him from penalties he might have incurred in waylaying and robbing certain merchants of between 400–500 crowns.)[12]

The clergy suffered as well, frequently finding that their cloth was no protection. Churches, monasteries and hospitals were all sacked and pillaged, often with bloodshed. As the sole source of poor relief in the fifteenth century was the Church, which provided what might be called the social services, this caused much misery among the swarms of beggars who roamed the streets after losing their livelihood as a result of the war. During his researches into petitions to Rome for relief on behalf of ecclesiastical property destroyed at this time, Henri Denifle was struck by how 'the King of England and the Duke of Bedford, who did not hesitate to ask the pope for favours for their own people, never once asked him to help a ruined French church. Yet so many churches had been left in ruins by the English!'[13] He concluded that they deliberately omitted to do so because they did not want to contribute, however indirectly and however little, to the resources of Charles VI or the dauphin.

Juvénal recounts in his letter what happened to clerics who supported the dauphin:

> And as for the poor priests, churchmen, monks and other poor workers staying faithful to you, they take them and imprison them, putting them in irons, in cages, in pits and ugly places full of vermin and leave them there to die of hunger, as indeed several have died. And God knows the dreadful things they do to them; they roast some, they tear out the teeth of others, while some are beaten with great rods; and they are never set at liberty until they have paid more money than their entire possessions are worth. And even when they are let go, their limbs are usually so crippled that they are never whole again.[14]

As has been seen, Henry himself was not above dragging dauphinist prelates off for ransom. Even clerics who had taken the oath of allegiance to him were not safe; in 1422 the canons of Rouen complained formally about being attacked on the Norman roads by English soldiers. No doubt a good deal of clerical harassment was by brigands but Jean Juvénal makes it clear in his letter that he blames the English troops most of all.

Henry's attitude towards the Church was inconsistent. 'What shall I say of your sacrilege, o cruel King Henry, prince of the sacrilegious,' cries Robert Blondel.[15] The king 'worried little about divine wrath' the Monk of St Denis tells us, 'and when his soldiers had looted with their sacrilegious hands churches consecrated to God, he would send home to England the relics they had stolen'.[16] This was certainly very different from his ostentatiously correct behaviour during the Agincourt campaign. Perhaps he had come to think that such incidents were unavoidable. In fairness to Henry and his men, it must be said that everyone's views on churchmen and church property had been distorted by the papal schism which had only recently ended. Previously schismatics had been regarded as no better than infidels, and French and English had supported different popes.

There was particular sympathy for the peasants among those in high places, to a surprising extent for so hierarchical a society. Pity was perhaps to be expected from churchmen but scarcely from fashionable poets who wrote for the ruling classes, even if it was theoretically a knight's chivalrous duty to protect the weak. Alain Chartier, born a Norman at Bayeux in 1388 and the brother of Jean Chartier the chronicler, was successively secretary to Charles VI and the dauphin. (One often finds Alain's signature next to that of the dauphin at the bottom of the latter's letters.) He was both near the centre of power and a poet who, in his own day at least, was compared to Petrarch. In his *Quadrilogus Invectif*, apparently written at the end of 1422, he roundly blames the French nobility for not doing enough to protect the peasantry, though at the same time he regards the entire French people, of every degree, as having to some extent contributed to the ruin of France. He mourns how in 1422 he has seen 'a foreign king gain glory from our shame and ignominy, batten on our plunder, cast scorn on our exploits and on our courage', and believes that 'the hand of God was on us and his anger set in motion this scourge of persecution' – an obvious reference to Henry V.[17] Indeed it was the French peasantry who, more than anyone else, suffered from the English king's ambition for a period of over thirty years.

Lancastrian France and the lands which bordered it became very like a desert during the years of occupation and warfare. To quote Bishop Basin yet again:

From the Loire up to the Seine and from thence to the Somme, the peasants had been killed or had fled until all the fields were for a long time, indeed for many years, left not only without being tilled but without any men to till them, save for a few rare patches of land . . . We ourselves have seen the vast plains of Champagne, of the Beauce, of the Brie, of the Gâtinais, Chartres, Dreux, Maine and Perche, of the Vexin (French as well as Norman), the Beauvaisis, the Pays de Caux, from the Seine as far as Amiens and Abbeville, the countryside round Senlis, Soissons and Valois right up to Laon and beyond towards Hainault absolutely deserted, uncultivated, abandoned, empty of inhabitants, covered with scrub and brambles; indeed in most of the more thickly wooded districts dense forests were growing up . . . All that people were able to cultivate in such areas at that time was in and around towns, fortresses or castles, sufficiently close to them for a lookout on the top of a tower or some other vantage point to see the raiders approaching. Sounding a bell, a horn or some other instrument he would signal to everyone working in the fields or in the vineyards to come back inside the fortifications.

This practice was so normal and widespread that nearly everywhere oxen and work horses, as soon as they were unharnessed from the carts when the lookout's signal was heard, would, at once and without being driven, return at a mad gallop to the place where they knew they would be safe. Sheep and pigs acquired the same habit. But in the aforesaid provinces, throughout the whole territory such towns and strong places were rare since so many had been burnt down, demolished or left in ruins by the enemy and since remained uninhabited. The very land tilled in the hiding places round the fortresses seemed very small and almost nothing in comparison to the vast extent of all those fields which stayed completely deserted, without a single soul to cultivate them.[18]

Henry attributed all this misery and destruction to the French having denied him his 'right'. In any case, as he had told Vincent Ferrer, he was 'the scourge of God sent to punish the people of God for their sins'. He is called a scourge by several contemporary French writers, such as Alain Chartier, though the only English mention of the term is in *The First English Life*.[19]

His relationship with the Burgundians was thoroughly uneasy. The English presence in France was deeply resented by them. We know from the chronicle of Georges Chastellain that the Burgundians disliked the English intensely. They included not only the Duke of Burgundy's subjects and clients but all those Frenchmen who detested the Armagnacs. And the Armagnacs made up the bulk

203

of the dauphinist party – indeed most people, like the Bourgeois of Paris, referred to the dauphinists as 'Armagnacs', or *'Ermynaks'* as the English termed them. They had no chance whatever of driving Henry out while he remained allied with Duke Philip. In consequence until the duke should change his mind about the English the inhabitants of the conquered territories had no alternative but to give their allegiance to the foreign king if they wished to stay there – unless they took to the woods. Although the Burgundian chroniclers testify to considerable respect for the Englishman's harsh justice and genuine admiration for him as a soldier, they are less admiring about other aspects of his character. Nor did they relish his ferocity towards Frenchmen of the other political faction, his ferocious handling of dauphinist prisoners.

Chastellain gives a good idea of what the Burgundians, and especially those around the duke, thought of Henry. Despite the prolixity and artificiality of his cumbersome prose, this poet, herald, soldier and courtier was a writer of penetrating and vigorously independent judgement, a realist with deep psychological insight:

> He [Henry] was foe to every brave and valiant man in the realm, and would have liked to exterminate them all, whether in battle or by some other more cunning means under a pretext of justice. Even those who were now fighting by his side and through whom he ruled and held sway in France, the Burgundians, he wished to supplant and keep down in subjection; he wanted the very name and race to be extinguished in order that he might live there alone with his Englishmen, and might be able to re-people and take possession of the entire land [of France] with his own people. And it is easy to conceive what a semblance of feigned affection he showed towards the young prince, Philip, whom he knew to be of a high and proud courage, powerful in lands and lordships, and truly a man quite bold enough to resist the greatest king on earth and say to him 'I do only what it pleases me to do.' . . . he [Henry] had never liked his father, the Duke John, since he was a proud man and opposed to him, so that he could not bend him to his will as he very much wanted, for he was the only man who could have thwarted his designs, at whose death he never knew greater joy.[20]

The same well-informed, balanced observer adds: 'Praise be to God! this kingdom has been delivered from a hard persecuter . . . the ancient enemy . . . a cruel man.' He also describes him as 'a tyrant and a persecuter'. Significantly, Chastellain recalls that 'it was by his hand, as though beneath *the scourge of God*, that the noble blood of France was so piteously shed at Agincourt.'[21] For it is too easily forgotten that probably as many Burgundians as Armagnacs had been killed during that battle, including Duke Philip's two uncles.

There was clearly a problem of communication between Burgundians and English. Some English gentry and clergy spoke and even wrote French of a sort, but while still used in administration and the law it had ceased to be the first language of the ruling class. No doubt after several months in France the men must have picked up a few words, like the Tommies' French of World War I (immortalized in 'Mademoiselle from Armentières'). Almost no Frenchmen can have had even a smattering of English, apart from returned captives or Henry's subjects in Guyenne. The fifteenth-century poet Jean Régnier describes seeing a wretched English prisoner surrounded by jabbering Frenchmen, unable to make himself understood or to understand and repeatedly crying out in terror, 'God and Our Lady help me!'[22]

The Burgundians would have been uncomfortably aware of the reputation for ferocity enjoyed by Henry and his subjects. Even during the previous century Froissart considered that 'underneath the sun there is no race more dangerous or more cruel than the English'. In 1411 Jean de Montreuil alleged that for a hundred years they 'have killed or caused the death of more Christians than any other nation'.[23] Robinet, the contemporary translator of the Norman refugee, Blondel's *Complaint of All Good Frenchmen*, described them as having 'eyes gleaming as treacherously as the devil's, foam flecking their teeth like a wild boar in rut'. He adds that wherever they found themselves they were not slow to shed blood.[24] At the end of the fifteenth century so restrained an observer as Philippe de Commynes commented that the English were extraordinarily savage tempered, especially those who had never been out of England.[25]

As always, the English were quite oblivious of what foreigners thought. In any case, unlike the French, the war did not affect their day-to-day lives at home. A modern historian has written: 'even a casual reading of the Paston Letters would suggest that it was as remote from the consciousness of English shire society in the fifteenth century as the Napoleonic wars and nineteenth century India are in the novels of Jane Austen.'[26] However, everyone must have met neighbours who had served in France and all admired their hero king, no doubt much in the way that their descendants would admire Nelson or Wellington.

Meanwhile there were many matters which demanded King Henry's urgent attention. Dauphinists on the Oise were threatening to cut one of the main links between Flanders and Paris. Jacques d'Harcourt, the dispossessed Norman magnate, was raiding throughout Picardy and into Normandy. The Duke of Brittany was proving tardy in ratifying the Treaty of Troyes and in recognizing Henry as his overlord. Down in the Pyrenees the Count of Foix, having extorted money to fight the dauphinists who were troubling the borders of Guyenne, was prevaricating before doing so. The Emperor Sigismund was far too busy coping with the nightmare menace of the terrible Hussite armies – Slav Lollards – in his new kingdom of Bohemia to spare the troops which he had once promised Henry, sending a polite but final refusal.

Moreover, although a brilliant piece of siegecraft, the capture of Meaux had solved nothing. No doubt it was an exceptionally strong town with an unusually strong garrison and generally recognized as such, so that a considerable moral victory had been won, and no doubt a number of other dauphinist fortresses had been cowed into surrendering. Nevertheless its possession was not of decisive importance. The heir and regent of France was faced by the prospect of an unending series of similar sieges, which were likely to last a lifetime if he persisted in trying to reduce his stubbornly hostile new subjects to obedience.

Such obedience was an impossibility. Amazingly, there are still modern English historians who believe Lancastrian France might have become an enduring reality had Henry lived. Yet nearly 150 years ago Pierre-Adolphe Chéruel, one of the much decried 'patriotic' school of French historians, published a history of Rouen under the English occupation. It contains the following letter:

We have recently learned from the great and piteous clamour that within the duchy of Normandy many who call themselves our officers, baillis, captains and etc. have committed and are committing great wrongs, excesses and abuses, taking advantage of their position to do so, to the prejudice of public welfare, such as: breaking into churches and stealing the goods therein; seizing and raping women, married and unmarried; cruelly beating the poor people, carrying off their horses with other beasts of burden and their seed corn; occupying the houses of churchmen, nobles and others against their will, demanding heavy tolls and quantities of merchandise at the city gates which they are supposed to guard; extorting levies of food from towns and parishes with law-abiding subjects; forcing men to perform more guard duties at towns and fortresses than is their obligation and making them pay huge sums if they go absent; seizing our poor subjects, beating them, judging them without trial and confining them in prisons or in their homes, robbing them of their goods, or seizing the same either without payment or else fixing the price. And, moreover, it is said that the baillis and captains do not keep the troops in their garrisons as they should do, that the baillis, often being at the same time captains of the [strong] places in their bailiwicks, farm out their clerkships, seals and lieutenancies to unworthy persons, and abuse the taking of provisions and other goods at their own price and pleasure.[27]

This letter is not fabricated by Chéruel. It was written by John, Duke of Bedford, the new 'Regent of France', on 31 January 1423 – a mere five months after his brother's death. If the dauphinist and Burgundian armies robbed, at least they spoke the same language. The people of Lancastrian France simply wanted the English to go away.

Henry's tools, his troops, were an insuperable barrier between him and his 'subjects'. His army doomed his regime from the very start. He knew that relations with the conquered population must be improved, and even the most 'patriotic' of France's nineteenth-century historians acknowledge that his efforts to do so were not far short of incredible. But it was all in vain. 'If the expression "bled white" was at any time accurate it best describes the state of the conquered provinces of France under the English garrisons' is McFarlane's comment.[28]

Even so, just after he died and his body had been taken back to England for burial, a French nobleman would joke grimly (so Monstrelet heard) that the king had left his boots behind.[29] The borders of Lancastrian France continued to expand for some years after his death. As late as 1433, when in reality the tide had turned against them, Bishop Jean Juvénal des Ursins could say in a notably gloomy and despairing letter that the English 'are waging a fierce war, gaining more territory in which no one stays or even makes a pretence of staying, save for the poor companions of the frontier [les povres compaignons des frontières] who love honour'.[30] Lancastrian France would take a surprisingly long time to die, outliving its creator by nearly thirty years.

Chastellain has a strange story – 'told me by a high and noble baron, the Seigneur de La Trémonille' – about a holy man who visited Henry sometime during 1421. He was the hermit of Sainte-Claude in

207

Flanders, John of Ghent, famous for his gift of second sight. (Later he prophesied the birth of Louis XI.) He warned the king to change his ways since God was growing displeased at the way he was treating the Christian people of France 'whose cries beneath your scourge have aroused his pity'. He explained that Henry had enjoyed divine favour because he had persecuted heretics so ardently when Prince of Wales, but that if he went on scourging the French like this he would have a very short life. At first Henry was somewhat shaken. Then he laughed.[31]

XIX
Death

'Glory is like a circle in the water,
Which never ceases to enlarge itself,
Till, by broad spreading, it dispenses to nought.
With Henry's death, the English circle ends.'

Shakespeare, Joan la Pucelle in *King Henry VI*, part I

'Thou liest, thou liest, my portion lies with the Lord Jesus Christ!'

Henry V on his deathbed

O n 7 July 1422 there were public prayers in Paris for the health
of King Henry, heir and regent of France. Waurin writes, 'I
have since been truly informed . . . that it was an inflammation
which seized him in the fundament, which is called the disease of St
Anthony.'[1] ('St Anthony's Fire', which is erysipelas.) We know from
the Bourgeois of Paris that smallpox was raging in and around the
capital, that many important Englishmen had caught it and that
some people believed that the King of England was among them.
One chronicler reports that Henry could not keep any food in his
belly, which might imply a duodenal ulcer. Basin tells us that: 'many
say he was smitten with this illness because he had ordered, or had
allowed, his troops to sack and devastate the oratory of St Fiacre and
its glebe near Meaux. Indeed one often calls his disease, which swells
the belly and legs hideously, St Fiacre's Evil.'[2] Plainly it was an
internal malady, and on balance the most likely diagnosis is dysentery – the scourge which had killed so many of his troops during
the siege of Meaux – eventually resulting in a fatal internal
haemorrhage. It was certainly not leprosy, as some contemporary

209

Frenchmen thought hopefully. Whatever it was, it was some time before the king would admit to himself that he was seriously, dangerously, ill.

Suddenly the Burgundians found themselves threatened by a totally unexpected dauphinist offensive. Duke Philip's town of Cosne on the upper reaches of the Loire, fifty miles from Orleans, was besieged in such overwhelming force that its garrison agreed to surrender if not relieved by 12 August. Should Cosne fall to the dauphinists they would be able to strike through the Nivernais at Dijon, the Burgundian capital. Philip force marched every man at his disposal towards Cosne, begging Henry to lend him archers. Not only did the king agree but he promised to come in person.

Henry set out for Cosne but soon had to substitute a litter for his horse. When he reached Corbeil, fifteen miles south of Paris, he took to his bed and handed over command to Bedford. He was forced to spend a fortnight at Corbeil. Learning that the dauphinists had beaten a hasty retreat from Cosne he decided to return to Paris. Although he felt a little better, he took his physicians' advice and travelled by barge down the Seine. However, he landed at Charenton and mounted his horse, but collapsed. He was carried back to the barge and taken to the castle of Bois-de-Vincennes, which he reached on or about 10 August.

The king must have known by now that he was dying. He was surrounded by the men whom he trusted most: his brother John, Duke of Bedford; his uncle Thomas, Duke of Exeter; his closest lieutenant Richard Beauchamp, Earl of Warwick; his standard-bearer Sir Lewis Robsart; and, his confessor again for the last eighteen months, Friar Thomas Netter. Among his intimate male companions Salisbury alone was absent, harrying the French.

The strangest absence was that of Queen Catherine. What is so curious is that she was within easy reach of Vincennes, at Paris only three miles away, and it was the normal custom even for medieval kings to have their wives by them when they were dying. It was not that she could not leave her baby; she had already done so and the child was in England. If her husband had summoned her she would have had to go to him. Plainly he did not summon her. The inference is that his feelings for Catherine were not quite so romantic as Shakespeare makes out, that he did not really think she had 'witch-craft' in her lips. Henry might well have anticipated Napoleon's jibe at his own dynastic match – 'It's only a womb I'm marrying.'

'I exhort you to continue in these wars until peace is gained,' he told those round his bed. He continued, on a familiar note, that he had been perfectly justified in invading France. 'It was not ambitious lust for dominion, nor for empty glory, nor any other cause that drew me to these wars, but only that by sueing of my right, I might at once gain peace and my own rights.' The disinheritor of the heirs of Richard II and Charles VI added: 'And before the wars were begun I was fully instructed by men of the holiest life and the wisest counsel that I ought and could begin the wars, prosecute them and justly finish them without danger to my soul.' However, he begged forgiveness from his stepmother, Joan of Navarre, for his ill treatment of her and also from Lord Scrope's children for having illegally confiscated entailed lands from them.

He provided for the government of the two kingdoms with his habitual thoroughness. The Duke of Gloucester was to be Lord Protector of England, but under the ultimate authority of the Duke of Bedford who was to be the future Henry VI's principal official guardian; the baby's other guardians were to be Bishop Beaufort, the Duke of Exeter, and the Earl of Warwick. Bedford, who was also to be governor of Normandy, must offer the regency of France to the Duke of Burgundy, to commit him more fully to the establishment of a Lancastrian dynasty in the land over which his forebears had reigned; if Philip declined, then Bedford was to take the regency himself – but at all costs he must preserve the alliance with Burgundy. Should the tide turn against the English, Bedford was to concentrate on saving Normandy. None of the higher ranking prisoners in England, especially the Duke of Orleans, was to be freed – to stop them organizing opposition to the English conquest.

The most recent French historian of the Hundred Years War, Jean Favier, commenting on Henry's instructions to Bedford about saving Normandy, thinks that he was tacitly admitting the dauphin's right to succeed to the French throne.[3] It was certainly extraordinary advice to come from someone who had always claimed that God supported his own right to the throne of France. It may indicate a loss of nerve induced by physical weakness.

According to the Arthurian tale told to Chastellain by M. de La Trémouille, the hermit, John of Ghent, came unexpectedly to the king's bedside. Henry was overjoyed to see the holy man. He asked him if he was going to recover from his illness. 'Sire,' answered the hermit, 'you are at your end.' Henry then inquired if his son would reign over France in his place. 'Never, never, shall he reign nor abide,' was the reply.[4] However fantastic this story may appear, it

211

really does seem that as he lay dying the king began to lose some of his confidence in the future of Lancastrian France.

His bed was in his chamber over the great hall in the donjon tower, built by Charles V some forty years previously, in which a single elegant column supported a high, vaulted ceiling. As a medieval king he had to die in public; courtiers thronged the room, though it is likely that to some extent he was shielded from curious eyes by screens placed around the bed.

Late in the evening of 20 August Henry asked his doctors how long he had to live, brushing aside soothing suggestions that God might still heal him. Then they told him the truth. 'Sire, think you on your soul. For, saving the mercy of God, we judge not that you can live more than two hours.' At this he summoned his confessor, Friar Netter, and together they recited the seven penitential psalms and the litany. After finishing the psalm *Miserere mei, Deus* he broke in, 'O good lord, thou knowest that if thy pleasure had been to have suffered me to live my natural age my firm purpose and intent was, after I had established this realm of France in sure peace, to have gone and visited Jerusalem and to have re-edified the walls thereof, and to have expulsed from it the miscreants thine adversaries [the Turks].'

The king received Communion and was anointed. At the very end, his iron self-righteousness faltered and for a moment he feared for his salvation. Suddenly he screamed, as though replying to some evil spirit, 'Thou liest, thou liest, my portion is with the Lord Jesus Christ!' Did he suspect that, as a usurper who insisted on being the rightful heir to England and France, he had committed the sin against the Holy Ghost, that persistent denial of the known truth for which there is no forgiveness? Even so, he died peacefully in Netter's arms at the end of the two hours given to him by the doctors, just before midnight. His last words were '*in manus tuas, Domine, ipsum terminum redemisti*'. He was not quite thirty-five. Had he lived another six weeks he would have survived Charles VI and inherited the crown of France.

There followed the grisly ceremonies which attended the death of a medieval king. His entrails were removed and buried in the church of Saint-Maur-des-Fossés at Vincennes (where they came to light in the early 1980s), his body was dismembered and then boiled down in the castle kitchens to remove the flesh from the bones, both being embalmed and sealed in a lead casket. In September his funeral chariot, drawn by four great horses, set out on its journey to

England. 'Above the dead corpse [in the caskets] they laid a figure made of boiled hides or leather representing his person as to the similitude of a living creature, upon whose head was set an Imperial diadem of gold and precious stones, and in his right hand he held a sceptre royal, and in his left hand a bowl [orb] of gold; and in this manner adorned was his figure laid in a bed in the said chariot, with his visage uncovered towards the heavens.' Beside the chariot walked mutes in white holding burning torches, behind came his household men gowned in black, behind them rode the Dukes of Bedford and Exeter and the King of Scots and, for part of the way, the Duke of Burgundy; and behind the princes rode 500 men-at-arms on black horses, their black lances reversed. Last of all came Queen Catherine in the white mourning of a king's consort. Whenever the cortège passed through a town of substance 'a canopy of marvellous great value such as is used to be borne over the Blessed Sacrament on Corpus Christi Day was borne over the chariot by men of great worship'.

The cortège did not reach London until 5 November, going by way of St Denis (the burial place of the Kings of France where Henry's effigy sat for a time in state), Rouen, Abbeville, Montreuil, Boulogne, Calais, Dover, Canterbury, Rochester and Dartford before it was met at Blackheath by the mayor, aldermen and guildsmen of London. As it processed to St Paul's there was a man standing outside the door of every house on the route holding a burning torch. After lying in state for two days the king's remains were taken to Westminster Abbey to be interred with a pomp memorable even by the standards of medieval England.

His magnificent tomb in the abbey, and the chantry chapel which houses it, were completed in the 1440s. The tomb was surmounted by his silver gilt effigy, with hands and head of solid silver. Above hung his tilting helm, sword, shield and saddle. The effigy has long since lost its silver and silver gilt, and the wooden core alone remains. But his helm, sword, shield and saddle still hang there.

Charles VI died on 11 October, living just long enough to cheat the ancient enemy of France of his throne. Jean Chartier records that a few time-servers cheered when the one-year-old Henry VI was proclaimed '*Henry, roy de France et d'Angleterre*'. He adds: 'But the more genuine wept and made moan because of the great kindness which had been in the said king of France [Charles VI] named Well Beloved, thinking on the many evils that might come upon them by changing their natural lord and how the said lordship was to be governed by foreign nations and customs, which was and is against reason and right, to the total destruction of the people and realm of France.'[5] No doubt Chartier, as historiographer to the dauphin, is biased. Yet the Bourgeois of Paris, who was also there and watched the crazy old king's cortège pass through the streets, is clearly telling the truth when he says that the ordinary people of Paris wept and cried, 'Most dear of princes! Never shall we find another prince so kind! Never shall we see you again! Cursed be death! We shall have nothing but war now that you have left us. You will find rest while we shall live among tribulations and miseries of every kind. For we are doomed to be captives like the children of Israel when they were led away to Babylon.' The Bourgeois adds that those in the streets or at the windows wept and cried as though the person each one loved most had died.[6] It was not the most promising way to greet the accession of France's first Lancastrian king.

Meanwhile in England, so Waurin admits, everyone continued to weep and lament and was in much sadness. He and Monstrelet, both writing in the 1440s, recount of Henry V how 'even now as much honour and reverence is paid at his tomb as if it were certain that he was a saint in heaven'.[7] The *Brut of England* records of 1422 that 'in that same year died most of the laurel trees in England'.[8]

The French writers of the day, including the most hostile, concede that though Henry had been their enemy he had been very great indeed. Waurin says of him; 'a most clever man and expert in everything he undertook',[9] Jean Chartier; 'a subtle conqueror and a skilful warrior.'[10] Chastellain too is magnanimous: 'It is not my intention to detract from or diminish in my writings either the honour or the glory of that valiant prince the English king, in whom valour and courage shone forth as befitted a mighty conqueror . . . of this King of England may high and glorious tales be told notwithstanding that he was the foe of France.'[11]

No one can deny that Henry V was a very great soldier and a very great king. Yet he was fortunate to die young. At his death there still remained two thirds of France to conquer, and had he lived he would have worn himself out in an unending series of sieges for which it would have become increasingly impossible to find the money. He was incapable of seeing where his wonderful gifts as a soldier and a diplomatist were leading him. Even with Henry V, even without Joan of Arc, the English could never have succeeded. The Burgundians were bound to turn against them. The king was basically an opportunist, albeit an opportunist of genius. As E. F. Jacob, one of

214

his greatest admirers among modern historians, writes: 'In the last analysis he was an adventurer, not a statesman; the risk he took in the creation of a double monarchy was too great, depended on too many uncertainties, and fundamentally misread the nature of France.'[12] Waugh, another admirer who forces himself to be objective if not always successfully, has to concede that: 'His will was doubtless set on purposes unworthy of a great or good man.'[13] McFarlane, the most fervent admirer of all, admits: 'It is the tragedy of his reign that he gave a wrong direction to national aspirations which he did so much himself to stimulate, that he led his people in pursuit of the chimera of foreign conquest.'[14] French historians have less difficulty in reaching the same conclusions.

The question may be asked why the Lancastrian conquest had no hope of enduring like that of William the Conqueror. But Anglo-Saxon England had been a much smaller country with a much smaller population in a more primitive age, while William had had no serious rivals after Hastings. In contrast Henry conquered a mere third of France, and that only because the kingdom was temporarily divided between two powerful factions with their own armies. Above all, the emergence of articulate French nationalism doomed his would-be dual monarchy.

Whether the king's brutality in war was simply in keeping with the military conventions of the age or the expression of an unusually savage nature is not easy to decide. What is indisputable is his impact on the French. They suffered more from his invasions than from any between the Vikings and the Nazis.

It is hard to pass judgement on Henry as a man, but it is generally agreed that his reputation is based on admiration and not on affection. He was ruthless in subordinating his feelings to his ambition; he was only speaking the truth when he said that had Clarence survived Baugé he would have had him executed for disobeying orders. The kindest thing that can be said is that those who worked with him (except Lord Scrope) seem to have been devoted to the king and to his memory. But, beyond question, the man always gave place to the warlord – there was something a little inhuman about him.

The admirers of Henry (and they include most people in the English-speaking world) ascribe any imperfections in him to his having been a 'late medieval man' since late medieval men were prone to superstition and violence. Unfortunately for this argument there was a 'late medieval man' who is a perfect yardstick by which to judge the king, his successor as ruler of Lancastrian France – his

215

brother Bedford, regent at Rouen and Paris from 1422 until his death in 1435. He too 'shed the blood of Frenchmen piteously' and won his own Agincourt; at Verneuil in 1424 he cut a Franco-Scots force to pieces, inflicting 7,000 casualties of whom 1,000 were dauphinists. 'Brave, humane and just,' Basin says of him, 'so much so that Normans and French men who lived in his part of the realm had great affection for him.'[15] The Bourgeois of Paris is no less complimentary – 'his nature was quite un-English, for he never wanted to make war on anyone, whereas in truth the English are always wanting to wage war on their neighbours. Which is why they all die an evil death.'[16] No contemporary French writer speaks of Henry in such terms. He was undoubtedly feared by his unwilling new subjects but he was certainly not loved by them.

In Henry's own brutal words, 'war without fire is like sausages without mustard.' Not only emergent French nationalism but French local loyalties were outraged by his invasions and campaigns of conquest. The horror unleashed by him was unforgiveable, and also unforgettable. No account tells the whole harrowing story, conveys how widespread and how savage was the misery which he inflicted on the French people. In the midst of all his hero worship Shakespeare somehow discerns the sheer callous cruelty of the king:

> *What is it to me, if impious war*
> *Array'd in flames, like to the prince of fiends*
> *Do, with his smirch'd complexion, all fell feats*
> *Enlink'd to waste and desolation?[17]*

But on the whole even Shakespeare succumbs to the legend. He could not know what had happened in France.

XX
Epilogue

'All the time of war during these forty year betwixt England and France, wist I not scant three or four men which wolden accord throughout, in telling how a town or a castle was won in France, or how a battle was done there.'

Bishop Reginald Pecock[1]

'For there may no king conquer a great realm by continual sieges.'

Sir John Fastolf[2]

At Formigny on 15 April 1450, six months after recapturing Rouen, the French under the command of a veteran of Agincourt annihilated an English army. It had just crossed the Channel in a desperate bid to relieve the beleaguered garrisons of Normandy; ironically, its archers were deployed in the same formation as at Agincourt. Caen fell in June. In August William Paston wrote, 'And this same Wednesday was it told that Cherbourg is gone and we have not now a foot of land in Normandy.' King Charles's men went on to conquer Guyenne, an operation completed by the autumn of 1451, Bordeaux having surrendered in June. A final English attempt to regain the duchy was humiliatingly defeated at Castillon in 1453. The only French soil remaining in English hands was Calais and the Channel Islands.

Hatred of the invader from across the Channel had united the various French *pays*, making them forget their regional differences. The revival of French morale had been begun by Joan of Arc, after whose brief, meteoric career the English failed to conquer more territory. Then in 1435 Philip of Burgundy deserted them,

217

recognizing Charles VII as King of France and his overlord. Henceforward the English increasingly suffered military and diplomatic reverses. Their occupation was doomed even though it took a reunited France another fifteen years to drive them out. To some extent they were defeated by the new French field cannon and handguns which, while still primitive, proved more effective than English bows.

Yet it was not just military technology which defeated the English. What broke them was lack of money. Henry VI's total annual revenue at this period was only £30,000 when his household alone was costing £24,000 a year; his father's pernicious practice of borrowing was continued so that the Crown's debts grew to nearly £400,000. In consequence there was no cash for military operations, nothing with which to pay ever smaller forces in the field or in the garrisons, arrears of pay causing mutinies, desertion and still more plundering of the local French population. The King's Ships were either sold off or left to rot at their moorings, while most of the English fortresses in France were allowed to grow so ruinous that it was impossible to defend them. All this came of embarking on a programme of overseas adventure and foreign conquest beyond England's resources.

When the French possessions were lost there was an outcry in England, which had come to regard Normandy as English territory, Rouen as much an English city as Bordeaux. Henry VI's three principal ministers were lynched. The kingdom sank rapidly into bloody anarchy. The nobility and gentry had been turned into professional soldiers by the wars in France; after being driven out, they and their followers were only too ready to use at home – and, if necessary, on each other – the lethal professional skills they had acquired abroad. What were later to be called the Wars of the Roses began in 1455, English veterans fighting each other instead of the French. Henry VI was deposed in 1461, to be murdered ten years later, less than three weeks after his only son had been killed at Tewkesbury. It was the end of the Lancastrian usurpation.

Yet the House of Lancaster might have survived the incapacity of its last king, even the madness which by a bitter irony he had inherited from his Valois grandfather, had it not been for his father's bequest of 'Lancastrian France'. For all his brilliance, Henry V's ambition ended by bankrupting and discrediting his son, and by ruining his dynasty.

Looking back from the end of the fifteenth century, Philippe de

218

Commynes (not a Frenchman but a man of Flanders), although he can refer to 'the wise, handsome and very brave king Henry', clearly believes that the destruction of the House of Lancaster was God's judgement on it for what it had done in France. Writing of the fate of the dynasty, together with its Beaufort and Holland cousins and Yorkist kindred, he says:

> All have been killed in battle. Their fathers and their followers had pillaged and destroyed the kingdom of France and possessed the greater part of it for many years. But they all killed each other . . . And yet people say, 'God doesn't punish men as he was accustomed to in the days of the children of Israel and tolerates wicked princes and men!' . . . In the long run there is no lordship, and certainly no strong one, where the country does not remain in the possession of its own people. As may be seen from the example of France, where the English held much territory for 400 years, but now hold only Calais and two little castles which cost them much money to maintain. The rest they lost more quickly than they had conquered it since they lost more in a day than they had gained in a year.[1]

It is clear that he has no doubts that Lancastrian France had been doomed from the start.

In 1475 Edward IV rode out from Calais at the head of 12,000 troops, accompanied by almost every English peer who was fit enough to climb into a saddle. Once styled Earl of March, he had been born at Rouen when his father was lieutenant-general of Lancastrian France. The English army marched confidently towards the Somme, killing, burning, and looting in the traditional style. But, unlike Henry V, Edward realized that he could not afford a long war of conquest while, again unlike Henry, as a womanizer running to fat he could never have stood the strain of lengthy campaigning. He let himself be bought off by Louis XI for 75,000 gold crowns down and annual instalments of 50,000. Commynes observes that no one should be surprised at Louis paying such sums 'considering the great evils the English have committed in this realm all too recently'. In the event it was the last full-scale English invasion of France. Nonetheless Commynes tells us that even in the 1490s the French still regarded their neighbours over the Channel as a threat:

> All the English nobles, commons and clergy are ready at any moment to fight against this realm on the pretext of spurious claims to it, in the

hope of winning profit here since God allowed their forebears to win several great battles . . . they carried off great plunder and wealth to England, taken from both the poor people and the lords of France whom they imprisoned in large numbers.[2]

As late as 1525, when François I was defeated at Pavia, Henry VIII thought he had a good chance of reconquering what had been Lancastrian France. Calais was lost only in 1558.

For centuries the north-western French celebrated the expulsion of the English. Until 1735 the liberation of Paris in 1436 was celebrated annually by the 'Procession of the English'. The Earl of Warwick's banner, captured at Montargis in 1427, was borne in triumph through that town on the *Fête des Anglais* every year till 1792. Mass was said twice annually in every important church in France until the Revolution in thanksgiving for the freeing of Cherbourg in 1450 and the end of the occupation of Normandy; it continued to be said in some parishes of the Cotentin throughout the nineteenth century. Even now the occupation's memory lingers. In Maine, farmers near Lassay still refer to the 'time of the English' (or did till a few years ago), while further west within living memory country people spoke of 'going into England' when crossing what had once been the frontier of the conquest.

After Waterloo in 1815 and after Sedan in 1870, when Alsace-Lorraine had to be surrendered, the French were again invaded and occupied by foreigners. It revived ancient but nonetheless bitter folk memories in the French people of what they had endured at the hands of the English. The cult of Joan of Arc embedded their ancestors' sufferings still more firmly in the popular mind. No doubt two world wars have done much to make them forget the Hundred Years War. Yet it is no exaggeration to claim that by reviving the war Henry dug a chasm between French and English, a Chasm which has grown deeper down the centuries.

Henry V's truest and most lasting monument is not the beautiful chapel at Westminster, not Shakespeare's play, not the tale of Agincourt and Crispin's Day. Nor is it the Wars of the Roses. It is that antipathy and distrust which, sadly, all too many Frenchmen feel for those who speak English as their first language. That is the king's legacy for those of us who live in the last years of the twentieth century. Other men and other wars have deepened it but he was one of its original architects.

Glossary

apanage	royal lands granted by a French king to a younger son for his maintenance, with the title of duke or count.
bailli	royal officer responsible for the administration of justice and of revenue in a baillage or district.
ballinger	English sailing barge usually with from forty to fifty oars, shallow-draughted and clinker built.
barbican	fortified gatehouse with tower above or flanked by towers.
bassinet	conical helmet with 'hounskul' (or 'pig-face') pointed visor.
bastard	title borne by acknowledged eldest natural son of a noble.
bastille	wooden tower on wheels for assault, used in siege warfare.
bastion	round or polygonal tower projecting from walls.
blanc	French equivalent of groat but mainly of base metal instead of silver.
bombard	heavy cannon used in siege warfare, firing gunstones or metal cannon balls of up to 1,000 lb.
bowyer	bow maker.
brigantine	defensive jacket of metal plates on cloth.
brimstone	sulphur.

althrop	small metal ball with four (angled) projecting spikes placed on battlefield to maim horses.
captal	Gascon title for captain of a castle.
carrack	large square-rigged sailing vessel of Genoese origin, clinker built.
chambres des comptes	accounting office for French royal finances at Paris or for Norman ducal finances at Caen.
champion	officer charged with defending his lord's cause in trial by battle.
châtelet	principal criminal court at Paris.
close-helmet	round-topped helmet attached to neck armour.
cog	main type of square-rigged sailing vessel in use in north European waters, clinker built.
crown	French gold coin weighing 3.99 gm (though weight fluctuated), worth 20½ sols.
culverin	light cannon firing lead or bronze bullets – mounted on portable rest and the ancestor of the hand gun and the harquebus.
curtana	the sword 'curtana' was the pointless sword of mercy (as opposed to the pointed sword of justice) borne before the English king at his coronation.
destrier	warhorse.
donjon	keep of a castle.
estates	consultative assembly of representatives of the three estates of nobles, clergy and bourgeois.
fletcher	arrow maker.
gabelle	tax on salt – a commodity which could only be bought at royal (in Normandy, ducal) depots.

haro	cry to a lord for rescue.
havoc	the word announcing permission for troops to plunder.
jack	defensive leather coat, either of several layers or quilted, often reinforced with metal studs or small plates.
jupon	short leather tunic worn over chain mail.
lit de justice	plenary session of the *parlement* presided over by the king of France at which a royal edict was forcibly registered or a peer of France tried.
mangonel	siege engine firing stone shot.
march	borderland – a 'marcher lord' was lord of a frontier territory, as in Wales where he had considerable independence.
maul	or mallet – a hammer-type weapon, with a heavy leaden head on a five-foot wooden shaft.
mine	tunnel dug under foundations to undermine walls or towers.
misericorde	'mercy' dagger, so called from being used to dispatch enemy wounded.
morning star	form of mace, consisting of a spiked metal ball attached by a chain to a short metal shaft.
noble	principal gold coin of English currency, worth 6*s* 8*d*.
pantler	master of the pantry.
parlement	supreme court of appeal in the kingdom of France, situated at the Palais de Justice in Paris.
pâtis	protection money levied by troops on local population.
pavise	large, free-standing shield on hinged support used by archers and crossbowmen as protection when shooting.
pole-axe	combined axe and half-pike, with axe blade balanced by hammer head on five-foot metal shaft.

223

poundage	customs duty on weight of all imports and exports save bullion.
pourpoint	quilted doublet.
president	principal judicial officer of the *parlement* at Paris.
provost	royal officer responsible for overseeing administration of justice.
ribeaudequin	cart mounting several small culverins discharged together.
sallet	type of helmet, unattached to neck armour and with or without visor.
saltpetre	potassium nitrate, a component of gunpowder.
salut	Lancastrian French equivalent of the gold crown.
sol	silver or base metal coin (later known as *sou*) subdivided into 12 deniers.
sollerets	articulated armour for feet.
sow	a mobile shelter used in siege warfare, with a strong timber roof and covered in damp hides to make it fireproof.
trebuchet	siege engine or catapult hurling rocks or barrels of flaming tow, the principal form of heavy artillery before the bombard and afterwards used to supplement cannon.
tunnage	customs duty on wine imported in casks, levied at so much per tun.
vicomte	Norman administrative official equal or junior in rank to a *bailli*.

Notes

(See Bibliography for full details of sources)

Introduction

1. Kingsford (ed.), *The First English Life of King Henry the Fifth*, p. 131
2. Harriss (ed.), *Henry V*, pp. 209–10
3. Perroy, *La Guerre de Cent Ans*, pp. 204–5

Chapter I, 'The Usurpers'

1. *The First English Life of King Henry the Fifth*, p. 17
2. *'Franche dague, dit un Anglais/Vous ne faites que boire vin.'*
3. Froissart, cit. Ascoli, *La Grande Bretagne devant l'Opinion Française*, p. 33
4. Hardyng, *Chronicle*, p. 353
5. Adam of Usk picked it up, *Chronicon Adae de Usk*, p. 119

Chapter II, 'Prince Henry and Prince Owain'

1. Adam of Usk, op. cit., p. 42
2. Wylie, *History of England under Henry IV*, p. 107
3. Adam of Usk, op. cit., p. 57
4. Capgrave, *The Chronicle of England*, p. 279
5. Hingeston (ed.), *Royal and Historical Letters during the Reign of Henry IV*, Vol. I, p. 149
6. Capgrave, op. cit., p. 279, who adds, 'Many othir inconvenientis did thei that time.'
7. For Tiptopt's career, see *Complete Peerage* and *Dictionary of National Biography*

Chapter III, 'He Would Usurp the Crown'

1. Taylor and Roskell (eds), *Gesta Henrici Quinti*, p. 19: 'almost second to none in the King's confidence.'

2. Capgrave, op. cit., p. 291
3. Juvénal, in Dénifle, *La Desolation des eglises, monastères et hôpitaux en France pendant la Guerre de Cent Ans*, Vol. I, p. 505
4. Jean de Montreuil, cit. Lewis, *Essays in Later Medieval French History*, p. 194
5. *The First English Life of King Henry the Fifth* has a strange tale of how the prince wore a fantastic coat, the symbolism of which has been forgotten, for this second meeting, pp. 11–12
6. Taylor and Roskell (eds), op. cit., p. 13
7. *The First English Life of King Henry the Fifth*, p. 17
8. McFarlane, *Cambridge Medieval History*, Vol. VIII, p. 379
9. Foxe, *Book of Martyrs* in *The Acts and Monuments*, Vol. III, pp. 235–9

Chapter IV, 'No Lordship'

1. *Chronique du Réligieux de Saint-Denys*, Vol. IV, p. 770
2. *Vita et Gesta Henrici Quinti*, p. 24
3. *The First English Life of King Henry the Fifth*, p. 17
4. Huizinga, *The Waning of the Middle Ages*, p. 96; Taylor and Roskell (eds), op. cit., p. 181, prays that under a single ruler England and France may 'turn as soon as possible against the unsubdued and bloody faces of the heathen'.
5. 'It is upon admiration, not affection, that his historical reputation has always been based.' Allmand, 'Henry V the Soldier, and the War in France', in *Henry V*, (ed. Harriss) p. 132
6. Livius de Frulovisis (Tito Livio), *Vita Henrici Quinti*, p. 5; *The First English Life of King Henry the Fifth*, p. 17
7. Jacob, *The Fifteenth Century*, p. 480
8. For Netter, see Dictionary of National Biography; also Wylie and Waugh, *The Reign of Henry V*. Vol. I, pp. 239–41; for a more sympathetic portrait see Knowles, The Religious Orders in England, Vol. II, pp. 145–48
9. Knowles, op. cit., Vol. II, pp. 175–82
10. For Lollards, see Knowles, op. cit., Vol. II, *passim*; and McFarlane, *Wycliffe and the Beginnings of English Non-conformity*
11. See McFarlane, *Lancastrian Kings and Lollard Knights*
12. Taylor and Roskell (eds.), op. cit., pp. 10–11
13. ibid., p. 7
14. Catto, 'Religious Change under Henry V' in *Henry V* (ed. Harriss), p. 97
15. ibid., p. 115
16. The most recent and comprehensive study is Powell, 'The Restoration of Law and Order' in *Henry V* (ed. Harriss), pp. 53–74
17. Catto, 'The King's Servants' in *Henry V* (ed. Harriss), pp. 82–3
18. Rymer, *Foedera, Conventiones*, Vol. IX, pp. 300–1

19. Taylor and Roskell (eds.), op. cit., p. 19
20. Capgrave, op. cit., p. 309
21. Wylie and Waugh, *The Reign of Henry V*, Vol. I, pp. 517–39; the best short account of the Southampton Plot is in Taylor and Roskell, op. cit., App. III, pp. 188–90
21. McFarlane, *Nobility of Later Medieval England*, p. 246

Chapter V, 'The English Armada'

1. Wylie and Waugh, op. cit., Vol. I, pp. 447–8
2. See J. Palmer, 'The War Aims of the Protagonists and the Negotiations for Peace' in *The Hundred Years War* (ed. Fowler), pp. 66–70
3. Strecche, *Chronicle*, pp. 150–1
4. Taylor and Roskell (eds.), op. cit., pp. 17–19
5. Wylie and Waugh, op. cit., Vol. I, pp. 113–4
6. Harriss (ed.), *Henry V*, p. 40
7. McFarlane, *Nobility of Later Medieval England*; and Postan, *Economic History Review*
8. Hewitt, 'The Organisation of War' in *Henry V* (ed. Harriss), pp. 82–3
9. See Richmond, 'The War at Sea', in *The Hundred Years War* (ed. Fowler), pp. 96–121
10. Taylor and Roskell (eds.), op. cit., p. 21

Chapter VI, 'Our Town of Harfleur'

1. Jacob, *Henry V and the Invasion of France*, p. 85
2. Taylor and Roskell (eds.), op. cit., p. 39
3. Capgrave, op. cit., p. 311
4. ibid., p. 13
5. Allmand, *Lancastrian Normandy*, p. 51

Chapter VII, 'That Dreadful Day of Agincourt'

1. Taylor and Roskell (eds.), op. cit., p. 67
2. Livius de Frulovisis (Tito Livio), op. cit., p. 14
3. Taylor and Roskell (eds.), op. cit., p. 77
4. Monstrelet, *Chroniques d'Enguerran de Monstrelet*, Vol. III, p. 102
5. Waurin, *Receuil des croniques et anchiennes istories de la Grant Bretaigne à present nomme Engleterre, 1399–1422*, Vol. II, p. 208
6. Taylor and Roskell (eds.), op. cit., pp. 85–7
7. Livius de Frulovisis (Tito Livio), op. cit., pp. 19–20
8. Halle, *The Union of Two Noble and Illustre Families of Lancastre and Yorke*, p. 70
9. *The First English Life of King Henry the Fifth*, p. 64

Chapter VIII, 'To Teach the Frenchmen Courtesy'

1. Printed in Taylor and Roskell (eds.), op. cit., App. IV (formerly ascribed to John Lydgate).
2. ibid., p. 113
3. ibid., p. 175
4. Wylie and Waugh, op. cit., Vol. II, Ch. 45, 'The Navy'
5. Taylor and Roskell (eds.) op. cit., App. III, pp. 189–90
6. 'Il se savait remarquablement secondé par son frère Jean, le duc de Bedford.' Favier, *Guerre de Cent Ans*, p. 437
7. Harriss (ed.) op. cit., p. 45
8. See Powicke, 'Lancastrian Captains', *Essays in Medieval History*, op. cit.
9. Taylor and Roskell (eds.), op. cit., p. 151.

Chapter IX, 'The Fall of Caen'

1. *The Brut of England*, p. 382
2. Chartier, *Chronique de Charles VII, roi de France*, Vol. I, p. 6
3. 'Propter horrorem nominis Anglorum . . . ferocissime belue quam homines.' Basin, *Histoire de Charles VII*, pp. 62–4
4. *Chronique du Réligieux de Saint-Denys*, Vol. VI, p. 100
5. ibid., Vol. VI, p. 104
6. Wylie and Waugh, op. cit., Vol. III, p. 61
7. Morosini, *Chronique d'Antonio Morosini: Extraits rélativs à l'histoire de France, 1414–1428*, Vol. II, pp. 146–9
8. *Chronique du Réligieux de Saint-Denys*, Vol. VI, p. 134
9. ibid., Vol. VI, p. 161
10. Juvénal, *Histoire de Charles VI*, p. 539
11. *The First English Life of King Henry the Fifth*, p. 102
12. *Chronique du Réligieux de Saint-Denys*, Vol. VI, p. 165
13. ibid., Vol. VI, p. 165
14. ibid., Vol. VI, p. 381

Chapter X, 'The Fall of Rouen'

1. Monstrelet, op. cit., Vol. III, p. 278
2. Page, 'The Siege of Rouen' in *The Historical Collections of a Citizen of London*, pp. 4–5
3. Riley (ed.), *Memorials of London and Lower Life in the XIIIth, XIVth and XVth Centuries*.
4. Page, op. cit., p. 18
5. *The First English Life of King Henry V*, pp. 134, 135
6. *The Brut of England*, p. 422
7. Monstrelet, op. cit., Vol. III, p. 308

Chapter XI, 'The Norman Conquest – In Reverse'

1. Allmand, *Lancastrian Normandy*, pp. 52–3
2. Juvénal, op. cit., p. 545; *Chronique du Réligieux de Saint-Denys*, Vol. VI, pp. 311–13
3. As recently as the 1960s, in *La Résistance à l'Occupation anglais*, p. 18, Jouet argued, 'En effet, les Anglais ont volontairement et clairement usé du terme préexistant de "brigand" pour designer une réalité nouvelle, le partisan. Manoeuvre habile . . .'
4. Basin, op. cit., Vol. I, pp. 166–8
5. 'So alarmed were the English authorities that they attempted to restrict, then to prevent the emigrants from leaving, and finally to entice them to return . . . by remission of rent and tax concessions.' Fowler, *Hundred Years War*, p. 14
6. Newhall, *The English Conquest of Normandy*, p. 226
7. *The First English Life of King Henry the Fifth*, pp. 132–4

Chapter XII, 'The Murder of John the Fearless'

1. Monstrelet, op. cit., Vol. III, p. 320
2. ibid., Vol. III, pp. 321 ff
3. Vaughan, *John the Fearless*, p. 230
4. *Journal d'un Bourgeois de Paris*, pp. 126–7
5. ibid., p. 129
6. McFarlane, *Nobility of Later Medieval England*, p. 33
7. Stevenson (ed.), *Letters and Papers*, Vol. II, pp. 579–81
8. Vaughan argues convincingly that the dauphin was well aware of the trap, *John the Fearless*, pp. 274–86
9. *The First English Life of King Henry the Fifth*, p. 153
10. Hearne (ed.), op. cit., pp. 80, 81

Chapter XIII, 'Heir and Regent of France'

1. Ascoli, op. cit., pp. 12–13, who takes it from Doncieux *Romancero Populaire de France*, showing it refers to the marriage of Catherine to Henry V and not to that of Henrietta Maria to Charles I.
2. *Chronique du Réligieux de Saint-Denys*, Vol. VI, p. 163
3. Monstrelet, op. cit., Vol. III, p. 406
4. Juvénal, op. cit., p. 561
5. Waurin, op. cit., Vol. II, p. 429
6. Juvénal, op cit., p. 561
7. ibid., p. 561

Chapter XIV, 'The Fall of Paris 1420'

1. *Journal d'un Bourgeois de Paris*, p. 145
2. ibid., pp. 146, 156
3. Chastellain, *Oeuvres*, Vol. I, pp. 198–200
4. Monstrelet, op. cit., Vol. IV, pp. 9–10; Chastellain, op. cit., Vol. I, p. 179
5. Monstrelet, op. cit., Vol. IV, p. 17; Tutuey (ed.), op. cit., p. 145
6. Monstrelet, op. cit., Vol. II, p. 305
7. Perroy, op. cit., pp. 232–3
8. Vale's brilliant *Charles VII* does belated justice to him, altering the traditional picture.

Chapter XV, 'Lancastrian Normandy'

1. Le Cacheux, *Rouen au temps de Jeanne d'Arc et pendant l'occupation anglais (1419–1449)*
2. Blondel, *Complanctorum bonorum Gallorum*, ch. xix
3. Blondel, *Oratio Historialis*, ch. iii
4. Newhall, op. cit., pp. 240–2
5. Rymer, op. cit., Vol. X, pp. 160–1
6. Newhall, op. cit., p. 236
7. At the truce of Tours of May 1444 the English agreed to end *pâtis*, *courses*, *sauvegardes*, *billets* and *congés* in Normandy, Anjou, Maine and Perches, and at Mantes and at Le Crotoy.
8. Allmand, op. cit., p. 30
9. Puiseux, *L'Emigration Normande et la colonisation anglaise en Normandie au XVe Siècle*, pp. 56–7
10. Favier, 'La Tourment' in *Histoire de la Normandie* (ed. Boüard), pp. 233–4
11. Favier, *Guerre de Cent Ans*, p. 467. In 1430 the ecclesiastical judges at Rouen gave a ruling that 'son of an Englishman' was an insult as grave as 'son of a whore'.

Chapter XVI, 'Rending of Every Man Throughout the Realm'

1. Wylie and Waugh, op. cit., Vol. III
2. Harvey, 'Architectural History from 1291 to 1558' in *A History of York Minster*, pp. 181–6.
3. McFarlane, *Cambridge Medieval History*, Vol. VIII, p. 387
4. Newhall, op. cit., p. 266
5. Juvénal, op. cit., p. 565
6. Strecche, *Chronicle*, p. 278
7. Adam of Usk, op. cit., p. 133
8. Harriss (ed.), op. cit., p. 177
9. Newhall, op. cit., p. 150–1, and Jacob, op. cit., pp. 204–10

10. Rymer, op. cit., Vol. X, p. 131
11. Knowles, op. cit., Vol. II, pp. 182–4

Chapter XVII, 'Meaux Falls'

1. Chastellain, op. cit., Vol. I, p. 220
2. Juvénal, op. cit., p. 566
3. Chartier, op. cit., Vol. I, p. 6
4. Chastellain, op. cit., Vol. I, p. 282
5. Burne, *The Agincourt War*, p. 179
6. Walsingham, op. cit., Vol. II, p. 343
7. *Chronique du Réligieux de Saint-Denys*, Vol. VI, p. 381
8. ibid., Vol. VI, p. 381
9. Juvénal, op. cit, p. 561
10. *Journal d'un Bourgeois de Paris*, p. 171 ff
11. *Chronique du Réligieux de Saint-Denys*, Vol. VI, p. 450
12. *Journal d'un Bourgeois de Paris*, p. 178
13. ibid., p. 163
14. Waurin, op. cit., Vol. II, p. 361
15. Clephan, 'The Ordnance of the Fourteenth and Fifteenth Centuries', *Archaeological Journal*, pp. 49–84
16. Letter in Bib. Nat. fr. 26044, no. 5712 – cit. Newhall, op. cit., p. 264
17. *Calendar of Patent Rolls, Henry V* (8 April, 1421), p. 384
18. *Journal d'un Bourgeois de Paris*, p. 170
19. Juvénal, op. cit., p. 563
20. *Chronique du Réligieux de Saint-Denys*, Vol. VI, p. 563
21. '*ac hospitalus fuit in castro delectabilissimo du boys de Vincennes per Seneam distante*', ibid., p. 466
22. *The First English Life of King Henry the Fifth*, p. 178
23. *The Brut of England*, Vol. II, p. 493
24. Chastellain, op. cit., Vol. I, p. 313
25. *Journal d'un Bourgeois de Paris*, p. 174 ff

Chapter XVIII, 'Lancastrian France'

1. Wylie and Waugh, op. cit., Vol. III, p. 143
2. Perroy, op. cit., p. 219. '*Henri V se fit brutal, lésa sans remords tous les intérêts. Expulsions, confiscations, amendes, firent regner un régime de terreur.*'
3. Favier, op. cit., p. 463
4. Walsingham, *Historia Anglicana*, Vol. II, p. 336
5. Chartier, op. cit., Vol. I, p. 13
6. Basin, op. cit., Vol. II, pp. 9–10
7. Puiseux, op. cit., Allmand, *Lancastrian Normandy*
8. Basin, op. cit., Vol. I, pp. 106–7
9. Le Cacheux, *Actes de la Chancellerie de Henri VI*, Vol. 1, pp. 253–5
10. Juvénal, in Dénifle, op. cit., Vol. I, pp. 502–12

11. ibid., p. 511
12. Stevenson (ed.), *Letters and Papers*, Vol. I, pp.10–19
13. Dénifle, op. cit., Vol. I, xvi
14. Juvénal, in Dénifle, op. cit., Vol. I, p. 506
15. Blondel, 'De Reductione Normanniae', in *Narratives of the Expulsion of the English from Normandy*, p. 179, 'Quid de tuis sacrilegiis, Henrie, rex immanissimo, omnium sacrilegorum princeps.'
16. *Chronique du Réligieux de Saint-Denys*, Vol. VI, p. 165
17. Chartier, op. cit., p. 4
18. Basin, op. cit., Vol. I, pp. 86–8. The great Lancastrian lawyer Sir John Fortescue, who was in France during the late 1460s, reports, 'there was never people in that land more poor than were in our time the commons of the county of Caux, which was then almost desert for lack of tillers.' (The Pays de Caux had once been the granary of eastern Normandy.)
19. *The First English Life of King Henry the Fifth*, p. 131
20. Chastellain, op. cit., Vol. I, p. 221
21. ibid., Vol. I, pp. 221–22, 308
22. cit. Ascoli, op. cit., p. 18
23. cit. Lewis, *Essays in Later French Medieval History*, p. 194
24. Robinet, cit. Ascoli, op. cit., p. 43
25. Commynes, *Mémoires*, Vol. II, p. 37
26. Fowler, *The Hundred Years War*, p. 23
27. Cheruel, *Histoire de Rouen sous la domination anglaise au quinzième siècle*, pp. 86–8
28. McFarlane, *The Nobility of Later Medieval England*, p. 35
29. Monstrelet, op. cit., Vol. IV, p. 117. The nobleman was 'Messire Sarasin d'Ailli, uncle to the Vidame of Amiens'.
30. Juvénal, in Dénifle, op. cit., Vol. I, p. 500
31. Chastellain, op. cit., Vol. I, pp. 337–9

Chapter XIX, 'Death'

1. Waurin, op. cit., Vol. II, p. 426
2. Basin, op. cit., Vol. I, p. 79
3. Favier, op. cit., p. 455. '*Dans ce réalisme des derniers instants, Henri V reconnaissait implicitement la légitimité du futur Charles VII.*'
4. Chastellain, op. cit., Vol. I, pp. 339–40
5. Chartier, op. cit., Vol. I, p. 28
6. *Journal d'un Bourgeois de Paris*, p. 178
7. Waurin, op. cit., Vol. II, p. 428; Monstrelet, op. cit., Vol. IV, p. 116
8. *The Brut of England*, Vol. II, p. 430
9. Waurin, op. cit., Vol. II, p. 429
10. Chartier, op. cit., Vol. I, p. 6
11. Chastellain, op. cit., Vol. I, p. 312
12. Jacob, op. cit., p. 202

13. Wylie and Waugh, op. cit., Vol. III, p. 426
14. McFarlane, *Cambridge Medieval History*, Vol. VIII, pp. 384–5
15. Basin, op. cit., Vol. I, p. 89
16. *Journal d'un Bourgeois de Paris*, p. 320
17. Shakespeare, *King Henry V*, Act III, scene iii

Chapter XX, Epilogue

1. Commynes, op. cit., Vol. II, p. 256
2. ibid., Vol. II, p. 240

Select Bibliography

CHRONICLES AND OTHER CONTEMPORARY SOURCES

Adam of Usk, *Chronicon Adae de Usk* (ed. E. M. Thompson), London, 1904.

Basin, Thomas, *Histoire de Charles VII* (transl. C. Samaran), Paris, 1964–65.

Blondel, Robert, *Oeuvres*, Rouen 1891.

Blondel, Robert, 'De reductione Normanniae' in *Letters and Papers Illustrative of the Wars of the English in France* (ed. J. Stevenson), see below.

Bouvier, Gilles Le, *Histoire Chronologique du roy Charles VII*, Paris, 1658.

The Brut; or the Chronicles of England, (ed. F. Brie), Early English Text Society, 1906–08.

Cagny, Perceval de, *Chroniques de Perceval de Cagny,* (ed. H. Moranville), Paris, 1902.

Calendar of Patent Rolls, Henry V, London, 1910–11.

Calendar of Signet Letters of Henry IV and Henry V, London, 1978.

Capgrave, John, *The Chronicle of England* (ed. F. C. Hingeston), London, 1858.

Chartier, Alain, *L'Histoire mémorable des grands troubles de ce royaume soubs le roy Charles VII*, Nevers, 1594.

Chartier, Alain, *Le Quadrilogue invectif*, Paris, 1923.

Chartier, Jean, *Chronique de Charles VII, roi de France* (ed. V. de Viriville), Paris, 1858.

Chastellain, Georges, *Oeuvres* (ed. Kervyn de Lettenhove), Brussels, 1863–66.

A Chronicle of London 1189–1483 (ed. N. H. Nicolas), London, 1827.

Chronique du Réligieux de Saint-Denys (1380–1422) (ed. F. Bellaguet), Paris, 1839–54.

Commynes, Philippe de, *Mémoires* (eds. J. Calmette and G. Durville), Paris, 1924–25.

Cronicques de Normandie (ed. A. Hellot), Rouen, 1881.

Fauquembergue, Clément de, *Journal de Clément de Fauquembergues, greffier du Parlement de Paris, 1417–1435* (ed. A. Tuetey), Paris, 1881.

Fenin, Pierre de, *Mémoires*, Paris, 1837.

The First English Life of King Henry the Fifth (ed. C. L. Kingsford), Oxford, 1911.

Fortescue, Sir John, *The Governance of England* (ed. C. Plummer), Oxford, 1885.

Froissart, Jean, *Oeuvres: Chroniques* (ed. Kervyn de Lettenhove), Brussels, 1867–77.

Gesta Henrici Quinti: The Deeds of Henry the Fifth (trans. and ed. F. Taylor and J. S. Roskell), Oxford, 1975.

Halle, Edward, *The Union of the two Noble and Illustre Families of Lancastre and Yorke*, London, 1809.

Hardyng, John, *Chronicle* (ed. H. Ellis), London, 1812.

Historical Poems of the XIVth and XVth Centuries (ed. R. H. Robbins), New York, 1959.

Hoccleve, Thomas, *The Regement of Princes* (ed. F. J. Furnivall), Early English Text Society, London, 1897.

Journal d'un Bourgeois de Paris, 1405–1449 (ed. A. Tutuey), Paris, 1881.

Juvénal des Ursins, Jean, *Histoire de Charles VI* (ed. J. A. C. Buchon, Paris, 1836.

Juvénal des Ursins, Jean, *Ecrits politiques de Jean Juvénal des Ursins* (ed. P. S. Lewis), Paris, 1978.

Lannoy, Guillebert de, *Oeuvres* (ed. C. Potvin), Louvain, 1878.

Le Fèvre, Jean, Seigneur de St Remy, *Chronique* (ed. F. Morand), Paris, 1876–81.

Letters and Papers Illustrative of the Wars of the English in France during the Reign of Henry the Sixth, King of England (ed. J. Stevenson), London, 1861–81.

Lettres des rois, reines et autres personnages des cours de France et d'Angleterre (ed. J. J. Champollion-Figeac), Paris, 1839–47.

Libelle of Englyshe Polycye (ed. G. Warner), Oxford, 1926.

Liber Metricus: Elmham liber metricus de Henrico quinto in *Memorials of Henry the Fifth, king of England* (ed. C. A. Cole), London, 1858.

Livius de Frulovisis, Titus, *Vita Henrici Quinti* (ed. T. Hearne), London, 1716.

Monstrelet, Enguerrand de, *Chroniques d'Enguerran de Monstrelet* (ed. L. Douët d'Arcq), Paris, 1857–62.

Morosini, Antonio, *Chronique d'Antonio Morosini: Extraits rélatifs à l'histoire de France, 1414–1428* (ed. G. Lefèvre-Pontalis and L. Dorez), Paris, 1899.

Narratives of the Expulsion of the English from Normandy MCCCCXLIX–MCCCCL (ed. J. Stevenson), London, 1863.

Original Letters illustrative of English History (ed. H. Ellis), London, 1824–46.

Otterbourne, Thomas, *Chronica Regum Angliae* (ed. T. Hearne), Oxford, 1732.

Page, John, 'The Siege of Rouen' in *The Historical Collections of a Citizen of London*, Camden Society, 1876.

Royal and Historical Letters during the Reign of Henry IV, (ed. H. C. Hingeston), London, 1860.

Rouen au temps de Jeanne d'Arc pendant l'occupation anglaise (1419–1449) (ed. P. Le Cacheux), Rouen and Paris, 1931.

Rymer, Thomas, *Foedera, Conventiones*, The Hague, 1739–45.

St Albans Chronicle, 1406–1420 (ed. V. H. Galbraith), Oxford, 1937.

Strecche, John, *The Chronicle of John Strecche for the reign of Henry V (1414–22)* (ed. F. Taylor), Manchester, 1932.

Upton, Nicholas, *The Essential Portions of Nicholas Upton's De Studio Militari before 1446* (ed. F. P. Barnard), Oxford, 1931.

Vegetius, *Knyghthode and Bataile: A XVth Century Verse Paraphrase of Flavius Vegetius Renatus' Treatise 'De Re Miltari'* (ed. R. Dyboski and Z. M. Arend), Early English Text Society, 1935.

Vita et Gesta Henrici Quinti (ed. T. Hearne), London, 1727.

Walsingham, Thomas, *Historia Anglicana* (ed. H. T. Riley), London, 1863–64.

Waurin, Jean de, *Receuil des croniques et anchiennes istories de la Grant Bretaigne a present nomme Engleterre, 1399–1422* (ed. W. Hardy), London, 1868.

SECONDARY WORKS

Allmand, C. T., *Lancastrian Normandy: The History of a Medieval Occupation*, Oxford, 1983.

Allmand, C. T., 'The Lancastrian Land Settlement in Normandy, 1417–50', *Economic History Review*, Second series, XXI (1968).

Allmand, C. T., (ed.), *Society at War: The Experience of England and France during the Hundred Years War*, Edinburgh, 1973.

Allmand, C. T., (ed.), *War, Literature and Politics in the Late Middle Ages*, Liverpool, 1976.

Ascoli, G., *La Grande Bretagne devant l'opinion française*, Paris, 1927.

Aylmer, G. E. and Cant, R. (eds.), *A History of York Minster*, Oxford, 1977.

Beaucourt, G. du Fresne de, *Histoire de Charles VII*, Paris, 1881–91.

Beaurepaire, C. de Robillard de, 'Les Etats de Normandie sous la domination anglaise', *Travaux de la Société d'Agriculture de l'Eure*, 3me série V, Evreux, 1859.

Boüard, M. de, *Histoire de la Normandie*, Toulouse, 1970.

Burne, A. H., *The Agincourt War: A Military History of the latter part of the Hundred Years War from 1369 to 1453*, London, 1956.

Calmette, J., *Les grands ducs de Bourgogne*, Paris, 1949.

Chéruel, P-A, *Histoire de Rouen sous la domination anglaise au quinzième siècle*, Rouen, 1840.

Clephan, R. C., 'The Ordnance of the Fourteenth and Fifteenth Centuries' *Archaeological Journal*, 2nd Series, 18, London, 1911.

The Complete Peerage (eds G. E. Cockayne and V. Gibbs), London, 1910–59.

Contamine, P., *La Guerre de Cent Ans*, Paris, 1968.

Contamine, P., *La Vie Quotidienne pendant la Guerre de Cent Ans*, Paris, 1976.

Contamine, P., *Agincourt*, Paris, 1964.

Contamine, P., *La Guerre au moyen age*, Paris, 1980.

Coville, A., *Récherches sur la misère en Normandie au temps de Charles VI*, Caen, 1886.

Coville, A., 'Les Premiers Valois et la Guerre de Cent Ans 1328–1422' in *Histoire de France* (ed. Lavisse), Tom. IV (i), Paris, 1902.

Dénifle, H., *La désolation des églises, monastères et hôpitaux en France pendant la Guerre de Cent Ans*, Paris, 1897–99.

Désert, G., *Histoire de Caen*, Toulouse, 1981.

Favier, J., 'La Tourmente' in *Histoire de la Normandie*, (ed. M. de Boüard), Toulouse, 1870.

Favier, J., *Nouvelle histoire de Paris. Paris au XVe siècle, 1380–1500*, Paris, 1974.

Favier, J., *La Guerre de Cent Ans*, Paris, 1980.

Fowler, K. E., *The Age of Plantagenet and Valois*, Elek, 1967.

Fowler, K. E. (ed.), *The Hundred Years War*, London, 1971.

Foxe, J., *The Acts and Monuments*, New York, 1965.

Harriss, G. L. (ed.), *Henry V*, Oxford, 1985.

Huizinga, J., *The Waning of the Middle Ages*, London, 1965.

Jacob, E. F., *Henry V and the Invasion of France*, London, 1947.

Jacob, E. F., *The Fifteenth Century*, Oxford, 1961.

Jouet, R., *La Résistance à l'occupation anglaise en Basse-Normandie (1418–1450)*, Caen, 1969.

Keegan, John, *The Face of Battle*, London, 1976.

Kingsford, C. L., *Henry V*, New York, 1901.

Kingsford, C. L., *English Historical Literature in the Fifteenth Century*, Oxford, 1913.

Le Cacheux, P., *Actes de la Chancellerie d'Henri VI concernant la Normandie sous la domination anglaise*, Rouen, 1907.

Lewis, P. S., *Later Medieval France: The Polity*, London, 1968.

Lewis, P. S., (ed.), *The Recovery of France in the Fifteenth Century*, London, 1971.

Lewis, P. S., *Essays in Later Medieval French History*, London and Ronceverte, 1985.

Lewis, P. S., 'War Propaganda and Historiography in Fifteenth Century France', *Transactions of the Royal Historical Society*, Fifth Series, 15, 1965.

McFarlane, K. B., *The Nobility of Later Medieval England*, Oxford, 1973.

McFarlane, K. B., *Lancastrian Kings and Lollard Knights*, Oxford, 1972.

McFarlane, K. B., 'England: the Lancastrian Kings, 1399–1461' in *Cambridge Medieval History*, Vol. VIII, Cambridge, 1936.

McFarlane, K. B., *John Wycliffe and the Beginnings of English Non-conformity*, London, 1952.

Myers, A. R., 'The Captivity of a Royal Witch', *Bulletin of the John Rylands Library*, Manchester, 1940.

Newhall, R. A., *The English Conquest of Normandy*, New Haven, 1924.

Newhall, R. A., 'Discipline in an English Army of the Fifteenth Century', *The Military Historian and Economist*, ii, 1917.

Newhall, R. A., 'Henry V's Policy of Conciliation in Normandy, 1417–1422', *Anniversary Essays in Medieval History of Students of C. H. Haskins* (ed. C. H. Taylor), Boston, 1929.

Nicolas, N. H., *History of the Battle of Agincourt and of the Expedition of King Henry the Fifth in France in 1415*, London, 1832.

Palmer, J. J. N., *England, France and Christendom, 1377–99*, London, 1972.

Perroy, E., *La Guerre de Cent Ans*, Paris, 1945.

Postan, M. M., 'Some Social Consequences of the Hundred Years War', *Economic History Review*, First Series, xii, 1942.

Postan, M. M., 'The Costs of the Hundred Years War', *Past and Present*, 27, 1964.

Powicke, M. R., 'Lancastrian Captains', *Essays in Medieval History presented to Bertie Wilkinson* (eds. T. A. Sandquist and M. R. Powicke), Toronto, 1969.

Puiseux, L., 'Prise de Caen par les Anglais en 1417', *Mémoires de la société des antiquaires de Normandie*, 3me. sér., xxii, 1858.

Puiseux, L., *L'Emigration normande et la colonisation anglaise en Normandie au XVe siècle*, Caen, 1866.

Puiseux, L., *Caen en 1421. Appendice au siège de Caen par les Anglais en 1417*, Caen, 1860.

Puiseux, L., 'Des insurrections populaires en Normandie pendant l'occupation Anglaise au XV siècle', *Mémoires de la société des antiquaires de Normandie*, 2me, sér., ix, 1851.

Roskell, J. S., *The Commons and their Speakers in English Parliaments*, Manchester, 1965.

Rowe, B. J. H., 'Discipline in the Norman Garrisons under Bedford, 1422–35', *English Historical Review*, xlvi, 1931.

Rowe, B. J. H., 'John, Duke of Bedford, and the Norman "Brigands"', *English Historical Review*, xlvii, 1932.

Sarrazin, A., *Jeanne d'Arc et la Normandie au quinzième siècle*, Rouen, 1896.

Steel, A. B., *Richard II*, Cambridge, 1941.

Vale, M. G. A., *English Gascony, 1399–1453. A Study of War, Government, and Politics during the later stages of the Hundred Years War*, Oxford, 1970.

Vale, M. G. A., *Charles VII*, London, 1974.

Vaughan, R., *John the Fearless*, London, 1966.

Vaughan, R., *Philip the Good*, London, 1970.

Vickers, K. H., *Humphrey, Duke of Gloucester*, London, 1907.

Wedgwood, J. C., *History of Parliament, Biographies of Members of the Commons House, 1439–1509*, London, 1936.

Wylie, J. H., *History of England under Henry IV*, London, 1884–98.

Wylie, J. H. and Waugh, W. T., *The Reign of Henry the Fifth*, Cambridge, 1914–29.

Index

Charles V, King of France, 6, 193, 212

Charles VI, King of France, 69, 73, 94, 108, 116, 132, 152, 174, 183; alliance with Owain Glyn Dŵr, 21; madness, 53, 90; and Henry V's invasion, 53, 54; battle of Agincourt, 89; Henry V becomes heir to, 137, 139, 140, 144–6, 156; at the siege of Melun, 150; and Henry V's occupation of Paris, 154, 156; Henry V's treatment of, 195; death, 212, 213–14

Charles the Bad, King of Navarre, 177

Chartier, Alain, 202, 203

Chartier, Jean, 100, 184, 198, 202, 213–14

Chartres, 179, 182, 183

Chastel, Tanneguy de, 112, 136

Chastellain, Georges, 154–5, 157, 182–3, 184, 195, 196, 201, 203–5, 207–8, 211, 214

Château Gaillard, 139, 151

Chaucer, Geoffrey, 7, 39

Chaucer, Thomas, 178

Chaumont, Bertrand de, 151

Chepstowe, John, 165

Cherbourg, 109, 110, 123, 162, 163, 168, 217, 220

Chéruel, Pierre-Adolphe, 206–7

Chester, 11, 15

Cheyne, Sir Thomas, 43

Chichele, Henry, Archbishop of Canterbury, 46, 118–19, 170, 171, 172, 176, 177

Chissay, Guichard de, 186

Chronicles of London, 177

Cinque Ports, 91, 170

Clarence, Thomas, Duke of, 33, 38, 48, 127, 130, 145, 151, 152; expedition to France, 31–2, 43; and Henry V's invasion, 55, 56; excluded from Henry V's will, 62; siege of Harfleur, 65, 66; abilities, 93; and the fall of Caen, 100–4; captures Pont-de-l'Arche, 112; siege of Rouen, 114; French lands, 122; moves towards Paris, 139; occupation of Paris, 158; occupation of Normandy, 160; death, 173–5, 215

Claydon, John, 45

Clifford, Lord, 22, 47

Clux, Sir Hartung von, 141

Colchester, 175

Coldharbour, 33

Colles, Roger, 177

Cologne, 140

Colvyl, Sir John, 53

Commynes, Philippe de, 205, 218–20

Compiègne, 195

Constance, Council of, 88, 178

Constantinople, 15

Conwy Castle, 10, 16, 20

Corbeil, 150, 152, 210

Cornwall, Sir John, 70, 72, 95, 112, 187

Cornwall, Richard, Earl of, 95

Cosne, 210

Courtecuisse, Jean, Bishop of Paris, 198

Courtenay, Richard, Bishop of Norwich, 46, 53, 66

Coutances, 123

Coventry, 32

Crécy, battle of, 7

Crépy-en-Valois, 193

Creton, Jean, 9

Croniques de Normandie, 184

Curwen, Sir Christopher, 122–3

Cyprus, 4

Danzig, 141

Dartford, 213

Denifle, Henri, 201

Deschamps, Eustache, 7

249

Rouen—*cont.*
  refugees, 101; siege of, 111,
    112–20, 121, 130; English
    occupation of, 123, 159–60;
    currency, 128, 153; wealth,
    134
Rougemont, 184
Royal Council, 28–9, 31, 46–7, 134
Ruisseauville, 75
Ruthin, 17
Rutland, Earl of *see* York, Edward,
    Duke of

St Catherine, 114
Sainte-Claude, 207–8
St Denis, 145, 213
'St George's Bridge', 114
St Germain, 139
St Médard, 200
Ste Suzanne, 134
St Vaast, 104
Salisbury, John Montacute, 3rd
    Earl of, 9, 13
Salisbury, Thomas Montacute, 4th
    Earl of, 38, 55, 56, 94, 100,
    111, 114, 122, 160, 174, 179,
    210
Sarthe, River, 174
Saundish, John, 53
Saveuse, Sieur Guillaume de, 78–9
Scandinavia, 141
Scotland, 15, 17, 36–7, 171
Scrope, Henry, 3rd Lord, 28–9, 40,
    46, 47–9, 93, 211, 215
Scrope, Richard, Archbishop of
    York, 22, 27, 34, 49
Seine, River, 64, 91, 102, 112–13,
    114, 116, 121, 136, 139, 145,
    149, 160–1, 165, 166, 185,
    210
Senlis, 195
Sens, 148
Sheen, 41–2
Shipton Moor, 22
Shrewsbury, 19–20, 74, 173, 180

Sigismund, Holy Roman Emperor,
    54, 87–90, 140, 141, 206
Somerset, Earl of, 174
Somme, River, 70, 71–2, 95
Soper, William, 62
Southampton, 47–8, 54, 62, 91, 96,
    98, 181
'Southampton Plot', 47–50
Southampton Water, 61, 91
Spencer, Hugh, 123
Springhouse, Sir Edmund, 104
Stafford, Earl of, 20
Stamford, 175
States General, 153
Statute of Provisors, 178
Stewart, John, 174
Stiff, John, 55
Stow, John, 33
Strecche, Canon John, 53, 173, 175
Suffolk, Earl of, 66, 81, 121–2, 163,
    183
Sweden, 141
Swynford, Sir Thomas, 14
Syon, 42

Talbot, Gilbert, Lord, 21, 94, 95
Talbot, Sir Thomas, 43
Ternoise, River, 73
Teutonic Knights, 4, 94, 141
Thomas, Prince, 28
Tille, John, 34
Tiptoft, Sir John, 23, 141–2
Touques, River, 100–1
Touraine, 183
Tower of London, 36, 43, 51–2, 59,
    82, 106, 158, 177
Tramecourt, 75
Très Riches Heures du duc de Berry, 193
Trier, 140
Trim Castle, 9
Trinity Royal, 63, 91
Troyes, 102, 143, 144, 145, 148
Troyes, Treaty of (1420), 137,
    145–6, 153, 160, 175–6, 206
Tudur, Owain, 147